Service Workers in the Era of Monopoly Capital

Studies in Critical Social Sciences

Series Editor
David Fasenfest
(*Wayne State University*)

VOLUME 202

New Scholarship in Political Economy

Series Editors
David Fasenfest
(*Wayne State University*)
Alfredo Saad-Filho
(*King's College London*)

VOLUME 12

The titles published in this series are listed at *brill.com/nspe*

Service Workers in the Era of Monopoly Capital

A Marxist Analysis of Service and Retail Labour

By

Fabian van Onzen

BRILL

LEIDEN | BOSTON

Cover illustration: Bust of Karl Marx, 1939, by S.D. Merkurov, at the Fallen Monument Park (Muzeon Park of Arts) in Moscow, Russia. Photo courtesy of Alfredo Saad-Filho.

The Library of Congress Cataloging-in-Publication Data is available online at https://catalog.loc.gov
LC record available at https://lccn.loc.gov/2021041815

Typeface for the Latin, Greek, and Cyrillic scripts: "Brill". See and download: brill.com/brill-typeface.

ISSN 2666-2205
ISBN 978-90-04-33705-3 (hardback)
ISBN 978-90-04-46962-4 (e-book)

This book is printed on acid-free paper and produced in a sustainable manner.

Contents

Preface

This book is a political work designed to stimulate discussion about service workers and retail employees using Marxist theory. Although significant numbers of people work in the service and retail industry, Marxist economic theory often still tends to focus solely on factory workers. There is increasingly a need for Marxist theory to respond to the today's labour conditions under which millions of working people live and work. My hope is that this book equips socialists who are organising service workers with the theoretical tools needed to make sense of service labour and retail employees. It is primarily a theoretical work, which shows how the main works of Marxism—Marx's *Capital*, Lenin's *Imperialism*, etc.—can be used to reveal tendencies of exploitation in the service industry, and potential sites of political struggle for service workers.

The ideas for this book arose primarily through my own political practice, which I will briefly discuss to give the reader a sense of this book's background. When I was twenty-three (in 2010), I joined a socialist organisation in Houston, Texas. For the next five years, I became an active member and was later elected to the post of Director of Marxist Education. I helped to organise a weekly Marxist reading group, which introduced comrades to the works of Marx, Engels, Lenin, and other Marxist writers. One of the things that was very noticeable was the way that Marxist study strengthened the political understanding of my comrades. Some of them, after attending the political education course, started to base their comments, suggestions, and recommendations at meetings on Marxist theory instead of 'common sense'. As a result, they enquired into each problem before posing it and considered the ways that a particular tactic affects the long-term strategy. These comrades became more disciplined, dedicated, and were of a better quality than before. It was this experience that first taught me the importance Marxist theory to addressing basic political problems. A major principle of this book is that Marxist theory should be able to respond to the actual conditions in which working people find themselves in order to provide them with tools to transform society. This requires a 'concrete analysis of the concrete situation' rather than an apriori approach of deduction from purely theoretical principles.

In the summer of 2012, my comrades and I spent a lot of time supporting a janitor's strike in Houston, which lasted an entire summer and involved significant amounts of militant civil disobedience. During the janitor's strike, I discovered that many comrades were unable to apply Marxist theory to cleaning workers. Although everyone was supportive of the janitor's strike, no one seemed able to apply the Marxist concepts of surplus-value and productive labour to understand their labour-process. In the Marxist education courses that I organised, comrades were sometimes hostile to viewing service workers as productive labourers and were often unwilling to engage in theoretical enquiry. Most comrades viewed *all* janitors as unproductive workers who contribute to the process of social reproduction, but do not themselves produce value. Because the janitors are outsourced to private companies such as Pritchard Industries, the idea that they were unproductive seemed problematic to me. It caused me to start thinking about better ways that Marxist theory could be applied to workers that do not produce physical goods, but services such as cleaning. Through reading the work of Nicos Poulantzas, particularly his *Classes in Contemporary Capitalism*, I discovered the unpublished appendix to Marx's *Capital*, which was my starting point for thinking about how some service workers could become productive labourers. When one read's Marx's *Capital*, it is easy to get the idea that only workers who produce physical goods are part of the working class and that service workers are 'unproductive'. Although Marx devotes significant attention to transport workers in Volume Two of *Capital*, he does not analyse the process by which service workers produce surplus-value. In many guides to Marx's *Capital*, such as David Harvey's *Companion to Marx's Capital* and Ernest Mandel's *Marxist Economics*, this problem is not addressed in significant detail. Mandel does devote an entire chapter to service workers in *Late Capitalism* but holds the view that they are largely unproductive and unable to produce surplus value. While not all service workers perform productive labour, some of them—such as the janitors on strike in Texas in 2012—do produce surplus-value. It was this lack of significant theorising of service workers in Marxism, and the noble struggle of janitors in 2012, that inspired me to begin thinking about this problem in more detail. This book will try to adjust some of the basic principles of Marxist theory so that they account for service workers, as well as retail employees.[1]

In addition to being a socialist activist, I spent many years teaching introductory courses in philosophy at community colleges around the Houston area, which had a huge impact on my theoretical development. In these courses, I often included modules on Marxist philosophy, which introduced students to the theory of surplus-value and the labour theory of value. When discussing Marx's *Capital*, my students—most of whom were employed in the service and retail industry—said they found it hard to relate to Marx's work.

1 I would add that since writing this book, other Marxist-inspired theoreticians have started addressing this problem—the greatest being Jamie Woodcock, who has written books on call centre workers and a recent book on the video game industry. Although Woodcock provides brilliant case studies, his use of Marxist theory remains somewhat limited at times.

They would raise important questions, such as 'do workers at Starbucks coffee produce surplus-value? If not, what is their role in the capitalist production process?' In *Capital*, Marx's examples are gained from nineteenth century capitalism in Victorian England and its industrial working class, which is quite different from today's service and retail workers. While teaching these courses, I spent a lot of time thinking about how to make Marx's theory of surplus-value relevant to my predominantly working-class students. My students played a significant role in helping me to think through the problems raised in this book and constantly challenged me to go beyond simplistic formulations. Although their input often came in a practical form, I often found the contributions of my working-class students significantly more interesting than the abstract theorising I encountered in graduate school. I found that the American style community college is a far better place to produce new theory in the terrain of Marxism than other sites of theoretical production. Working class students who become interested in Marxism often make very deep insights into the workings of capitalism and sometimes pose the most interesting questions. If I had to name the central figures who influenced my thinking—in addition to Marx, Poulantzas, Sweezy, and Lenin—it was my predominantly working-class students and the questions, comments, and remarks they made during class discussions.

While I was teaching, I also spent a lot of time thinking about my own labour-process, which was that of a part-time adjunct professor. Between 2012 and 2017, I worked at three institutions simultaneously—Lone Star College, Houston Community College, and the University of Houston Downtown—and usually taught between six and nine courses a semester. The pay was extremely low and the exploitation severe. My days were usually spent driving from campus to campus, often during rush-hour and sometimes with less than an hour between courses. Although I had some autonomy giving me the ability to organise my own courses, there were few prospects for a stable career. I loved my teaching job, but I detested the conditions of my employment, which was one of constant anxiety and the threat of termination. After discovering that adjunct professors around the United States faced similar conditions, I spoke with my co-workers at Houston Community College about forming a union, which we called the Higher-Education Workers Association (HEWA). We held meetings with our students, who were often deeply frustrated when they learned about the exploitative conditions under which their teachers worked. Although we did not have a union, we built a strong solidarity network consisting of students, co-workers, and some community members. This solidarity network made the adjunct instructors feel more confident about organising a union and reduced some of their anxieties of the risks of union organising.

Knowing that they could depend on the solidarity network if management went on the offensive empowered them to take action to organise themselves. Some of the ideas that I develop in chapter ten about the worker-consumer alliance and building solidarity networks have their origin in this experience. During the years that I taught face-to-face courses (2012–2017), I spent a great deal thinking about the process by which workers in higher education are exploited. I again discovered that Marxist theory needed to be adjusted so that it could provide adjunct professors—and all those employed in service jobs—with the theoretical tools to understand their own labour-process so that they may change it. In this book, I do not specifically focus on workers in higher-education because this would take away from its primary task, which is to demonstrate how Marx's theory of surplus-value can be used to think about service and retail workers. Therefore, while I make references to adjunct professors in some of the sections, I do not devote a specific chapter to their labour-process.

In 2015, I began a PhD programme at the European Graduate School and wrote my dissertation under the guidance of Mladen Dolar. My dissertation—titled the *Proletarian Standpoint: Surplus-Value and Revolutionary Subjectivity*—contained a chapter on service workers that I would later transform into this book. I defended the dissertation in the presence of Mladen Dolar, Slavoj Zizek, and Alenka Zupancic at the University of Ljubljana in 2018 after which I received my PhD. Most of the content for this book was written in Scotland, where I moved to in 2017 and completed in the Netherlands during the 2020–2021 coronavirus lockdown. Although the lockdown shut down libraries and places to do research, it nonetheless provided me with the free time to complete this work.

I hope that these brief introductory remarks clarify the purpose of this book, and its general political orientation. Before I begin, I would like to acknowledge some of the people that were influential in the writing of this book. First, I would like to acknowledge all the students who attended my philosophy courses, for their participation often challenged me to think about the problems raised in this book. Second, I would like to thank Mladen Dolar and the Faculty of Philosophy at the University of Ljubljana. It was through many hours of discussion with Mladen and his colleagues that I was able to write this book. Third, I would like to thank the following comrades, who influenced my thinking significantly: Bernard Sampson, Allison Hubbard, David Stiles, Joe McLeod, Caglar Karaca, and my partner. Particularly, I would like to thank Paul Mullan, who read sections of this manuscript and gave tremendously helpful feedback. Fourth, I must acknowledge my parents: although they hold very different views from me, they always provided me with the love and support needed to complete this work. I dedicate this book to the international working class, with the hope that it makes a small impact in the fight for a socialist world.

Figures and Tables

Figures

Tables

CHAPTER 1

Introduction

1 Centrality of Service Work in Contemporary Capitalism

In today's capitalism, millions of people are employed in the service industry and the production of service-goods. As a result of deindustrialisation and neoliberalism, most available jobs in the capitalist centres do not involve the production and manufacture of physical goods. Although manufacturing has not entirely disappeared from the advanced capitalist nations, most working people are employed as cleaners, transportation providers, restaurant workers, retail employees, I.T. specialists, and in logistics. While this is mostly true of the imperialist centres, such as Britain, the United States, the European Union, and Japan, many working people in peripheral nations are also employed in service-industry jobs. Some Caribbean nations, such as Jamaica and Trinidad, have a very high proportion of their workforce employed in tourism and other service jobs.

The service industry is central to contemporary capitalism, for as Renata Kosova and Francine Lafontaine point out,

> The retail and service sectors are increasingly important parts of the economy in developed countries. According to the Bureau of Labor Statistics, as of December 2008, about 13 million of the 112.5 million non-farm employees in the private sector in the U.S. worked in manufacturing, while 92 million workers were involved in private service industries, including 15 million in retailing and another 13.3 million in the leisure and hospitality sector. Moreover, most of the productivity growth in the U.S. since the mid 1990's has been traced back to improvements in the efficiency of the wholesale, retail, and service sectors.[1]

Many jobs that were traditionally unprofitable, such as cleaning, public transportation, teaching, logistics, and technical support are today profitable industries conducted on a capitalist basis. Companies such as Molly Maid, Phoenix University, UPS, and WGC specialise in the production of services that turn out super-profits each business cycle. Cleaning is a major source of employment for

1 Kosová and Lafontaine 2010, p. 543.

 | DOI:10.1163/9789004469624_002

many working people, which employs millions of people worldwide to clean homes, workplaces, hotels, and offices. The cleaning industry is particularly interesting because it is mostly conducted by commercial cleaning companies, which make huge profits through the super-exploitation of labour. Cleaners, many of whom are immigrant women, are some of the lowest paid workers. In Britain, they are often given zero-hour contracts and either work too much or struggle to get enough hours to survive. Because the cleaning industry is representative of the service industry, significant attention will be given in this book to analysing the labour-process of cleaning workers.

In contemporary economics, particularly Value Chain Analysis, there has been significant theoretical work on service labour. International organisations, such as the United Nations Conference on Trade and Development (UNCTAD) have published numerous documents that analyse how the growth of the service industry has impacted working people around the world. The IMF points out that

> manufacturing jobs are waning. In many emerging market and developing economies, workers are shifting from agriculture to services, bypassing the manufacturing sector. In advanced economies, the rise in service sector employment typically reflects the outright disappearance of manufacturing jobs.[2]

While mainstream economic science has produced significant research on service labour, Marxist economics still lags a bit behind. Marx wrote about service workers in volumes two and three of *Capital*, discussing transportation workers, and argued that they are productive labourers who produce surplus value. With great insight, he perceived that workers who transport commodities from the factory to shops occupy a different place in the chain of production than workers who manufacture goods. Marx also discusses a variety of service workers such as retail employees, salespersons, and warehouse workers. However, because it was not relevant to Marx's immediate project of understanding the dynamics of capital accumulation, he did not further explore the nature of service jobs.

Marxist economics after Marx has produced a very small amount of work on the nature of service labour. There have been some decent attempts by Marxists to make sense of the service industry, such as Ernest Mandel's *Late Capitalism*, Sweezy and Baran's *Monopoly Capital*, Poulantzas' *Classes in*

2 Gruss and Novta, 2018

Contemporary Capitalism, Tregenna's article "What Does the 'Services Sector' Mean in Marxian Terms?" and Braverman's *Labor and Monopoly Capital*. In the late sixties, a group of Marxists in Japan attempted to account for the role of productive labour in the service industry and engaged in a lively debate through their academic journals. While these writers observed significant changes to the composition of the working class and the growth of service labour, they did not devote book-length works to an examination of service workers. To an extent, the absence of detailed Marxist theoretical work on service labour is understandable. Marx's central category of surplus-value, which Lenin called the 'cornerstone' of his political economy, was designed to understand the exploitation of productive labourers. A productive labourer produces a commodity containing surplus value, which is appropriated by capitalists to make a profit. Until the 1970's, most service workers were not productive labourers. They were employed by capitalists to perform tasks necessary to capitalist production and social reproduction but did not produce surplus value. Consequently, service workers were generally only analysed in relation to the circulation of physical commodities and some Marxists thought that service workers could not produce value under any conditions. As a result, service workers have not occupied a significant place in Marxist theory.

There are some Marxists, such as Nicos Poulantzas, who deny that service workers are proletarians and claim they are 'petty-bourgeois'. Throughout *Classes in Contemporary Capitalism*, Poulantzas claims that only productive workers who produce surplus value are part of the working class. As Poulantzas puts it,

> The working class is not defined by a simple and intrinsic negative criterion, its exclusion from the relations of ownership, but by productive labour: 'every productive worker is a wage-earner, but it does not follow that every wage-earner is a productive worker'.[3]

Thus, according to Poulantzas, all service workers, such as retail employees, cleaners, administrative staff, and waiters, are wage labourers but are not members of the working class. On the basis of this assumption, Poulantzas argued that service workers, irrespective of the labour they do, are part of the new petty-bourgeoisie and have their own unique class interests.

There is a major problem with Poulantzas assumption that service labour cannot result in surplus-value. In today's capitalism, many of these formerly

3 Poulantzas 1978, p. 210.

in-house services, such as cleaning, I.T. work, transportation, and even job training, have been outsourced to private companies and are conducted on a capitalist basis. The commercial cleaning company Molly Maid, for example, extracts significant surplus value from the labour of cleaning workers. Their cleaners produce clean spaces as a commodity and produce far more value than they are compensated for. The capital relation is present between Molly Maid and its cleaners even if their labour does not result in a physical commodity. Poulantzas makes a fatal error in assuming that service workers cannot be subjected to the capital relation and that only labour resulting in physical goods is productive. His mistake may be attributed to his own historical conjuncture, which did not have a large commercial service industry, but this mistake cannot be continued today. In today's capitalism, even scientists and software developers can work for companies who employ them on a capitalist basis and use their labour to get a product that results in surplus-value. Although Poulantzas goal was to develop a socialist strategy that could unite the working class with the 'new petty-bourgeoisie', the result of such a position is that his followers[4] have often neglected a serious attempt to understand service workers.

It has only been recently that service workers, and even some retail employees, have become productive labourers. Millions of working people perform service labour for corporations that exploit their labour in order to get a profit. Their employment is characterised by the capital relation, in which a capitalist purchases their labour-power and appropriates the value produced by them. In the 1970's, commercial cleaning companies like Molly Maid, WCG, and Noonan emerged, which sought to transform cleaning from a necessary task into a profitable business. This made it possible for capitalists to outsource cleaning tasks in order to cut labour costs and make greater profits. What began with cleaning was later generalised to many other labour processes, such as security-work, domestic housekeeping, transportation, tourism, entertainment, and education. With the deindustrialisation policies of the 1980's in many parts of the capitalist North, millions of working people found themselves only able to get service jobs. Although manufacturing is primarily located in the global South, the expansion of the service industry has also characterised many Southern nations such as the BRICS countries, Indonesia, Thailand, and the Philippines.

4 Poulantzas ideas were very popular in the French and US Maoist movement. While this had a positive effect, encouraging a strong theoretical foundation for politics, it was negative in that it oriented Maoists towards only organising workers in factories. Some of Poulantzas' followers, such as Erik Olin Wright and Bob Jessop, were highly critical of his understanding of the working class.

A Marxist analysis is needed that offers an account of these changes to the composition of the working class. This is not an intellectual exercise, but a political intervention. Marxism equips working people with tools to produce knowledge of the system of production that exploits them and profits from their labour. As many working people today are service workers, Marxist theory must be capable of offering a clear explanation as to how they are exploited and what their role is in the international division of labour. I will show that the primary categories of Marxism, such as surplus-value and the rate of profit, are appropriate for analysing the labour process of service and retail workers. It is no longer the case that these categories apply only to workers who produce physical goods, but extends to cleaners, teachers, bus drivers, and security guards. I will argue that the value structure of the service industry differs considerably from the industries that produce means of production and consumer goods. There are significant differences in the relationship of the service worker to the product of their labour, to the consumer, and to their employers. For those who are trying to organise service workers, such as trade unionists and socialists, it is vital to have a clear understanding of these differences. I will demonstrate that an understanding of how service workers differ from industrial proletarians can help develop new strategies for organising them into a militant political force.

In addition to productive service workers, the retail sector also plays a more significant role than it did in the earlier stages of capitalism. For Marx, retail labour was viewed as a necessary cost of circulation, but not as an integral part of the capitalist production process. He does analyse the role of retail employees in volume two of *Capital*, but only in order to elaborate on the circuit of capital. In some ways, this was justified, as there was not mass consumerism or a large retail sector in Marx's time. Consumerism was limited to the wealthy who could afford to spend some of their income on luxury goods and entertainment. Personal credit was not widely available to working people until the sixties, and this ensured that the working class would have limited consumption. It therefore made sense to ignore retail labour, as it was not an integral part of capitalism. This situation changed significantly with the development of monopoly capitalism and neoliberalism. As Sweezy and Baran showed in *Monopoly Capital* the sales effort is very important in the era of monopoly capitalism because of the rising economic surplus. Capitalists invest a lot of money into advertising, salespeople, and retail employees in order to realise the surplus-value contained in their goods. They are not just after personal consumers, but also corporate clients who are important to the stimulation of demand.

There have not been many Marxist works that deal specifically with the retail sector. Jamie Woodcock wrote an excellent book, *Working the Phones*, which examines the role of call centre workers in selling commodities. While this work explores the lived experience of working in a call centre and the stress that its employees face, it does not engage significantly with Marxist theory. Besides Woodcock, Wolfgang Fritz Haug wrote *Commodity Aesthetics* in the 80s, in which he analyses sales employees and tactics they use to sell commodities. This book is noteworthy because it engages with Marxism, although from a somewhat limited Frankfurt School perspective. There have been some Marxist feminists, such as Alexandra Kollontai, Angela Davis, Kirsten Ghodsee, and Maria Mies who have discussed the labour process of cleaners and care workers. However, their focus has been primarily concerned with the gendered component in the exploitation of service workers and their role in social reproduction, which is tremendously important but does not give us insight into how concepts such as surplus value can be used to understand the exploitation of service labour. Other Marxist writers, such as John Smith, Andrew Brooks, and Harry Braverman have mentioned the retail sector in their work, but not devoted significant theoretical work to it. This is unfortunate, as many young people today, both in the capitalist North and South, are employed in the retail sector in shops such as H&M, Primark, Starbucks, and Ikea. Marxism must be able to speak to them so that it gives them the tools to organise themselves into a radical force capable of transforming society.

We need to articulate how a retail employee relates to surplus value, and how their self-organisation can strengthen the international working class. Such a theoretical intervention should demonstrate the relationship of retail employees in the imperialist centres with industrial workers in the peripheral nations. Without the labour of workers in the peripheral nations, retail employees would not have goods to sell, and without the labour of the retail employees, the continued production of goods by peripheral workers would come to a halt. Because production is today internationalised as a result of globalisation, a transnational organising model is needed that organises workers across the value-chain rather than only in one nation. A Marxist analysis of retail workers should provide us with the tools to create international solidarity between retail workers in the imperialist centres and industrial proletarians in the peripheral nations of the global South. Such transnational labour organizing is not frequently used by trade unions, but there have been some successful attempts in Germany by the Transnational Information Exchange, which organised a functional relationship between the workers in German H&M shops and garment workers in Bangladesh. This allowed for the coordination of political actions between workers in Germany and Bangladesh and the strengthening of international solidarity. I will examine the work of the Transnational Information Exchange in detail in chapter ten.

Besides retail shop employees, the other important sector of the service industry are workers employed in restaurants, cafes, pubs, and coffeehouses. What distinguishes food-service workers from retail shop employees is that they produce goods containing new surplus-value. A barista in a coffee-shop adds additional value to the coffee-beans, milk, and paper cups used to produce cappuccinos, lattes, and other coffee drinks. They are connected to working people in the peripheral nations of the global South through the use of raw materials produced by them. Coffee grown by farmers in Colombia, Tanzania, Kenya, and Brazil is used by baristas at Starbucks to produce a cup of coffee or make a latte. The labour of the barista ensures a continued market to realise the surplus-value produced by farmers in the global South. At the same time, when they produce a coffee drink, the barista produces additional surplus-value, which is appropriated by Starbuck's in order to accumulate funds for expansion. A Starbucks coffee shop is similar to a high-street shop but differs in that its workers produce surplus value under conditions of very low capital intensity, which creates new funds for investment and expansion.

It is notoriously difficult to organise baristas at Starbucks, and there are few Starbucks shops that are unionised. Although there are multiple reasons for this, one major cause is that trade union organisers often employ the same strategies for organising service workers that they use to organise those employed in manufacturing. What all working people share is separation from the means of production and wage-labour, but this does not mean that they should all be organised in the same way. One must be attentive to management strategies, which in companies like Starbucks is designed to create an ideology of belonging to the company and being part of a big family. The workers are constantly bombarded with propaganda about 'fair trade' and told about the humanitarian projects that the company engages in. As many corporations, Starbucks likes to present itself as a humanitarian corporation that is fair, concerned with 'sustainability' and protecting the environment. Such a management ideology is generally absent on the farms in Colombia where farm labourers work under constant threat of violence and suffer extremely high levels of exploitation. Unless socialists intervene, Southern proletarians will be filtered through Starbucks's corporate propaganda, which alienates the barista from the coffee farmer.

To organise workers employed in a coffee shop like Starbucks (or Costa, Nero, or any other), it is vital to break the grip of this management ideology. As I will show later, doing this requires creating concrete bonds of solidarity between workers in peripheral nations and baristas in the imperialist centres in the global North. This is not as simple as distributing a leaflet highlighting the exploitation suffered by workers in the South, but rather organising them to make direct contact with the producers through their trade unions. Furthermore, service workers in the North must be educated about the revolutionary traditions of the people in the oppressed nations where most of the goods they consume are produced. They must learn about the history of Southern peoples, how neo-colonialism operates in their nations, and about the struggles of Southern workers to emancipate themselves from imperialism. Transnational networks of solidarity must be built, which is only effective if it takes the form of direct communication between workers in the South and the North.

Socialist activists sometimes tend to privilege workers who produce physical goods over service and retail workers. There is a widespread belief that point-of-production workers are more class conscious because they work collectively and have the ability to stop production. It is indeed true that the collectivity of the production of physical goods makes it easier for this section of the workforce to organise itself against capital. They can more easily organise a strike, stopping the production of goods and directly confronting the bourgeoisie. This does not mean that non-industrial workers are 'less' capable of organising collectively, nor are they in a lesser position to confront the bourgeoisie. Rather, their position in the international division of labour is different from industrial workers, and therefore the struggle to organise them will differ. A retail employee in a high street shop occupies a different position in the division of labour than the workers that produce the goods that she sells. They have a relationship to the surplus-value, but their relationship to surplus-value differs from those who directly produce it. Retail employees generally do not *produce* surplus-value but facilitate its *realisation* (although some, such as Starbucks workers produce small increments of surplus-value). Without their labour, it would be impossible to continue the production of surplus-value. A worker in retail is vital to social reproduction, as they ensure the continual reproduction of the process of production.

2 Overview of Book

Chapter two discusses the method of historical materialism, which will be used in this book to produce knowledge of the service industry. This chapter will discuss an important distinction between mode of production and social formation, which is vital for detecting changes to capitalism. Using an Althusserian formulation, I will argue that social formations contain multiple modes of production, in which one mode of production is dominant and exercises a dissolution effect over others. I will show how Althusser's formulation is helpful for analysing the transformation of formerly unproductive tasks—cleaning, maintenance, etc.—into profitable businesses. Chapter two will also discuss Marxist approaches to accounting and show that company accounts are extremely important sources of information when researching the service industry. I will present—in a very brief way—a method that I have used to translate bourgeois company accounts into Marxist economic categories such as constant capital, variable capital, and the rate of profit. I view this as a kind of Althusserian theoretical practice, using company accounts as raw material that must be worked on in order to produce scientific knowledge.

The third chapter will produce an analysis of the class structure of contemporary capitalist social formations. It will begin by showing why class analysis is vital to Marxist research and lay out the primary classes in capitalist societies. My approach to Marxist class analysis is heavily influenced by Nicos Poulantzas, whose distinctions such as class fraction, social category, and class place are helpful for understanding classes. This chapter will also show how service and retail workers—as well as service employees such as administrators, managers, and franchisees—fit into Marxist class categories. This analysis is provided at the beginning of the book so that the reader will have a clear understanding of what I mean by the term's bourgeoisie, proletariat, petty-bourgeoisie, monopoly capitalism, and imperialism. My hope is that this chapter stimulates an interest in Marxist class analysis and that the reader perceives its importance in socialist political organising.

Chapters four and five will engage with volumes one and two of Marx's *Capital* in order to demonstrate how the categories of commodity, profit, and surplus-value can be used to analyse the service and retail industry. The goal of these chapters is to contend with the commonly held belief that only workers who produce physical goods are productive workers. Following David Harvey, I will argue that surplus-value is not a thing, but a social relation, and that a worker is productive if the capital-relation is present. This will help us to see how domestic cleaners, outsourced maintenance workers, and computer programmers produce commodities containing surplus-value. What I will show, however, is that the form that service workers produce surplus-value is significantly different from industrial proletarians who produce physical goods. Chapter five will focus on volume two of Marx's *Capital*, and show how Marx's categories of circulation time, costs of circulation, working period, working time, and turnover are helpful for theorising the retail industry. I will produce a set of new but related categories—consumption time and consumption period—which are designed to analyse labour processes that are related to consumption, such as computer programming and maintenance work.

The sixth and seventh chapter will introduce the reader to the Marxist theory of monopoly capitalism through the work of Paul Sweezy and Paul Baran. Although Marx grasped the tendency for capital to become concentrated in volume three of *Capital*, he lived in a time when monopoly capital only existed in an embryonic form. Following Braverman, I will show that the growth of the service and retail industry is the product of the growth of monopoly capitalism. Chapter six will also introduce the reader to the Marxist theory of imperialism through the work of Lenin, Harry Magdoff, Intan Suwandi, Samir Amin, and John Smith. The theory of imperialism is particularly important when analysing the retail industry, as retail employees usually help sell commodities for multinational companies. In order to articulate the position of retail employees in the international division of labour, I will construct a two-stage, transnational model in chapter seven. The first stage is located primarily in the peripheral nations of the global South and is where most physical goods are produced. Stage two is located primarily in the imperialist centres and is where commodities are sold. This model will demonstrate how retail workers in the imperialist countries are related to workers in the developing nations through the products they sell. My goal here is to help the reader visualise the imperialist chain in order to properly position a worker within it and reveal the relationships between links in the chain. Its purpose is to construct a model that can be effective in creating international proletarian solidarity by uniting workers across the supply chain.

Chapter eight will provide a Marxist analysis of outsourcing as it operates within the imperialist centres. Whereas John Smith has analysed outsourcing in peripheral nations, my goal will be to explore the outsourcing of unprofitable maintenance tasks to large corporations in the capitalist centres. I will define outsourcing as the capitalist transformation of unproductive tasks into productive labour that result in surplus-value and new sites for capital investment. This chapter will offer a case study of the outsourcing company, Bidvest-Noonan, which specialises in a variety of outsourced services such as security, administration, cleaning, and recycling. Chapter nine will shift the focus from outsourcing to service companies that specialise in the production of service-goods. Because cleaning is representative of this process, I will provide a case study of the domestic housekeeping company, Molly Maid. This chapter will explore not just the domestic cleaner, but also the franchisee, who I view as a member of the petty-bourgeoisie.

In chapter ten, I will examine ways that service and retail workers have organised themselves against their employers. I will argue that because their position in the division of labour differs from manufacturing workers, the tactics to organise service workers will differ as well. This chapter will offer a brief case study of a campaign by trade unionists in Germany to organise workers at H&M. The study is interesting because it shows how anti-imperialism can be used to empower retail employees to organise themselves. The chapter will also discuss SEIU-led Justice for Janitors campaign, which reveals a great deal about how to organise precarious workers. This is one of the few campaigns that has produced new organising tactics for uniting and empowering workers in the era of neoliberalism.

In the final chapter, I will examine service and retail labour in socialist social formations that have gone beyond capitalism. The chapter will introduce the reader to the Marxist theory of socialism, building heavily on the work of Albert Szymanski, Roger Keeran, Thomas Kenny, Paul Baran, Clive Thomas, Paul Sweezy, Kirsten Ghodsee, and Victor Grossman. I will show how an exploration of socialism as it existed in the former Soviet Union, the Polish People's Republic, and the German Democratic Republic can reveal what service labour might be like under socialism. I want to show how socialism can transform the nature of service and retail worker in order to offer a compelling argument for socialist revolution.

This book is designed to provide a systematic Marxist account of the service and retail industry. My hope is that it makes a small contribution to socialist organising and helps open a space for further debate. As the theorist Louis Althusser often pointed out, the function of historical materialism is to produce knowledge of capitalist social formations. This knowledge is not solely for intellectual purposes, but to give us insight into the structures of social life so that we can transform them. Marx's *Capital*, for example, was written to give working people a clear understanding of the structures and tendencies of the capitalist system. Using this knowledge, they could critically evaluate capitalism, identifying its principal contradiction and main social forms. With this critical intervention, working people can begin to envision an alternative to capitalism. Because the service industry accounts for the employment of millions of people, it is vital that we use Marxist theory to produce knowledge of it. The point of this book is therefore not simply to interpret the service industry using Marxist theory, but to open up possibilities for how we might change it.

CHAPTER 2

Historical Materialism

1 Method of Historical Materialism

Throughout this book, I will be using the method of historical materialism to conduct my research into the service and retail industry. As there are a variety of approaches to historical materialism, I need to clarify how I understand it and why I intend to utilise it as my methodology. In this chapter, I will discuss the basic concepts of historical materialism and show how I will be using it.

The founders of historical materialism were Marx and Engels, who first used the term in the *German Ideology*. Neither of them provided a detailed exposition of the method, but rather put historical materialism into practice to produce their major works. A historical materialist approach can be found in Marx's *Capital* and Lenin's *The Development of Capitalism in Russia*. Engels' book, *The Origin of the Family, Private Property, and the State* used historical materialism to examine the origins of patriarchy and women's oppression, as well as the nature of the state.

One of the foundational concepts of historical materialism is 'mode of production', which is the method by which people produce their goods and distribute them to society. Marx identifies five modes of production: primitive communalism, ancient slavery, feudalism, capitalism, and socialism. The first of them, primitive communalism, is marked by a low level of technological development combined with egalitarian ownership and distribution. Ancient slave societies, feudalism, and capitalism are societies divided into classes, in which a dominant class appropriates the surplus produced by the working population. Socialism is a transitional mode of production, in which the working class holds state power and plans production in order to meet the needs of society. While there are still class divisions under socialism, its goal is to gradually abolish class divisions and transition to communism, which is classless and stateless.

Historical materialism studies societies through a scientific examination of their mode(s) of production. It utilises four key concepts that make such a study possible: productive forces, relations of production, class struggle, and social formation. The productive forces are the means of production that a society uses to produce goods and services. Although science is not a directly productive force, it plays an important role in transforming the means of production through the introduction of new technology. A correlate to the

 | DOI:10.1163/9789004469624_003

productive forces is the relations of production, which are the social relations that structure the production process. These include the division of society into classes, but also forms of social inequality such as racism and misogyny. Relations of production do not autonomously arise but are conditioned by the level of development of the productive forces. In the *Poverty of Philosophy*, Marx discusses the relationship between the relations of production and the productive forces, saying that

> social relations are closely bound up with productive forces. In acquiring new productive forces men change their mode of production; and in changing their mode of production, in changing the way of earning their living, they change all their social relations.[1]

Each new scientific advance produces new personifications of economic categories. Marx says that, "The hand-mill gives you society with the feudal lord; the steam-mill, society with the industrial capitalist."[2] It is only when there is a steam mill that an industrial capitalist emerges who owns it and exploits the labour-power of the workers who work in the mill. With each transformation of the productive forces, there are new corresponding economic personifications, and hence changes to the relations of production. At a certain stage, the relations of production come into conflict with the productive forces and no longer correspond to it. When this happens, there is the chance that a revolutionary situation might develop, although it is no way guaranteed.

Historical materialism "studies production relations in their interaction with the productive forces ... the productive forces and the production relations as a unity constitute the mode of production."[3] Productive forces and relations of production are therefore always studied in relation to each other and how they interact. Marx points out in the *Poverty of Philosophy* that "The production relations of every society form a whole."[4] The goal of historical materialism is to connect the production relations of a social formation in order to gain knowledge of the totality. Historical materialism gives one the ability to draw important connections between phenomena that may appear disconnected on the surface. Referring to Marxist value-theory, Alfredo Saad-Filho points out that Marx's historical materialist approach

1 Marx 1847 [1955], chapter 2.
2 *Ibid.*
3 Economics Institute of the Academy of Sciences of the USSR, 1957
4 Marx 1847 [1955].

> can help the reader identify *connections* between aspects of reality that other theories tend to analyse separately. Using value theory, it becomes easier to see systemic relationships across history and between and within societies. [5]

For example, the oppression of racial minorities may appear *only* as an issue of racist social structures and chauvinistic attitudes. A historical materialist would acknowledge that racist politicians and legislators create laws that discriminate against people of colour and national minorities. Most Marxists would agree with the work of race theorists, such as Michelle Alexander's *the New Jim Crow*. What a historical materialist adds are additional questions that connect the source of racism to a society's mode of production. Marxism tries to demonstrate how racism arose with the emergence of capitalism, and how a racist ideology serves the interests of the capitalist class. Historical materialism would point to capitalism's colonial and imperialist history, which has resulted in oppressed nations that are subjugated to the imperialist centres. As Lenin shows in multiple works, imperialism produces national chauvinistic ideas and beliefs, which accelerate the oppression of national and racial minorities.

Historical materialism theorises the relationship between a society's mode of production and the superstructure that is built upon it. Phenomena such as racism, misogyny, national chauvinism, and other oppressive structures are superstructural. This does not mean that they are just a reflection of the mode of production or that we can ignore them. They have a concrete, objective existence in a social formation, and must be addressed by Marxist theory. Historical materialism only adds an additional layer to existing theory by pointing to the mode of production as an important element.

One of the theorists after Marx and Engels to produce significant theoretical work on historical materialism was Louis Althusser. He argues that the superstructure, though determined by the economic mode of production, has its own autonomous structures (which he calls 'relative autonomy').[6] This means that systemic racism or sexism can operate in a structural way and develop their own tendencies independently of the mode of production that produced it. Historical materialism places great value on mass movements that confront racism and patriarchy even if they do not overtly confront the capitalist class. These movements combat the bourgeoisie in a mediated way by confronting

5 Saad-Filho 2019, p. 2.

6 See appendix two in Althusser (2014) for a discussion on the relative autonomy of the superstructure.

one of its superstructural forms. For example, the Black Lives Matter movement in the United States confronts capital through its struggle against police brutality and the racist power-structure that sustains it. Such movements are not just 'reformist', for they seek to overturn a superstructural form created by the capitalist class. It is not surprising that some black nationalists, such as Amiri Baraka and Kwame Ture later became communists, for their confrontation with racist power structures revealed the deeper class contradictions in which they found themselves. It is also not surprising that many young people engaged in the BLM movement are turning to Marxism to broaden their political vision. Historical materialism is thus not reductive, as is sometimes claimed, but is sensitive to the multiplicity of contradictions that structure the social horizon.

2 Mode of Production and Social Formation

Another important concept of historical materialism is the notion of 'social formation'. Whereas 'mode of production' is a *general* concept, 'social formation' defines the particular form in which a mode of production exists. A pure mode of production does not exist, for it must be articulated within a historically mediated social formation. When we analyse a capitalist social formation, we assume the basic knowledge acquired through Marx's *Capital*, as well as other Marxist economists. However, studying a social formation includes additional elements, such as the composition of the class structure, occupational shifts, gender and race relations, consumerism, and other historical peculiarities. Social formation analysis explores "the specific ways in which different forms of capitalist relations are combined within a given society."[7]

One can study a mode of production in abstraction from a social formation in order to gain knowledge of its basic structure and tendencies. Marx's *Capital* is a historical materialist analysis of the capitalist mode of production (CMP), whose purpose is to disclose the inner laws and tendencies of the CMP. This is a highly abstract level of analysis, which abstracts from the concrete social formation in which the CMP is operative in order to analyse the basic elements of capitalism. Throughout *Capital*, Marx abstracts from secondary, accidental, and contingent factors of the CMP in order to examine its *general* structure. This often involves making certain assumptions, such as the presupposition that commodities are sold at their value, or that supply and demand are in

7 Wright 1985, p. 11.

equilibrium. The purpose of these assumptions is to disclose the inner laws of the CMP without having to analyse its external manifestations.

In his monumental study of social classes, Erik Olin Wright provides a helpful analogy from chemistry for understanding the difference between a mode of production and social formation. He says,

> In the scientific study of the chemistry of a lake, the highest level of abstraction involves specifying the particular way that the basic elements that go into making water, hydrogen and oxygen, combine to make water, H2o. The study of the different forms of water—ice, liquid water, evaporation, etc.—would all be at this most abstract level. The middle level of abstraction corresponding to social formation analysis involves investigating the ways in which this compound, H2o, interacts with other compounds in lakes.[8]

The study of a mode of production is thus a highly abstract level of analysis, which is necessary for gaining knowledge of the basic structure of capitalism. Social formation analysis is more concrete, as it examines how the elements of a mode of production exist within a particular historical situation. Some Marxists, such as Althusser, include a third level of analysis with the concept of conjuncture, which explores the concrete effects of combining a mode of production and a social formation. According to Althusser, social formation is a general concept defining a particular stage of a mode of production, such as 'competitive capitalism', 'monopoly capitalism', and 'neoliberalism'. Conjuncture names a particular social formation, such as 'American capitalism', 'really-existing socialism', and 'European imperialism'. Although the distinction between social formation and conjuncture is helpful, it can create confusion and misunderstanding. In order to avoid this, I will use the concept 'social formation' to refer to the historical articulation of a mode of production within a particular historical situation. Much of what Althusser includes under the concept of 'conjuncture' I will include as part of social formation analysis.

This book is mainly concerned with examining how monopoly capitalism and neoliberalism have expanded the service sector and thereby transformed the capitalist mode of production. It is an exploration of how service workers have been transformed into productive workers that directly produce surplus value. Also, it seeks to define the importance of the retail sector, which has come to occupy a central position in the era of monopoly capitalism. This book

8 Wright, 1985, p. 12.

is mainly concerned with how the capitalist mode of production has been articulated within contemporary capitalist social formations. Although some of my analysis will involve making abstractions similar to those in *Capital*, I am operating on a level of theory that is sensitive to the particularities of neoliberalism and monopoly capitalism. At the same time, I seek to examine the abstract features of the labour-process of service workers, irrespective of the social formation in which they find themselves.

One additional point that is important to social formation analysis is the theory of the multiple modes of production. In his *Reproduction of Capitalism*, Althusser argues that every social formation is characterised by multiple modes of production that are in an antagonistic relationship to each other. One mode of production is always dominant and exercises a dissolution effect over the others. In a capitalist social formation, the capitalist mode of production is dominant, but it is not the only method of production. Modes of production that predate capitalism can and often do coexist within a capitalist social formation. They exist in an antagonistic relationship to capitalism because the CMP is constantly threatening their existence. Also, non-capitalist modes of production, such as traditional handicraft work, crofting, and sharecropping assume a unique form within a capitalist social formation. A capitalist social formation is one where the capitalist mode of production is dominant, and where pre-capitalist modes of production such as feudalism are either dissolved or assume a new form under the dominance of the capitalist mode of production. For example, the form in which feudalism exists under the dominance of the capitalist mode of production is petty-bourgeois small-scale commodity production, which is constantly declining as capitalism develops. With the further development of capitalism, some pre-capitalist modes of production will be displaced and disappear, while others will struggle to survive.

I found Althusser's insight helpful in articulating the process by which the service industry develops in the era of monopoly capitalism. As I will show, many service jobs have only recently come to be conducted on a capitalist basis, and some continue to survive in their pre-capitalist form. Cleaning work, for example, was traditionally conducted on a non-capitalist basis by self-employed people with small cleaning firms. The rise of commercial cleaning companies transforms non-capitalist cleaning work into a profitable capitalist business and threatens the existence of small, private cleaners. Interestingly, this is directly reflected in the adverts of companies like Molly Maid, who constantly compare themselves to private cleaners, their main form of competition. The theory of multiple modes of production is helpful as a tool to explore these processes within capitalist social formations.

Although pre-capitalist modes of production can exist within a capitalist social formation, it is also possible that socialism exists in an embryonic form. Socialism is unable to fully develop in a capitalist social formation because the capitalist mode of production dominates its structure. An example of this is the National Health Service in Britain, which in Scotland is free at the point of use and centrally managed by the UK government. Because the NHS has to operate in a capitalist social formation, its potential is significantly hindered. It must still interact with capitalist pharmaceutical companies and is vulnerable to being underfunded. A socialist revolution that puts the working class in command of the British state and transforms society would fully unleash the potential of the NHS. The fact that socialism can exist within a capitalist social formation is important because it can allow socialists to demand the expansion of socialism. Institutions like the NHS in Britain can become key sites of political struggle, as they point to the possibility of non-capitalist, non-commodified modes of production.

3 Historical Materialist Research

Historical materialism allows us to gain knowledge of how a mode of production is articulated within a concrete social formation. It allows us to study modes of production abstractly in order to gain knowledge of its basic tendencies, social forms, and contradictions. As Erik Olin Wright points out in *Class, Crisis, and the State*, the concepts of historical materialism and Marxist economics—mode of production, social formation, productive forces, relations of production, surplus-value, etc.—are not just descriptive categories.[9] Historical materialism is a tool that can be used to conduct research and gain knowledge about our social formation. Although its categories and concepts involve abstractions, they are empirically verifiable and have an objective existence in social reality. In this book, I will be using historical materialism and Marxist economics to deconstruct empirical and statistical material on the service industry. I will here discuss what data I used and how I analysed it.

One of the richest sources of information on the capitalist class is the UK government website Companies House, which publishes detailed financial information on most large corporations operating in Britain. The online register was formed in accordance with the Companies Act of 2006, which requires companies to publish their annual accounts, listing their annual expenditures,

9 Wright 1978, pp. 12–14.

revenues, and profits. An interesting feature of a company account is the opening section where the board of directors discuss what they perceive as their company's main risks and concerns. This gives us very revealing information into the vulnerabilities and weaknesses of the bourgeoisie, as well their business strategy. One can spend hours sifting through company accounts of large companies to gather valuable information about a corporation. In my case studies of Bidvest-Noonan and Molly Maid, I will use the statement of economic risk as an indication of why these corporations utilise a particular class strategy over another and demonstrate how the working class can exploit these weaknesses in an organising campaign.

Company accounts also supply data that can be used to calculate the primary Marxist economic variables: constant capital, variable capital, surplus-value, the rate of surplus-value, and the rate of profit. In his *Accounting for Value in Marx's Capital*, Robert Bryer points out that Marx himself used company accounts to deduce these variables. Bryer points out that

> Marx used his theory of value to explain accountants' principles and practices, the foundation of his explanation of capitalism as a system of social control, how the law of value "asserts itself," through markets, but also through its system of accounting control.[10]

As companies did not reveal their balance sheets in his time, Marx was largely dependent on Engels, who used data from his father's business to conduct his analyses. His information was very limited, and he was often forced to use imaginary figures in order to make his analyses, especially in Volume 3 of *Capital*. This does not mean his discoveries were false, but only that he lacked the data to go beyond a logical analysis. Marx, sitting in the British Library writing *Capital*, would have been impressed by Companies House and probably would have spent a lot of time researching company accounts.

Investors, bankers, and corporate CEOs are usually the people who read company accounts, which they use to assess the performance of a corporation. A Marxist who studies a company account approaches it with different concerns than a member of the capitalist class. The purpose is to gain empirical figures for a particular company in order to calculate the mass and rate of surplus-value, as well as the rate of profit. The goal is not to get exact figures, but rather a general picture of the level of exploitation and the class strategies used by a particular corporation. One does not need to be professionally

10 Bryer 2017, p. 28.

trained as an accountant to deduce the variables of Marxist economics from a company account. Rather, one needs to translate the categories used by capitalist accountants into Marxist economics. This is not difficult to do and only requires an understanding of Marxist economic concepts. A company's financial statements are usually standardised, and it is easy to read them once one has gotten beyond the jargon.

When reading a financial statement, one must first locate the monetary value of the constant capital, as this is the first variable in the formulas for the rates of surplus-value and profit. As Marx shows in *Capital*, constant capital is the means of production, which includes machinery, plant equipment, raw materials, and other tools that are used in the production process. A part of it is fixed capital, which is used in multiple business cycles until it expires, and includes things like a factory, machinery, vacuum cleaners, and vehicles. The other part is circulating capital, which is used up in a single business cycle, and includes things like cotton, fuel, and cleaning fluids. In company accounts, constant capital is listed as 'non-current assets' or 'tangible assets'. A tangible, non-current asset is viewed by a business as a long-term investment, which they intend to use for productive purposes rather than sell.

A Marxist theorist must use judgement to decide whether a particular tangible or non-current asset belongs to the category of 'constant capital'. Financial accounts include information in tangible and non-current assets that do *not* correspond to constant capital. In most cases, financial statements will list under tangible and non-current assets: 'property, plant, and equipment', 'investment in subsidiaries', 'goodwill', and 'deferred tax assets'. The first, 'property, plant, and equipment' is identical to constant capital, but 'deferred tax assets' and 'investment in subsidiaries' will correspond to other elements that are not relevant when calculating constant capital. Some might consider including 'goodwill' as part of constant capital. Goodwill includes things like a company's investment in marketing, branding, and advertising. It is also referred to as 'intangible capital' because it is not material, but an integral part of the production process.

Marx probably would not have included intangible assets such as goodwill into the category of constant capital. During his time, capitalists did not invest significant capital into advertising, marketing, or product design. The value of these intangible assets would have been low and would have been viewed as unproductive expenditures necessary to the circulation of commodities. Sweezy and Baran show in their work, *Monopoly Capital* that the sales effort takes on a greater importance in the era of monopoly capitalism than in Marx's time. Advertising, marketing, and product design are directly incorporated into the production process and are necessary to engage in capitalist production. Especially in the service industry, in which the stimulation of demand takes place before production, advertising becomes a directly productive force. I would therefore argue that some of a company's intangible assets can correspond to constant capital.

Once one has identified the constant capital in a company account, one can proceed to locate the variable capital, which is the second element needed to calculate the rate of surplus value and profit. For Marx, variable capital is not equivalent to total labour costs, but only the cost of productive labour that produces surplus-value. Using company accounts to find this information can be challenging because they generally include the total labour costs, and even include the salaries of top management. Sometimes it will not be possible to use a company account to identify variable capital, and one will have to use rough estimates rather than precise figures. If this information is not available in the company account, one can find out what the average wage is of its productive employees. This number can then be multiplied by the total number of productive workers employed by the enterprise, which is usually listed in the financial statement. With this number, one then only needs to subtract it from the total labour costs to arrive at an estimate of the variable capital.

Another way to estimate variable capital costs is to examine how many employees in the company have managerial or administrative jobs. If this information is available, it is necessary to estimate their yearly salary. Although salaries are usually not public, one can look through job adverts to get a rough figure. Once a rough yearly salary has been identified, this number should be multiplied by the number of managerial and administrative employees, and then subtracted from the total labour costs in the company account. When this procedure has been followed, the remaining amount is the variable capital.

In addition to the constant and variable capital, company accounts provide information on the total value of goods and services produced. For companies that sell multiple products and services, they will sometimes list the value produced in each sector. This information is generally in the section that lists 'revenue' in the financial report. If one finds this information, one will have attained the three figures needed to calculate the mass of surplus-value, the rate of surplus-value, and the rate of profit.

As Marx shows in *Capital*, one can calculate the surplus-value by subtracting the cost of variable capital from the total value produced. Although the company account will not give an exact figure, it provides information to give a rough estimate of the mass of surplus-value produced by the workers. Using Marx's formula S/V, dividing surplus-value by variable capital, one can calculate the rate of surplus-value. Furthermore, one can divide the surplus-value by the total capital, S/C+V, in order to calculate the rate of profit.

Some might say that this method is problematic because it is impossible to get exact figures from a company account. It is true that the information will be an estimate, but a company account will still be able to give us a fairly accurate picture of the level of exploitation in the business. We do not need perfectly exact figures to make these calculations, as our aim is to get a sense of how the process of value production takes place and the degree of exploitation happening in a company. With a value calculation, changing any of the variables by a few thousand or even million will not have a significant impact on the result. For example, if we calculate that a company invests £10mn into labour, it will not make a huge difference on our calculation if this figure is actually £5mn or £15mn in actual practice. Neither the rate of profit nor the rate of exploitation will be significantly impacted by such differences, and therefore estimates are appropriate.

In *Capital*, Marx was not trying to help the capitalist class make decisions about the future of their business, but to reveal mathematically the composition of value. His equations are helpful because they can be used to show how wage increases or decreases affect the rate of exploitation. If we compare company accounts over a period of time, we can observe changes to the rate of profit, which tends to fall overtime in capital intensive industries. Therefore, it is perfectly legitimate to use company accounts to conduct value calculations *for the purposes* of historical materialist research. We can compare the findings of a company account with other sources of data, such as statistics on wages, profits, revenue, etc., gathered by financial institutions and trade unions. Studying company accounts should be a part of every historical materialist investigation and should become an integral part in the training of Marxist political economy. In this book, I will be using the above method to analyse company accounts, which may sound boring and uninteresting, but is actually extremely illustrative. My hope is that other Marxist theorists use company accounts as a way to gain empirical insight into the capitalist labour process.

One of the foundational techniques of historical materialism is class analysis. The centrality of class in historical materialism is what distinguishes it from non-Marxist theories such as structuralism. Marxism does not just point out how society is divided into classes but shows that social relations are organised according to a society's class structure. Because class analysis is foundational to historical materialism, I will devote the entire next chapter to an analysis of the class structure of contemporary capitalism.

CHAPTER 3

Marxism, Class and the Service Industry

1 Marxist Class Analysis

Class analysis has always played a prominent role in historical materialist research. Marxism identifies the major classes and the forms of struggle between them in order to reveal the class dynamics operative in a social formation. This knowledge can be used to formulate a socialist strategy that advances the long-term interests of the working class and its allies. What distinguishes a Marxist socialist strategy from other political tendencies is that it is scientific. The class categories used in historical materialist research are not just descriptive categories, but empirically verifiable realities in the material world.[1] They can be used to disclose real tendencies in the social structure, identify objective contradictions in a social formation, and formulate a strategy based on the real material conditions of society. Marxist class analysis thus aspires to be scientific and bases its formulations on evidence and facts, rather than ideas and descriptions.

A Marxist class analysis will be of interest to many different people: socialists, trade unionists, workers, researchers, feminists, and anti-racist activists. Trade unions often conduct a high level of research before launching a campaign or calling a strike. They research things like income levels, the structure of management, the grievances of their members, gender/racial discrimination, and occupationally specific problems. Often, trade unions view class in terms of occupation, income, or power, which guides their research and affects the way they formulate their demands. Generally, they are able to clearly identify the *phenomenal* forms of social class but lack a grasp of the class *structure* of capitalism. This is because they use non-Marxist definitions of class, which guides their research and organises the way that they interpret data. Income inequality and precarious employment, for example, are ways that the working class *experience* its class-belonging. Struggling for a higher wage or better employment conditions is an important way that working people can learn about their capabilities as a class. Every victory of the working class puts them in a better position against capital, and therefore improving the immediate

1 See Wright (1985) for a discussion of how Marxist class categories are empirically verifiable, as well as a method for strengthening historical materialism's ability to conduct empirical research.

 | DOI:10.1163/9789004469624_004

material conditions of working people is important. Trade unionists can benefit from historical materialism because it allows them to go *beyond* the phenomenal forms of class, to scientific knowledge of its structure. Through a Marxist class analysis, trade unions can improve their research in order to become important vehicles of proletarian politics.

As I argued in the previous chapter Marxism is not class reductionist. There have been Marxist writers who have made the mistake of reducing everything to class, and fail to properly analyse racial and national oppression, sexism, and homophobia. This was often the case in orthodox Marxist-Leninist organisations, such as the Revolutionary Communist Party, which refused to support the gay liberation movement and denounced feminism as bourgeois.[2] Unfortunately, these groups have given Marxist class analysis a somewhat bad name, and it has now become an accepted view that Marxism is 'class reductionist'. This has made some feminists, anti-racist activists, and gay liberationists suspicious of Marxism. Instead of a scientific historical materialist analysis, progressive activists have often adopted purely descriptive categories from intersectional theory. Their motivations are justified, for intersectional theory is sensitive to the multiple ways that people experience oppression under capitalism. Some of their observations and analyses are helpful, such as Patricia Hills Collins *Black Feminist Thought*. However, a genuine Marxist analysis of class structure is capable of being just as sensitive as intersectional theory while providing a broader theoretical framework. Because many feminists and anti-racist activists have abandoned Marxism, they have often formulated social conflicts through *liberal* categories such as privilege, and reduced class to a mere identity. Class has disappeared from their analysis and becomes a marker of one's identity within a racial, ethnic, national, or gender group. The result is often a highly subjective focus that utilises personal narratives, accounts of one's privileges, and how one experiences oppression. In principle, there is nothing wrong with this, as autobiography is an important component of building group solidarity and unity of the people. Some of the most moving socialist books were written in the form of autobiography, such as Trotsky's *My Life* and Harry Haywood's *Black Bolshevik*. Marxist class analysis can bring additional layers of depth to this and demonstrate the structural tendencies that operate through our autobiographies. It can show how our subjective experiences are the results of objective structures, which we can transform through collective

2 For an overview, see Max Elbaum's *Revolution in the Air*. He discusses the ways that New Communist Organisations often reduced social conflicts to class, and thereby became hostile to non-proletarian movements.

interventions and the intensification of class struggle. Hence, Marxist class analysis will be of interest to anti-racist and feminist activists, in addition to trade unionists and communists. It is not 'class reductionist', but sensitive to the way that the class structure operates through multiple oppressions such as racism and sexism. In order to demonstrate this, I will begin with a discussion of the Marxist definition of class as formulated by Lenin and Poulantzas. After this, I will examine the primary classes in a capitalist social formation and the tendencies that they exhibit. My hope is that this chapter generates an appreciation for Marxist class analysis, especially by anti-racist activists and feminists.

2 Marxist Definition of Class

In an article titled, 'The Great Beginning', Lenin offers a very helpful definition of social classes, which contains the generality needed for defining class. Lenin says that classes are

> large groups of people which differ from each other by the place they occupy in a historically determined system of social production, by their relation (in most cases fixed and formulated by law) to the means of production, by their role in the social organization of labor, and, consequently, by the mode of acquisition and the dimensions of the share of social wealth of which they dispose. Classes are groups of people one of which can appropriate the labor of another owing to the different places they occupy in a definite system of social economy.[3]

This definition is helpful because it identifies the primary features of the Marxist definition of social class. Class is defined by the relationship that one has to the means of production, which includes raw materials, machinery and equipment, logistical systems, and anything else needed to engage in productive labour. Some classes, such as landlords and capitalists, own the means of production and appropriate the economic surplus produced by peasants and workers. Others, such as the working class, are separated from the means of production, produce an economic surplus, and have no legal title to the products of their labour. There are also classes that own their own means of production but lack the means to exploit the labour of others

3 Lenin 1919

(i.e., the petty-bourgeoisie). In every mode of production, there are usually two primary classes that exist in an antagonistic relationship to each other. This antagonistic relationship is determined by the objective needs of the dominant class, which involves the appropriation of the surplus produced by the exploited class.

In his *Classes in Contemporary Capitalism*, Nicos Poulantzas provides a definition of classes that demonstrates the structural nature of classes. He says that classes are

> groupings of social agents, defined principally but not exclusively by their place in the production process, i.e. in the economic sphere. The economic place of the social agents has a principal role in determining social classes.[4]

Poulantzas explains that class places are structural and exist objectively, although they assume a particular form in a social formation. When we analyse a mode of production, we can identify the main places through which classes will be reproduced. These class places identify the exploiting class and the exploited class, as well as non-exploiting classes, which must align themselves with either the exploiting or exploited class. In a capitalist mode of production, the place occupied by the bourgeoisie allows them to exploit the labour of the working class by appropriating the products of their labour. On the other hand, the place occupied by the working class excludes them from the means of exploitation and thereby forces them into a relationship of exploitation with the bourgeoisie. The petty-bourgeoisie does not exploit labour-power but is forced to align itself either with the working class or the bourgeoisie. What the notion of a class place makes possible is an understanding of the *structural* dynamics of class struggle in a capitalist mode of production. If one only explains class by one's relationship to the means of production, one will miss the complex dynamic of social reproduction of class places. It is because one occupies a *class place* that one will have a relationship to the means of production. This relationship is a *deduction* from the concept of *class places*, and therefore must be included in a definition of class in order to perceive its essential features.

4 Poulantzas 1978, p. 14.

3 Two Approaches to Class Analysis

The distinction between mode of production and social formation results in two different approaches to class analysis. When we analyse how classes operate in a mode of production, we are concerned with the structural elements of classes independently of the historical specificities in which the class structure is operative. When we analyse the main classes of a capitalist mode of production, we abstract from the particular capitalist social formation in which these classes exist. Instead, we can analyse classes more generally as they operate within *any* capitalist mode of production irrespective of its historical particularity. This does not mean we take an a-historical approach to class analysis, for we still have to account for the historical specificity of the classes in a capitalist mode of production. Classes—such as the bourgeoisie and the proletariat—do not always exist, but only within a historically determinate capitalist mode of production. When we analyse the bourgeoisie and the proletariat, we therefore still have to account for the *historical* conditions that give birth to them. Furthermore, we can analyse the historical progression of the capitalist mode of production by distinguishing distinct stages, such as mercantilism, competitive capitalism, monopoly capitalism, etc. Each of these stages contain their own specific class forces, which will operate in unique ways depending on the social formation. For example, in the stage of monopoly capitalism, the bourgeoisie is divided into monopoly and non-monopoly sectors. The monopoly bourgeoisie exercises a *dominant* role, while the non-monopoly bourgeoisie is *dominated* by the monopolies. It is necessary to analyse the *main* elements of the bourgeoisie in order to perceive their essential features in the stage of monopoly capitalism. Hence, when we analyse the pure capitalist mode of production, we only abstract from the *specific* capitalist social formation and therefore operate on a high level of generality. We will then perceive how the historical conditions that give rise to a capitalist class structure operates in every capitalist social formation, irrespective of its specific particularities.

When we analyse a capitalist social formation, our analysis will begin with an *a priori* assumption of a *general* capitalist class structure. The analysis will demonstrate how a mode of production operates within a *historically* singular social formation. As Poulantzas says,

> A social formation is the locus of existence of an articulation of several modes and forms of production. This is expressed: (a) in the existence within a social formation of other classes besides the two classes based on the dominant mode of production, classes which derive from other

> modes and forms of production present in that formation; (b) in the effects of class decomposition and restructuring of the over- and under-determination of class, i.e. by effects of the articulation of these modes and forms of production on the classes which derive from them in a social formation.[5]

A multiplicity of factors will be brought into the analysis that go *beyond* the elements of a pure capitalist mode of production. These factors are the relationship between classes and the state, the effects of foreign policy on the accumulation of capital, the *social* definition of the value of labour-power, trade union organisation, and tax policy. It is not necessary to include these factors when we produce an analysis of the capitalist mode of production because they do not tell us anything about its *structural* operations. They become necessary when we want to analyse how the class struggle in a social formation directly affects the laws and tendencies of a mode of production. These elements create the social horizon in which the class struggle unfolds, but the class struggle can itself intervene to transform these laws.

A social formation is the unique product of a system of accumulation, which organises social classes through the mediation of capitalist institutions, which include the state, transnational corporations, and international organisations such as the IMF. These institutions play an important role in determining the forms of capital ownership, the relations between finance capital and industry, and the scope of possibilities for working class political action. Although a capitalist social formation contains the structural features of a capitalist mode of production (CMP), it articulates the unique historical existence of the CMP. The product of this historical articulation is the emergence of a unique class structure, which is specific to the historical conditions in which this class structure emerged.

4 Main Classes of Capitalist Mode of Production

Analysing this class structure does not involve simply highlighting the forms of ownership in a capitalist conjuncture. Although this is an integral part of historical materialist analysis, we must also demonstrate the relationship between the class structure and the state in order to perceive how state institutions have distributed social subjects to places within the class structure.

5 Poulantzas 1978, pp. 199–200.

Furthermore, we must be sensitive to the way that the system of accumulation (SoA) puts pressure of the state to enact policies and create institutions that are compatible with the dominant SoA.[6] These policies and the institutions that sustain them play a very important role in the historical articulation of the CMP and its organisation of the class structure. Generally, these pressures are made by the ruling class, but are enforced through the dominant fraction of capital and their organisations. International capitalist organisations such as the IMF and the World Bank, for example, play an important role in pressuring capitalist states to enact neoliberal policies and create state institutions to enact them. As a result of this, the system of accumulation is an important concept of Marxist class analysis, for it helps us to understand the particular ways that the CMP has been articulated within a social formation. This historical articulation determines the form of classes within a conjuncture, which has no existence apart from this historical process.

Using social-formation analysis also allows us to analyse the fractions of each social class. A fraction of a class is a subcategory of a social class, which has a *different* role than other fractions in the process of social production. In each social formation, a fraction of the ruling class is the dominant fraction, which effects all the other fractions. In a capitalist social formation, there is only one bourgeoisie, but it has multiple fractions. The dominance of a fraction of the bourgeoisie will subordinate other fractions to it, which can have long term effects on a capitalist social formation. What unites these different fractions is a basic class unity as members of the bourgeoisie irrespective of the particular fraction that they belong to. The purpose of analysing the fractions of the bourgeoisie is to disclose contradictions within the bourgeoisie and show how these contradictions operate in a social formation. This can allow us to formulate political strategies crafted to respond to the particular political situation. This is particularly important when we analyse social phenomena such as fascism or military dictatorships, which will require a well-thought-out political response.

Marx himself was aware that the bourgeoisie is divided into different fractions: industrial capital, finance capital, commercial capital, circulation capital, and rentier capital. Each of these fractions of the bourgeoisie play an important role in the extraction of surplus value from the working class. The industrial bourgeoisie exploits the labour power of working people in order to directly appropriate surplus value from them. A commercial capitalist purchases goods *below* their market value in order to *realise* a portion of the

6 For an excellent discussion of the concept of System of Accumulation see Saad-Filho (2019)

surplus value contained in these goods. Finance capital gives the industrial capitalist a loan and then captures a portion of the surplus value through *interest*. The interest rate is directly determined by the productivity of labour and plays a role in stimulating production in order to allow banks to capture more surplus value from the workers. A landowner who rents land to the bourgeoisie will capture surplus value in the form of rent. In monopoly capitalist social formations, a fraction of the bourgeoisie will be part of monopoly capital, while other fractions will tend to be non-monopoly in character. In the era of imperialism, the world is divided into imperialist centres located in the North, and peripheral nations in the global South. Retail workers occupy the link that connects these two geographical locations and have the potential to strike significant blows at the capitalist class.

Marxist class analysis provides us with knowledge of the complexities of the social structure. It allows us to see the multiplicity of social forces and how they interact with each other. Most importantly, class analysis allows us to perceive the process of exploitation and the forms taken by the economic surplus. Every capitalist mode of production contains two primary classes, the capitalist class (bourgeoisie) and the working class (proletariat). It also contains the petty-bourgeoisie, which is a historical remainder from feudalism.

4.1 *The Working Class*

The working class are all the people who do not own the means of production and must sell their labour-power in exchange for a wage. Because they do not own the means of production, working people must work for someone else. A worker transforms their abilities into a commodity that they sell in order to earn enough money to pay their bills, gain access to leisure and entertainment, and provide goods and services for their family. A worker has no legal title to the products of their labour, as this is the property of the person for whom they work. Working people do not command the labour of others, and do not possess the ability to terminate another person's employment. While some workers may have a level of autonomy at work, all working people are managed and required to follow the rules created by management. I make this point in order to specify that separation from the means of production and wage labour are not sufficient to define the working class. A manager, even if they are at a very low level, is not part of the working class because they have the power to command the labour of others and represents the interests of management. However, they share with the working-class separation from the means of production and wage/salaried labour. In some cases, workers who are most committed to the corporation are recruited into lower-level management positions.

Being a member of the proletariat is not the result of ignorance, a lack of schooling, or bad life decisions. One does not choose to be part of the working class, and it is rare for a proletarian to become part of the capitalist class. This is because the *objective* place of the proletariat is *structural* and is reproduced through the institutions of capitalism. Those who belong to the working class may increase their income and learn new skills through education, but this increased income will not remove them from the class place that they occupy. Reforms to a capitalist social formation may improve the lives of working people, but it will not eliminate the objective place of the proletariat. The place of the proletariat reproduces the structural *exclusion* of the working class from ownership of capital, and thus their separation from the means of production. Capitalism can only function if there is a working class, for it is the source of surplus value and profit. Therefore, the *place* of the working class is inscribed into the very structure of capitalism and will exist so long as capitalism exists.

Working people are hired to do a multiplicity of jobs that valorise the profits of the capitalist class. The working class produces our food, extracts metals and minerals needed to make complex goods, manufactures electronics and cars, produces machinery, and makes clothing. Some sections of the working class directly produce surplus-value, while others help to realise it. In the era of monopoly capitalism, some service workers produce surplus value, such as cleaners employed by a commercial cleaning company. They often work for very little pay on insecure job contracts, with no guarantee of employment. Whereas cleaning work traditionally did not result in surplus-value, today's commercialisation of service work has made cleaning a productive form of labour.

In addition to producing goods, a large section of today's working class is employed in services such as transportation, logistics, and retail. Working people transport goods to storage facilities, distribution centres, and shops. Just as the workers who produced the shirts, these workers do not own the means of production and have very little control over the labour process. They work for a wage and produce far more value in services than they are compensated for. In today's capitalist social formations, large sections of the workforce are employed in the retail sector. Their job is not to produce commodities, but to help the capitalist class realise the surplus-value contained in them. Some of them work in retail shops, in which the commodities produced at an earlier stage are sold, while others produce new commodities *and* help to sell them (i.e., baristas in a coffee-shop, cooks in a restaurant, etc.).

Although most retail workers do not produce surplus-value, they are still exploited, as the capitalists give them a wage that is far smaller than the actual surplus-value that they help them realise. They can face long working hours, management bullying, and high levels of exploitation. Retail employees have the power to stop the realisation of surplus-value, and this can have an effect on the direct production of goods. This became clear during the 2020 Coronavirus crisis, in which many retail workers were classed as 'essential workers'. Although they are often undervalued, retail employees are essential to the distribution of goods and the realisation of the surplus-value contained in them. If they are properly organised, they have the ability to stop goods from being sold, which to the capitalist class is just as serious as if they were not produced.

A major argument of this book is that service and retail workers have a different relationship to the labour process than workers that produce physical goods. Because they are closer to the direct consumption of the commodity, service and retail workers have a much more immediate relationship to the consumer than workers in a factory or farm. In fact, they share with the consumer an alienation from the producers of physical goods, and an ideological attachment to the service or product that they sell. Because of this, there is a potential for an alliance between service workers and consumers in a shared struggle against the company that exploits them. Furthermore, it is possible to organise a transnational alliance between retail employees in a Northern clothing shop with garment workers in the global South. Thus, while Marxism recognises the class identity of service workers with industrial proletarians, it acknowledges that they require different organising strategies. I return to this in chapter ten of the book.

To sum things up: someone who belongs to the working class does not own the means of production, works for a wage or salary, has no legal title to the product of their labour, and does not command the labour of others. The Marxist definition of the proletariat does not say anything about the type of labour performed or income levels. It does recognise that some workers possess specialised skills or training that gives them a higher-wage, and that this can affect their political consciousness. Lenin once called the materially well-off section of the working class the 'aristocracy of labour' because they tended to oppose industrial actions and were willing to collaborate with management. Their lived experience of the capitalist labour process differs significantly from low-wage, unskilled workers on zero-hour contracts. Someone who barely earns enough to survive and is constantly bullied by management is likely to relate differently to the labour process than someone with a permanent contract and a high wage. Despite their differences, Marxism recognises that they belong to the same class. Unless trade unionists and socialists organise them, there is a chance that their immediate experience of the labour-process will prevent them from uniting with other members of their class.

In 2011, Guy Standing introduced the concept of the 'precariat', which refers to workers that lack permanent employment and have temporary or zero-hour contracts with extremely low wages. As he points out,

> the precariat is defined by short-termism, which could evolve into a mass incapacity to think long term, induced by the low probability of personal progress of building a career.[7]

Marxism would not consider the precariat a class, but a stratum of the working class. Standing's work is helpful for understanding the specific conditions faced by people with precarious employment. We must be sensitive to this, as it is integral for uniting the working class. For example, in colleges and universities, significant teaching staff work on temporary contracts as 'adjunct professors' or 'bank lecturers'. They lack the stability and permanence enjoyed by full-time staff and have very few opportunities for career advancement. It is common to hear tenured professors complain about standardised testing, classroom observations, and the curriculum, while remaining silent about the struggles of precarious part-time staff. This is detrimental to a trade union campaign because its campaigns become organised *solely* around academic freedom and higher income for full-time staff. A trade union, such as Unison or the American Federation of Teachers, must not solely make demands for full-timers, but articulate the needs of precarian temporary staff. One of the most effective ways to do this is to demand the immediate transfer to permanence of temporary employees and an end to zero-hour contracts. If the full-time lecturers who lead the union only demand higher wages, those on precarious employment contracts will not benefit, as they may not be there next semester to enjoy better pay. Only if the trade unions put the interests of the most vulnerable employees on the forefront of their agenda will they succeed in building class unity. This often requires a struggle, as trade unions are often staffed with leaders that collaborate with management and make a career by only representing the upper strata of the working class.

4.2 *The Bourgeoisie*

The other major class in a capitalist mode of production is the capitalist class, also known as the bourgeoisie. Marxism has traditionally defined the capitalist class through their ownership of the means of production and the exploitation of labour. While this definition is correct, it sometimes fails to articulate

7 Standing 2011, p. 21.

the different sections of the bourgeoisie. The way that I would like to define the bourgeoisie is as someone who owns capital used to appropriate the surplus-value produced by working people. Capitalists are the people that own factories, large farms, oil rigs, and commercial cleaning companies, and command the labour of working people on an international scale. The capitalist class also controls the process of circulation and distribution of commodities, which includes transportation of goods to distribution centres, the storing of commodities in warehouses, and logistical systems necessary for accounting and bookkeeping. Besides industrial and circulation capital, the capitalist class also includes merchant capitalists, who use merchant capital to purchase goods below their value in order to capture a portion of the surplus-value contained in them. For example, the large retail chain stores and restaurants such as WalMart, Asda, Starbucks Coffee, Nandos, and Ikea are all representative of merchant capital.

Sweezy and Baran point out in *Monopoly Capital* that in contemporary capitalism, groups of capitalists form giant corporations in which capital is centralised and heavily concentrated.[8] The monopoly bourgeoisie has control over the entire production process, from the extraction of raw materials to the sale of the commodity. A characteristic feature of monopoly capitalism is the dominance of finance capital, which is possessed by large banks such as HSBC, Chase, and ABN Amro. Lenin points out in *Imperialism: the Highest Stage of Capitalism* that

> a personal link-up, so to speak, is established between the banks and the biggest industrial and commercial enterprises, the merging of one with another through the acquisition of shares, through the appointment of bank directors to the Supervisory Boards (or Boards of Directors) of industrial and commercial enterprises, and vice versa.[9]

A CEO of a bank will sometimes sit on the board of directors of a large corporation and has the power to influence important business decisions. By charging interest, banks are able to appropriate a portion of the surplus-value produced by industrial workers. These banks control the funds of the bourgeoisie and are integrated with large multinational corporations. Through foreign direct investment and arm's length outsourcing in developing nations, the monopoly bourgeoisie is able to control the production process on an international scale.

8 Sweezy and Baran (1966).

9 Lenin 1916, chapter 3.

This splits the capitalist class into an imperialist bourgeoisie, which is centred in the imperialist nations of the global North, and a national bourgeoisie that is centred in the developing countries of the South. In the developing countries, the bourgeoisie is itself split between a comprador bourgeoisie, which is aligned with imperialism and serves its interests, and a domestic bourgeoisie, which is opposed to imperialism and seeks to make itself independent from imperialist domination.[10]

The industrial bourgeoisie own capital that allows them to employ workers in order to directly appropriate the surplus-value contained in the goods that they produce. These are capitalists that own factories, farms, and machinery, which enables them to purchase labour-power at a low-cost. Workers in their factories produce far more value in goods than they are paid for. The industrial bourgeoisie appropriates this excess of value and reinvests it in order to expand production and accumulate capital. This section of the capitalist class is adequately captured by the traditional Marxist definition of the bourgeoisie, as they own the means of production and exploit the labour-power of working people. Other sections of the bourgeoisie, such as merchant capital, own capital and thereby appropriate surplus-value, but do not directly command the production process. A commercial capitalist that primarily owns merchant capital is able to purchase goods produced by industrial proletarians at a price below their value. They are able to appropriate the surplus-value contained in these goods by selling them at a significantly higher-price. In *Volume 3* of *Capital*, Marx calls this process 'commercial profit', as it involves the appropriation of surplus-value by exploiting price differentials between nations. It is no surprise that most industrial capitalists are geographically located in the global South, while merchant capitalists are in the global North. Large capitalist retailers, such as Nike, Starbucks, and H&M are merchant capitalists that have contracts with producers in Southern nations like Bangladesh, India, and China.[11] Their ownership of merchant capital gives them access to cheap advertising, the command of markets in the imperialist centres, and the ability to sell goods significantly above their value. As is well-known, these companies do not produce anything, but outsource their production and exploit the unequal exchange that results from their geographical position in global capitalism.[12]

For the above reasons, I define the bourgeoisie as the class of people who own capital that enables them to appropriate surplus-value from the working

10 Poulantzas [1973] 2008, p. 200.

11 Suwandi 2019; Smith 2016

12 Smith 2016, pp. 146–151.

class. This capital can take many forms and is in no way limited to industrial or agrarian production. It allows us to more clearly define the capitalist class and identify them by the *place* they occupy in the extraction of surplus value. Belonging to the bourgeoisie is not a subjective identity, but an objective *place* within the social process of capitalist production. To belong to the bourgeoisie means that one has access to a capital-fund that can be used to appropriate surplus-value from the working class. Although the fractions of the bourgeoisie may have specific interests, they nonetheless are united as a class and make decisions that will benefit the interests of the entire bourgeoisie.[13] The institutions of a capitalist social formation, such as the state, the legal system, and its repressive organs are organised to ensure the social reproduction of the place of capital.

As I have now shown, the two main classes in a capitalist social formation are the proletariat and the bourgeoisie. The bourgeoisie has capital at its disposal and exploits the labour-power of working people to extract surplus value. They are "the class of the owners of the basic means of production, which lives by exploiting the hired labour of the workers"[14]. The working class is separated from the means of production and must sell its labour-power on the market in exchange for a wage. They have no autonomy and are objects of managerial control. They have a relationship to surplus value, which is either its production or realisation. As Otto Kuusinen explains,

> The creator of the colossal wealth appropriated by the bourgeoisie is the working class, the chief productive force of capitalist society. At the same time it is a class deprived of ownership of the means of production and compelled to sell its labour-power to the capitalist.[15]

It is through the separation of the worker from the means of production that labour-power becomes commodified in a capitalist mode of production. Hence,

> Two conditions are necessary for capitalist production: firstly, the concentration of the basic means of production as the private property of capitalists, and secondly, the absence of means of production among the majority, or a considerable portion of the members of society. This

13 For an excellent discussion of divisions and unity of the bourgeoisie, see Poulantzas (1978), pp. 138–151.
14 Kuusinen 1963, p. 189.
15 *ibid.* p. 153.

> compels those who possess nothing but their capacity to work to become wage workers in capitalist enterprises in order to keep starvation from their door.[16]

Only on the basis of the commodification of labour-power is it possible for the bourgeoisie to generalise the commodity form, which determines production, circulation, exchange, and distribution. Now that I have discussed the bourgeoisie and the proletariat, I will turn to a non-capitalist class that is nonetheless integral to the functioning of capitalism.

4.3 *The Petty-Bourgeoisie*

Because the capitalist mode of production must be articulated within a social formation, classes from pre-capitalist modes of production exist. Poulantzas points out that "a social formation is the locus of existence of an articulation of several modes and forms of production."[17] One of the classes from a pre-capitalist mode of production is the petty-bourgeoisie, which is the form taken by peasants, small shop owners, small-scale commodity producers in a capitalist social formation. The petty-bourgeoisie is the product of the historical articulation of the capitalist mode of production (CMP) and has a unique existence in a capitalist social formation. On the one hand, the petty-bourgeoisie is a remnant of a pre-capitalist mode of production, and its existence in a social formation reflects the fact that a conjuncture contains multiple modes of production. Even though the petty-bourgeoisie is not a class unique to capitalism, it assumes a unique form in a capitalist social formation. Its existence in a capitalist social formation is an effect "of class decomposition and restructuring of the over- and under- determination of class."[18] Although the petty-bourgeoisie exists in every capitalist social formation, there is a tendency for it to decline as a class. Its decline depends on the *particular* ways in which the capitalist mode of production exercises a dissolution effect on pre-capitalist modes of production within a concrete social formation. The existence of the petty-bourgeoisie demonstrates how the historical articulation of the capitalist mode of production creates a unique social class with its own particular determinations. As it is not a class specific to capitalism, its existence in a capitalist social formation will always be the unique product of history.

Traditional Marxism has defined the petty-bourgeoisie as the class of people that own the means of production, but do not exploit the labour-power of

16 *ibid.* p. 260.
17 Poulantzas 1978, p. 199.
18 *ibid.* p. 199.

working people. As Otto Kuusinen—one of the best representatives of traditional Marxism—says,

> These are people who have possession of small means of production, but unlike the big bourgeoisie, do not live by exploiting the labour of others. The petty bourgeois occupy an intermediary position in capitalist society. As owners of private property, they adhere to the bourgeoisie, but as representatives of the strata who live by their own labour and are exploited by the bourgeoisie, they adhere to the workers.[19]

Some sections of the petty-bourgeoisie employ workers, such as take-away restaurants, legal firms, and small independent shops. They may use capitalist management techniques, such as Taylorising the workplace in order to eliminate unnecessary labour-time. However, they do not possess capital that allows them to appropriate surplus-value, and therefore they compensate their workers out of revenue.[20] They themselves do most of the important work and gain a profit through selling their product or service slightly above its cost-price.

A defining feature of the traditional petty-bourgeoisie is the absence of a boss or manager, for their assets allow them to be their own boss. Some sections of the petty-bourgeoisie, especially those engaged in handicraft production or services (i.e., physiotherapy, cleaning, commercial painting, music, etc.), take pride in their work. What they value most is the quality of their product and the autonomy that their business gives them. Although they do consider profitability, they are more concerned with producing a high-quality product or service. They often lament the mass production of goods and services that characterise contemporary capitalism and try to produce commodities by 'putting their soul' into their product. Although the traditional petty-bourgeoisie does not have an immediate boss, this does not mean it is entirely autonomous in a capitalist social formation. For some sectors of the petty-bourgeoisie, such as farmers, there is tremendous pressure to meet targets for local clients. Farmers who accept contracts from larger commercial food companies are often under extraordinary pressure to increase production. Even though they manage their own business, their contract with a large corporation forces them to produce on a capitalist basis. The pressure exerted over them by the corporation results in a loss of their autonomy and their subsumption to monopoly capital.

19 Kuusinen 1963, p. 190.
20 See Marx [1867] 1976 p. 1041 for his distinction between labour compensated from revenue and labour compensated from capital.

Bukharin and Preobrazhensky very clearly perceived this, noting with reference to the petty-bourgeois artisan,

> Capital exploits him in various ways: the usurer exploits him; the shop for which he works, exploits him; and so on. The artisan feels himself to be a 'master'; he works with his own tools, and in appearance he is 'independent', although in reality he is completely entangled in the web of the capitalist spider.[21]

The independence of the petty-bourgeoisie is thus to a large extent illusory. While they are free to manage themselves, they must organise their production to ensure that they meet the targets set by the capitalist monopolies.

Furthermore, the petty-bourgeoisie is sometimes negatively affected by tax increases and is often fiercely opposed to the state.[22] Whereas large corporations are able to pay taxes from the surplus-value, the petty-bourgeoisie must pay taxes from their own revenue. The tax on their product is calculated as a loss and limit on their business growth. As a result, the petty-bourgeoisie tends to support neoliberal politicians who promise tax cuts and privatisation of public services. Writing about the Brazilian social formation, Alfredo Saad-Filho and Lecio Morais point out that the petty-bourgeoisie

> remain ideologically attached both to a neoliberal-globalist project that slows growth, and to a clientelistic politics, landowner interests and neoliberal ideology that gives them advantages over the poor.[23]

The narrow-mindedness of the petty-bourgeoisie prevents them from seeing how taxes and the public sector benefit their own production. Tax revenues are often used to provide small business grants from which the petty-bourgeoisie benefits. Although a higher tax may be calculated as an immediate loss, the long-term benefits of taxation disappear from the minds of the petty-bourgeoisie. Second, a large public sector generally makes life easier for the petty-bourgeoisie for a number of reasons. Privatisation strengthens large corporations, and thereby the expansion of capitalist production to formerly non-capitalist spheres. For example, whenever capitalist states privatise healthcare,

21 Bukharin and Preobrazhensky [1923] 1966, p. 87.

22 See Saad-Filho and Morais (2018), pp. 133–136 for a discussion of why the petty-bourgeoisie—in the Brazilian context— tends to adopt right-wing politics during moments of crisis.

23 Saad-Filho and Morais (2018), p. 135.

they are taken over by private corporations who transform medical care into a capitalist business. Many sectors of the petty-bourgeoisie that have a private practice benefit from there being a public health service and often receive funding from it. When this health service is privatised, they have to compete with large corporations, which will tend to displace them.

A frequent difficulty of the petty-bourgeoisie is the inability to compete with large corporations. Small clothing shops, for example, find it very difficult to maintain a stable customer base in an era of fast fashion. Especially during a capitalist crisis, in which the income of most people falls, few people will purchase higher quality, expensive clothing from small shops. Commercial clothing chains, such as H&M and Primark, sell cheaper clothing and tend to displace the small shops. The same does not necessarily hold for all small businesses, as some of them have a low elasticity of demand and are able to maintain a stable customer base even in the worst crises. For them, difficulties arise when there is a general increase in the cost of commodities, and they are forced to raise their prices in order to survive. The price increase may result in lower revenues and bankruptcy. Because of this, the petty-bourgeoisie can sometimes adopt an anti-capitalist consciousness, although not a revolutionary one. As Poulantzas notes, "even when the petty-bourgeois sectors adopt working class positions they often do so by investing them with their own ideological practices."[24] For this reason, revolutionary socialists—particularly Trotsky—were sometimes distrustful of the petty-bourgeoisie, which they believed was not a reliable class ally.[25] While Trotsky, as well as Lenin at times, believed revolutionary socialists should try to win the petty-bourgeoisie over to its programme, they nonetheless were cautious lest they betray them. Thus, Trotsky says "a sound policy will compel the proletariat to call to power the influential leaders of the urban petty-bourgeoisie",[26] while retaining the political independence of the proletarian leadership. It is extremely important to win the petty-bourgeoisie over to working class leadership, for it has a tendency to adopt fascist political views when it is left unorganised.[27]

The historical articulation of the capitalist mode of production has expanded the *place* of the petty-bourgeoisie. In earlier capitalist societies, the place of the petty-bourgeoisie was reserved for those who had their own

24 Poulantzas 1978, p. 289.

25 See Trotsky 2020, chapter 4–5 for a discussion on socialist strategy in relation to the petty-bourgeoisie.

26 Trotsky 2020, p. 215.

27 While there is a voluminous literature on the topic of fascism and the petty-bourgeoisie, the finest overview is Poulantzas classic work, *Fascism and Dictatorship* (1979).

means of production, but not enough capital to appropriate surplus value from the working class. One reason for this was Keynesian economic policies, which ensured a large state sector and sufficient profitability in the manufacturing industries. During the seventies in countries like Britain, Sweden, Japan, and South Korea, the state sector generally ensured that a large sphere of production was carried out on a non-capitalist basis. The primary source of surplus-value was derived from the production of the means of production and high-cost consumer goods, such as cars and electronics. Capitalists around the world also made super-profits through appropriating surplus-value from arms sales, which were sold to the capitalist militaries and used in the never-ending imperialist wars. Hence, the place of the petty-bourgeoisie was limited to small businesses and self-employed people.

As Poulantzas notes in *Classes in Contemporary Capitalism*, the place of the petty-bourgeoisie has expanded to include semi-autonomous employees, managers, and other professionals. As he points out

> from medicine through to the liberal professions (law, architecture, etc.), and including entertainment and the media, the agents providing services have overwhelmingly become employees of capital, which has seized hold of their activities.[28]

This new section of the petty-bourgeoisie shares with the working-class separation from the means of production and wage labour. However, they have qualifications, such as a university degree or a specialised skill, which gives them autonomy in the labour-process (they are what Erik Olin Wright calls 'semi-autonomous employees'[29]). In some cases, this results in their promotion to a managerial position, which gives them the ability to hire and fire staff. For example, a lecturer may begin their career at a college working as a wage labourer. However, their seniority results in their promotion to tenured professor, giving them the ability to hire new staff and manage their department. Although they have higher level management above them, they now occupy the position of a boss to the staff in their department. Their tenure also gives them a level of job security that part-time lecturers do not have, as well as the ability to choose their hours and courses.

This new section of the petty-bourgeoisie values the freedom that their class position gives them. They will often go to extraordinary lengths to hold onto

28 Poulantzas 1978, p. 215.
29 Wright 1985, pp. 47–51.

this freedom, and even take industrial action to do so.[30] Their greatest fear is proletarianization and the loss of their class position, which forces them to adopt a reformist politics and a careerist mentality. As Poulantzas notes,

> afraid of proletarianization below, attracted to the bourgeoisie above, the new petty bourgeoisie often aspires to 'promotion', to a 'career', to 'upward social mobility', i.e. to becoming bourgeois.[31]

As with the old petty-bourgeoisie, they value the quality that they are able to provide. The growth of the petty-bourgeoisie is the result of the particular features of the contemporary capitalist social formation. These include neoliberal reforms, which involve the sale of public assets and their replacement with private companies. Neoliberalism tends to displace small businesses and make former business owners into managers in large corporations. The old petty-bourgeoisie is shifted to transnational corporations, which generally require a certain level of education. Managers help to extract surplus value from the workers, but do not themselves have any real control over the labour-process.[32]

In contrast to the traditional definition of the petty-bourgeoisie, I define it as the group of people that command the labour-process, but do not appropriate surplus-value because they do not possess *productive* capital. Instead of distinguishing between an old and new petty-bourgeoisie as Poulantzas does, my definition is able to comprise both in a single definition while recognising occupational differences within the petty-bourgeoisie. Although some sections of the petty-bourgeoisie may be self-employed and possess their own means of production, they are unable to initiate the capital-relation that results in the appropriation of value. In mainstream economics, someone with a small business will be said to possess capital. While this is fine for accounting purposes, from a Marxist standpoint someone is only a capitalist if they are able to use their capital in order to appropriate surplus-value from the working class. Since the petty-bourgeoisie does not have this ability, they can only use their capital for non-productive purposes and are therefore not capitalists.

My definition of the petty-bourgeoisie is helpful because it includes within it those who work for the management of a capitalist business. As I indicated above, a manager is not part of the working class because they command the labour of others and have the power to terminate another's employment. While they may face enormous stress and have multiple levels of management above

30 Poulantzas 1978, pp. 290–292.
31 *Ibid.* p. 292.
32 *Ibid.* p. 228.

them, they are part of the petty-bourgeoisie. Managers control the labour-process, but do not possess the capital needed to appropriate the surplus-value produced by the working class. Often, people who own a small business become managers or franchise-owners of a large corporation. For example, someone who owned a small cleaning firm may find it more profitable to become a franchisee of a commercial cleaning company like Molly Maid. It might also happen that a person who once possessed their own take-away restaurant becomes a manager of a large food chain when they go bankrupt (i.e., McDonalds, Burger King, Starbucks). Their class background has given them the training to command the labour-process so that it is productive and efficient.

In order to demonstrate the strength of my definition of the petty-bourgeoisie, I would like to contrast it with Erik Olin Wright, who discusses this in his *Classes*. According to Wright, the petty-bourgeoisie own their own means of production but do *not* hire staff. They may own a small restaurant, coffeeshop, store, or cleaning business, but are only petty-bourgeois if they do not employ workers. Wright thinks that the moment a small business owner hires a few workers, they become part of the bourgeoisie.[33] The problem with this position is that while they might extract a tiny surplus from their employees, this is not the primary means by which a small business owner attains their income. Generally, the owner will themselves work, producing more value than the staff that they employ. If they do appropriate a small surplus, this is not yet surplus-value, for the value-form does not yet regulate the production process of the petty-bourgeoisie. They are unable to extract surplus-value because they do not possess *productive* capital that would enable this, for they do not occupy the place of the bourgeoisie.

There are plenty of employers that hire workers without being capitalists. First, charities and non-governmental organisations hire staff to run storefronts, raise funds, transport goods, and provide services. It is possible that the charity uses capitalist management techniques in order to maximise the efficiency of the labour that they employ, but they are not capitalists. Second, public sector services such as the NHS (in Britain) and public schools employ workers on a non-capitalist basis. Nurses, doctors, and teachers are compensated from taxes in order to produce services needed to maintain and train the workforce. Neither the NHS nor a public school are conducted on a capitalist basis, although they do interact with capitalist society and ensure its social reproduction. Wright is therefore wrong to say that a small employer

33 Wright 1985 pp. 42–51.

who hires workers is automatically a member of the bourgeoisie. I would contend that they are members of the petty-bourgeoisie because they lack the productive capital needed to organise production in a capitalist way. They direct the labour of others and might extract a small surplus, but this does not make them capitalists. Only if they gain access to productive capital, which they own and control, will they become members of the capitalist class.

Wright also significantly overcomplicates the issue of managers, as he denies they are members of the petty-bourgeoisie. His argument is similar to the one above, which says that the petty-bourgeoisie does *not* command the labour of others. Because managers control the labour-process of a section of the workforce, they cannot be said to be members of the petty-bourgeoisie. According to Wright, managers occupy a contradictory class location, as they are situated between the working class and the bourgeoisie.[34] It is certainly true, as Poulantzas recognised, that modern managers are qualitatively different from the traditional petty-bourgeoisie. While they may possess shares in the company they work for, they do not own its assets or its productive capital. What managers share with the traditional petty-bourgeoisie is control over the labour-process, but lack the productive capital needed to appropriate surplus-value from the workers.

My definition of the petty-bourgeoisie overcomes these problems, for it defines the *place* of the petty-bourgeoisie as (i) command over labour-process and (ii) non-ownership of productive capital. As I have shown, the petty-bourgeoisie includes self-employed people that own their own means of production but lack the capital necessary to appropriate surplus-value from the working class. Furthermore, it also includes those people who are employed by the bourgeoisie to manage the labour-process and help to extract surplus-value from working people. They lack ownership of the means of production but exercise a certain level of control over it and sometimes have hiring power. What this new section of the petty-bourgeoisie lacks is capital, and therefore has no legal title to the products of their labour. Rather, they are what Eve Chiapello and Luc Butanski called 'management cadres'[35] who promote the interests of the corporation, but lack ownership or control of its major assets. I also include those who operate small franchises as part of the petty-bourgeoisie, which manage their own business but are themselves managed by the larger corporation of which they are a franchise. This section of the petty-bourgeoisie extracts surplus-value from its workers but transfers it to the

34 Wright 1985 p. 45.
35 Boltanski and Chiapello 2018

larger corporation in the form of a franchising fee. At the end of the production process, they do not retain a significant portion of the surplus-value and can only continue operating as a franchise if they are productive. The primary way that they differ from managers is that they must invest their own capital in order to go into business but have no autonomy and are fully subordinated to the larger corporation.

4.4 *The Dissolution of the Petty-Bourgeoisie*

Lenin often noted out that the petty-bourgeoisie has no future as a class, for it is constantly being dissolved by monopoly capital. As Bukharin and Preobrazensky point out, "many of them are ruined in the course of capitalist development"[36] and thereby become part of the working class. A small section of the petty-bourgeoisie will become part of the capitalist class. This may occur because someone goes from being a middle-level manager to becoming part of the board of directors of a company. They already know how to command labour and have experience appropriating surplus-value for the bourgeoisie. Their position and dedication to the corporation make them candidates for the capitalist class. It is also possible that someone who starts with a small business becomes capable of using their capital *productively* so that they exploit the labour-power of their employees. This means they no longer pay them for their services with their revenue but purchase their labour-power with the goal of extracting surplus value. Thus, Poulantzas notes that some sections of the petty-bourgeois display "a particularly high level of movement into other social classes".[37]

In his *Reproduction of Capitalism*, Althusser provides a formulation that is helpful for grasping the process by which the petty-bourgeoisie is displaced, proletarianized, and deformed. He says,

> Every concrete social formation is based on a *dominant* mode of production. The immediate implication is that, in every social formation, there exists more than one mode of production: at least two and often many more. The dominated modes are those striving from the old social formation's past or the ones that may be emerging in its present. The plurality of modes of production in every social formation and the current dominance of one mode of production over those that are disappearing or coming into being make it possible to account for the contradictory

36 Bukharin and Preobrazensky [1923] 1966, p. 87.

37 Poulantzas 1978, p. 282.

> complexity of the empirical facts observable in every concrete social formation ....[38]

In a capitalist social formation, a multiplicity of modes of production co-exists but the capitalist mode of production is dominant. The capitalist mode of production exercises a dissolution effect over pre-capitalist modes of production, such as feudalism and slavery. These modes of production can exist in a capitalist social formation, but they have a tendency to dissolve or partially operate on a capitalist basis. For example, the countryside of a capitalist social formation may still produce food according to a feudal mode of production, in which landlords hold a monopoly on land ownership and use their property to exploit small peasants. However, they generally require that their peasants produce according to what is socially necessary to ensure that their products have the socially recognised market value. The peasants may rent land and be required to provide free labour directly to the landowner, but the form of their coerced labour is itself structured on a capitalist basis. As capitalism penetrates the countryside, these feudal landowners may be forced to sell their land to larger capitalists and become managers in a large capitalist agro-business; as a result, the feudal relations dissolve. Hence, even though non-capitalist modes of production can exist in a capitalist social formation, the capitalist mode of production is dominant over all other modes of production.

Althusser's formulation is helpful in articulating the process by which unproductive industries are transformed into productive enterprises organised to produce surplus-value. In an earlier stage of capitalism, maintenance activities, such as cleaning, housekeeping, and waste-management did not result in surplus-value. The cleaning of a factory, workshop, or office, for example, was paid for directly by the corporation as a necessary cost to ensure continued production. Cleaning machines, sweeping floors, and scrubbing toilets did not generate surplus-value, but was necessary to ensure that production could continue. This does not mean that cleaners were not exploited, as the form of exploitation is still present because the cleaner is a wage-labourer. She may work long hours, which allows the capitalist to capture far more surplus-value from the productive workers than she is compensated for. However, her labour itself is not paid from bourgeoisie's capital, but from their revenue and therefore cannot generate surplus-value. It was for this reason that Marx called their labour unproductive, as it did not result in new value due to the absence of capital-relation.

38 Althusser 2014, p. 19.

With the development of capitalism and the dissolution of non-capitalist social relations, cleaning is gradually transformed into a value producing labour process. In the eighties, large commercial cleaning companies began emerging, which specialised in cleaning and solely produced clean-spaces. Commercial cleaning companies are capitalist firms, which employ cleaning workers to get surplus-value. In some cases, corporations that produce cleaning products created commercial cleaning companies in order to generate an outlet to absorb their economic surplus. The development of capitalism therefore transformed cleaning from an unproductive activity related to social reproduction, to a productive one that results in surplus-value. The same process can be observed in other industries that were originally carried out on a petty-bourgeois basis, such as hospitality, social care, beauty treatment, and haircutting. Although the petty-bourgeoisie continues to co-exist alongside large corporations, many are displaced and disappear.

The dissolution of the petty-bourgeoisie can also be seen in higher-education, in which many tenured professors are being replaced by adjuncts instructors. Traditionally, lecturers in higher education would not have been thought of as productive workers, but as members of the petty-bourgeoisie. Although working for a salary, professors in a university or college have the ability to hire staff and manage their departments. They are compensated through a combination of public funds and tuition depending on the country. Their job is to conduct research in order to discover new technology that could increase the productivity of labour or stimulate demand for new commodities. Research can also contribute to the development of new management techniques, such as the discoveries of cognitive psychology. In addition to research, a professor trains the workforce in order to produce skills that are necessary for certain jobs. Colleges directly contribute to the production of a semi-skilled workforce capable of doing work in construction, retail management, and hospitality. Hence, professors and lecturers, although working for a salary, were traditionally members of the petty-bourgeoisie and contributed to the needs of social reproduction.

Although universities and colleges in Britain, the United States, and Canada still employ tenured professors, a significant portion of educational work is conducted by adjunct professors and temporary lecturers. An adjunct professor is hired on a temporary, part-time basis by a full-time member of staff in their respective department. In the United States, they are usually only compensated for the hours they teach, while in Britain, they generally receive payment for some additional tasks, such as grading papers and lecture preparation. In both cases, temporary teaching staff are paid significantly less than full-time professors and have no job security. If they decide to teach something controversial, their manager could decide not to give them classes in the future. Adjunct professors therefore lack the academic freedom enjoyed by full-time teaching staff and are often forced to teach heavily standardised material.

In the US, Canada, Britain, and the European Union, austerity has caused higher-education institutions to lose funds needed to pay staff. The primary reasons for hiring adjuncts and temporary lecturers is that it results in significant cost-reduction. Because universities and colleges receive less money, they will employ adjuncts and temporary lecturers to teach courses. Adjuncts generally receive five to ten times less to teach a course than a full-time professor, even though the former sometimes have more teaching experience than the latter. Sometimes, multiple courses assigned to a full-time professor are combined into a single one and given to an adjunct professor to teach. The result is that adjuncts sometimes teach courses with over fifty students while being given a poverty wage. In the US, there are adjuncts that teach 6–8 courses a semester with hundreds of students to assess.[39]

The adjunctisation of higher education has resulted in a significant decline of full-time teaching staff. In the United States, over 70% of all course instruction is conducted by adjunct professors and there are fewer permanent teaching jobs available.[40] This has resulted in hostility towards adjuncts, who are sometimes perceived by tenured professors as replacing them. Indeed, as colleges and universities employ more adjuncts to teach courses, the jobs of full-time professors are threatened. It is entirely possible that higher-education institutions will solely hire adjuncts in the future, while a few professors are employed to conduct research. As universities and colleges employ more adjuncts, professors who are part of the petty-bourgeoisie gradually disappear and are replaced with proletarianized lecturers. The dissolution of the petty-bourgeoisie and their transformation into workers can therefore be observed in higher education.

The above, extended analysis demonstrates two things. First, it shows that as capitalism develops and becomes dominant, non-capitalist modes of production gradually dissolve. The forces of capitalist society will eventually force the old petty-bourgeoisie to become part of the bourgeoisie or dissolve into the ranks of the *proletariat*. When this happens, they lose the autonomy and security that they enjoyed as members of the petty-bourgeoisie. If they can get access to capital, they can purchase a franchise and become part of a large corporation. Second, the above analysis demonstrates that those small businesses

39 For an excellent Marxist analysis of adjunct professors, see Berry (2005)

40 American Association of University Professors Information Leaflet.

that stay in operation must operate on a capitalist basis if they are to compete with the monopolies. The big corporations, with their business networks and large amount of capital, are the main competition to small businesses.

5 Summary

The purpose of class analysis is to give us an understanding of the terrain in which the class struggle unfolds. This will be useful to trade unionists and socialists who are organising the working class into a politically conscious social force. A class analysis shows who the allies of the working class are, as well its main enemies in order to reveal the *social* terrain. This can help us to produce a political strategy that reflects the real conditions of the class struggle operative in a social formation. On the basis of this, they can develop tactics for uniting the working class, building alliances with other classes, and tactics to defeat the bourgeoisie politically. I have argued that the capitalist class is defined by their access to productive capital, which enables them to appropriate surplus value from working people. The working class has been defined as those who don't own the means of production, work for a wage, and have no control over the production process. I also discussed the petty-bourgeoisie, which I defined as the class of people that do not have access to productive capital and therefore are unable to appropriate surplus-value. Although the petty-bourgeoisie will exist in all capitalist social formations, they tend to decline as monopoly capital develops.

In the next chapter, I will begin enquiring more deeply into the service and retail industry through an examination of Marxist value theory. I will demonstrate how the concepts of commodity, surplus-value, and profit are helpful for uncovering the tendencies in the labour of service and retail workers.

CHAPTER 4

Service Labour and Value Theory

1 Marxism, Services, Commodities

In Marx's nineteenth century, the service industry did not exist and services had a very different function than today. Service labour were necessary, but unprofitable tasks that had to be completed in order for production to continue. Cleaning and maintenance work were not conducted on a capitalist basis and were not industries in which capitalists invested to get a profit. Workers themselves often looked after the workplace, cleaning the machines themselves and sweeping the floors. Braverman points out that until the twentieth century, workers sometimes possessed skills to conduct basic maintenance. Although cleaners and engineers were hired in the nineteenth century, the emergence of special sectors specialising in these tasks did not exist. It was only with the emergence of monopoly capitalism in the mid twentieth century that commercial service companies appeared, which transformed service work into a profitable business.[1]

Marx wrote *Capital* against the background of nineteenth century capitalism in Victorian England. Fiona Tregenna points out that

> during Marx's time, services comprised a relatively small proportion of total economic activity, a situation very different from today where they account for most of both employment and GDP in most countries of the world. Furthermore, at that time, there was a much lower degree of outsourcing of services to specialised service providers than is currently the case, as these activities were typically undertaken in-house (e.g., in a manufacturing firm) rather than falling within a distinct services sector.[2]

Marx does not discuss service workers in significant detail, although he makes occasional references to them. The most sustained analysis of service work in Marx's writings is the posthumously published "Results of the Immediate Process of Production", in which Marx argues that any labour process can be conducted on a capitalist basis, including services. If labour-power is

1 Braverman 1974
2 Tregenna 2011, p. 282.

 | DOI:10.1163/9789004469624_005

exchanged against capital, then it has the potential to produce surplus-value and therefore become a site of profitable business activity. Because most service labour in the nineteenth century was not exchanged against capital, but rather the revenue of the capitalist, it did not occupy a significant place in Marx's overall analysis.

In the manuscript of *Capital* that was published in Marx's lifetime, most of Marx's examples are about workers in factories that produce physical goods such as linen, coats, and steel. When one reads *Capital*, one could easily get the idea that Marx only considered factory workers as productive labourers, and that service workers are not significant to capitalist production. Some passages in *Capital* make it appear that Marx held this view, such as "a service is nothing other than the useful effect of a use-value, be it that of a commodity, or that of labour. But here we are dealing with exchange value."[3] In Marx's time, it would have been unusual to think of cleaners and maintenance workers as productive, as they were largely employed on a non-capitalist basis. They performed a service for the capitalist that was paid out of his revenue, which was necessary but not profitable. Their services allowed capitalist production to continue, but the capital-relation was absent.

In this section, I will show that the propositions of Marx's *Capital* are not just historical observations of nineteenth century capitalism, and that they are relevant to grasping the nature of service labour. Following in the footsteps of Paul Sweezy, Harry Braverman, and Fiona Tregenna, I will demonstrate how the basic categories of Marxist economics can be used to articulate the nature of service labour and how service workers produce surplus-value. I will go through the major categories of *Capital*—commodity, abstract labour, labour-power, and surplus-value—and show how they bring out structural tendencies in the labour process of service workers. Once I have done this, I will show how the production and realisation of surplus value in the service industry is very different from industries that produce goods.

2 The Commodity-Form

The best place to begin is with the commodity form, which is a foundational category in Marxist economics. As Marx argued in the first chapter of *Capital*, a defining feature of capitalism is commodity production. Tregenna points out that services can be produced as commodities, for "commodities are not limited

3 Marx [1867] 1976

to physical goods, and similarly 'production' is not limited to the physical production of a tangible object."[4] A commodity is any good or service that is useful for some purpose *and* is produced to be sold. It must *appear* useful for some purpose, as this is what makes it an object of demand. I italise the word 'appear', for capitalists use complex advertising tricks to generate the appearance of use-value. A commodity could be inherently useless or of low-quality, but nonetheless be demanded by consumers because advertisers have convinced them they need it.

Many commodities do of course possess a natural use-value, such as food, fuel, housing, and coffee, but advertising is still necessary to create the *appearance* of use-value in a particular brand or model. For example, a sweater possesses natural use-value in that it provides warmth during the winter, but advertising is needed to create the *appearance* of use-value in a sweater designed by Gap. Advertising makes it appear that the Gap sweater contains *more* use-value because of its non-useful properties, such as its colour or design, or its difference from another brand such as Primark. In the era of monopoly capital, it is sometimes difficult to perceive what is actually useful in a commodity and what has been fabricated by advertising agencies.

The stimulation of demand for a service is integral to the service industry, as one must have customers that believe they need the service before production can take place. Some sections of the service industry depend entirely on an (affluent) consumer's belief in their inability to produce the service themselves. For example, one must believe that one is incapable of cleaning one's own house and have significant disposable income in order to seek out domestic cleaning services from a company like Molly Maid. In their marketing, they use carefully constructed images of dirty houses and overworked professionals to sell their cleaning service. Significant manipulation goes into convincing the consumer that their cleaning abilities are less than a Molly Maid cleaner, generating the demand for the service. Creating the *appearance* of use-value is therefore as important for the service industry as it is for goods-producing industries such as fast-fashion.

Use-value is a necessary condition for something to be a commodity, but not a sufficient one. Something can contain use-value without being sold as a commodity. These include services such as public healthcare (i.e., the NHS in Britain) and education (public schools). Although there are forces that want to privatise the NHS and transform education into a profitable enterprise, they are non-commodified and consumed solely for their use-value. In a socialist society, the state would organise production to maximise use-value

4 Tregenna 2011, p. 286.

and gradually move away from exchange value. Although advertising might be used to encourage consumers to try new products, socialism does not deceive consumers by providing unnecessary products that only appear to be useful. Socialist societies also change the way that demand is generated for commodities by involving the community in the creation of new products. Therefore, socialism removes the *appearance* of use-value from commodities and organises consumption so that people can live rich and creative lives.

In order for something to be a commodity, it must be produced in order to be sold on the market, which Marx calls its exchange value. Its exchange-value is not a natural property, but a social relation that appears through the material body of use-value. The Soviet Marxist Rubin notes that value

> does not characterize things, but human relations in which things are produced. It is not a property of things but a social form acquired by things due to the fact that people enter into determined production relations with each other through things. Value is a "social relation taken as a thing," a production relation among people which takes the form of a property of things.[5]

Through the physical body of a loaf of bread, or the clean space produced by the cleaning worker, the exchange value of the commodity appears. Working at a very high level of abstraction, Marx says that this equivalence appears between two commodities. The exchange value of commodity X appears through its relationship with commodity Y, although it is not reducible to either of them. For example, two loaves of bread exchange for one kg of rice, or every square foot of cleaned space is exchanged for two kgs of tea. Each of these commodities articulate their exchange-value through the mediation of another commodity. Marx does this in order to demonstrate that the exchange-value of a commodity is not determined by its use-value, but something abstracted from its utility. Exchange-value has nothing to do with the quality of materials, the thoroughness of the clean, or the rarity of the product.

To discover this immaterial value-content of the commodity, Marx says that we must engage in a process of abstraction. When we abstract from the material properties of a commodity, suspending its use-value and concrete-labour, the only thing that remains is a product of abstract labour. This process of abstraction reduces the commodity to an abstract labour-value rather than a concrete object of utility. When two commodities are exchanged, the

5 Rubin 2010, p. 69.

identity of the abstract labour contained in them appears through a concrete relationship of equivalence. For Marx, it is abstract labour that defines a commodity's value and not the specificity of the labour that went into its production. Abstract labour is something structural and general, rather than concrete and particular. However, in the exchange of commodities, the contradiction between concrete and abstract labour is resolved and the two opposites are united. Through exchange, a particular commodity, which is the product of a particular kind of labour, materialises a structural and general relationship to the capitalist totality.

Whether this commodity is a material good or a service is irrelevant, as both are the products of abstract labour. As Tregenna reminds us, a commodity is defined "not according to its physical characteristics, but rather according to the way in which it was produced."[6] The notion of abstract labour is important, as it allows us to define something as a commodity irrespective of whether it is a physical good or a service. A t-shirt or bag of tea is as much the product of abstract labour as a cleaned-house or a bus-trip. What matters is not the particularity of the labour that went into producing it, but only that it is labour in general. The concept of abstract labour is helpful for making sense of service labour and the production of service-goods. Since service workers produce service-goods, such as bus-trips, clean-houses, and haircuts, they produce a commodity whose exchange value is defined by abstract general labour. Although the concrete labour processes of domestic cleaning workers differ from garment workers, they are the same when reduced to the abstract labour contained in the commodity that they produce.

Having demonstrated that exchange-value is defined by abstract labour, Marx shows what determines the magnitude of the value contained in the commodity. The value of any commodity is determined by socially necessary labour time, which is "the labour-time required to produce any use-value under the conditions of production normal for a given society and with the average degree of skill and intensity of labour prevalent in that society."[7] There are a variety of factors that determine the socially-necessary labour-time required to produce a commodity. The technology, science, and management techniques used by most capitalists in a particular industry determine the average amount of time for the output. If there is a revolution in technology or management science that allows goods to be produced faster, the value of the commodity

6 Tregenna 2011, p. 285.

7 Marx [1867] 1976, p. 129.

will drop. Value is directly dependent on the productivity of labour, which causes fluctuations in the value of commodities.

One effect of imperialism is that the national bourgeoisie in the peripheral nations often only have access to obsolete technology and require more time to produce goods than other capitalists. As Samir Amin points out, on the global market, their products are valued according to the socially necessary labour time of the technology used by capitalists in the imperialist centres.[8] This puts tremendous pressure on them to intensify the exploitation of their workers and cut wages in order to survive against the capitalist monopolies. Unequal exchange creates the temptation for the bourgeoisie in the oppressed nations to become subsidiaries of the monopolies in order to gain access to their technology. As a result, there is a split in the bourgeoisie in the oppressed nations. A section of the bourgeoisie puts the needs of its people first and refuses to become an agent of imperialism. The national bourgeoisie suffers from the domination of the global economy by financial oligarchies that determine the socially necessary labour time required to produce goods and services. National oppression in peripheral nations transforms a section of the bourgeoisie into agents of the imperialists, which has been referred to as the comprador or lumpen bourgeoisie. They give the imperialists access to cheap labour and domestic markets, in exchange for access to better equipment and technology. Comprador bourgeoisies amass extreme wealth in developing nations such as Bangladesh at the expense of the working class, who are made poor through the betrayal of their own bourgeoisie.[9]

In his *Labor and Monopoly Capital*, Harry Braverman shows that modern management techniques such as Taylorism drastically increased the productivity of labour and reduced the socially necessary labour time to produce a commodity. Braverman notes that "Taylor set as his objective the maximum or "optimum" that can be obtained from a day's labor-power."[10] Taylor and his followers used the stopwatch to measure every movement on the production-line in order to eliminate unnecessary time between tasks. Using mathematics, Taylor was able to create models that articulated the precise socially necessary labour time needed to produce goods and services. The result of this was that the output increased on an astronomical scale, and thereby drastically reduced the value of commodities.

8 Amin 1974

9 For a sustained analysis of the contradictions of the bourgeoisie in oppressed nations, see: Smith (2016) and Suwandi (2019)

10 Braverman 1974, p. 67.

The value-form can be thought of as an *abstract* structure that regulates the *concrete* production of commodities. Workers are under tremendous pressure to produce goods and services below the social-average so that the capitalist can get more value out of the worker. The domestic cleaning company, Molly Maid, employs cleaners on a capitalist basis and has developed techniques to ensure that its cleaners clean houses as quickly as possible. On their website, they market themselves as 'highly professional', 'efficient', and define themselves against private cleaners who do not operate on a capitalist basis.[11] Molly Maid cleaners work in a highly stressful environment, where they are under constant pressure to produce as many clean homes as possible in a single day. Because it is organised on a capitalist basis, Molly Maid requires that its workers produce clean homes in the time that is socially necessary. To enforce this, they adopt Taylorised models of workplace organisation, with strict timetables and deadlines, standardised routines for each job, and an oppressive management structure. One former worker reported that,

> there are no lunch breaks at all, you must eat while you drive which is very dangerous. Employees are treated like cleaning machines, supervisors would often get upset if you ask for a day off work or even call in sick, and try an convince you to come into work.[12]

By making the workers 'cleaning machines', Molly Maid ensures that homes will be cleaned below the time that is socially-necessary. The law of value thus regulates capitalist production and puts pressure on workers to be as productive as possible, which is enforced by management.

In this section, I have discussed Marx's analysis of the commodity as it appears in the first chapter of *Capital*. A commodity is a good or service that is produced to be sold on the market. Its exchange value is not dependent on its use-value but determined by abstract labour. The magnitude of a commodity's value is determined by the socially necessary labour time required to produce it under a determinate set of conditions. Once a capitalist mode of production has become dominant in the social formation, the commodity-form is generalised and determines the mode of production, circulation, exchange, and distribution. From the beginning, in which goods and services are produced, to the end of its cycle in which it is purchased and consumed, the commodity-form is present. Now that I have discussed the commodity-form, I will turn to Marx's

---

11 Molly Maid Website, "Molly Maid versus Private Cleaning".

12 Indeed Job Review, August 18, 2018.

theory of surplus-value, which is central to conceptualising how working people are exploited by capital.

3 Surplus-Value and Service Workers

Marx first introduces the concept of surplus value in his analysis of the circuit of capital. Marx says that the general formula for capital is Money (M)—Commodity (C)—Money (M'). In the case of M-C-M', a capitalist begins with a quantity of money, which they use to attain a commodity on the market. After attaining this commodity, they go back to the market and end up with more value. The excess of money that the capitalist takes out of circulation is new value that did not exist at the beginning. This new value that arises out of M-C-M' is the surplus-value, which can only arise in such a relationship and has no existence outside of the capital relation. A capitalist is "any economic agent who puts money and use values into circulation in order to make more money."[13] As David Harvey points out in the *Limits to Capital*, for Marx, capital is value that has been put into circulation in the form of money in order to generate surplus value. Instead of viewing capital as a thing, Harvey notes that it is a process through which surplus-value is produced and accumulated.[14]

Marx observes that the monetary surplus value that the capitalist takes out of the circulation is not where surplus value arises. When the capitalist takes more money out of circulation than he began with, this is only *realised* surplus-value. In order to discover the origin of surplus-value, Marx says that we must turn our attention to the production of commodities. To do this, we must first look at the commodities that the capitalist purchases in order to initiate the production process. The capitalist uses his money to purchase constant capital, which consists of plant equipment, machinery, raw materials, and other means of production. In the cleaning industry, constant capital consists of transport vehicles, cleaning fluids, vacuum cleaners, and storage space. With outsourced security services, constant capital consists of specialised security cameras and software, weapons, and communication equipment. I would argue that in the service industry, a company's marketing system and its brand name are part of the constant capital. Franchisees rent access to a brand-name like 'Molly Maid', 'Uber', and 'Just Eat' in order to gain customers and engage in production. Intangible assets are therefore part of the means of production in

13 Harvey 2006, p. 21.
14 *ibid*, pp. 20–21.

the service industry, without which it is impossible to engage in production.[15] In *Capital* and the writings of Marxist economists, it is usually argued that constant capital does not generate any new value. Science and technology are not a directly productive force, and by themselves do not generate any new value. Surplus value is therefore not produced by machines, but rather transfers their value to the product. Where then does surplus-value come from?

The capitalist does not just purchase the means of production, but also labour-power, which Marx calls variable capital. David Harvey reminds us that "what the labourer sells to the capitalist is not labour (the substance of value) but labour power",[16] which Marx defines as

> labour-capacity, the aggregate of those mental and physical capabilities existing in the physical form, the living personality, of a human being, capabilities which he sets in motion whenever he produces a use-value of any kind.[17]

The sale of labour-power is only possible because the worker is separated from the means of production and must thereby commodify their labour-power in order to gain employment. The use-value of labour-power is first and foremost its ability to produce value, which is human labour-power embodied in commodities. The 'aggregate of those mental and physical capabilities existing in the physical form' are the workers' abilities that allow them to engage in productive labour. They are the skills they have accumulated in their lifetime and define their unique personality. The capitalist uses these skills to get goods and services from the worker, which result in surplus-value and its realisation.

What the capitalist pays the worker for is not the value that they produce, but only for the value of their labour-power, which is determined by the value of the goods that the worker needs to reproduce him or herself. As Marx puts it,

---

15 This is not a generally accepted view and it is controversial. Most Marxists would probably not include intangible assets in the category of constant capital. However, for those who rent access to the brand in exchange for regular franchise payments, brand name is a means of production. An Uber driver, for example, would not be able to produce taxi-rides were it not for the brand name and advertising system of 'Uber'. A Molly Maid franchisee chooses to become a franchise because the recognized brand gives them access to a larger consumer base than if they operated on an independent basis. Therefore, I claim that intangible assets, brand name, and goodwill in service industries is sometimes a means of production and can thus be included in the category of constant capital.

16 Harvey 2006, p. 23.

17 Marx 1976 [1867] p. 270.

> the labour time necessary for the production of labour-power is the same as that necessary for the production of those means of subsistence; in other words, the value of labour-power is the value of the means of subsistence necessary for the maintenance of its owner.[18]

As I discussed in the previous section, the value of commodities is determined by the time on average that it takes to produce them. This is determined by the level of development of the productive forces, the state of science, and management techniques such as Taylorism. Things that the worker needs to survive are called the means of subsistence, and their value is determined by the socially necessary labour-time required to produce them. For example, the value of bread or rice is determined by the average amount of time it takes to produce them using the existing farming techniques.

The value of the means of subsistence that the worker needs to produce and reproduce their labour-power on a daily, monthly, quarterly, and yearly basis constitute the value of their labour-power. With every change in the productivity of labour in the industries that produce means of subsistence, the value of labour-power will increase or decrease. If food production increases due to a good harvest, then it takes less socially necessary labour time to produce food and its value drops. As the value of food drops, the value of labour-power drops too. If there is a war in countries that produce oil, the production of oil will be halted and there will be an increase in its value. Since oil is essential for transportation in today's capitalist society, any increase in the value of oil will necessarily increase the value of labour-power (although this does not mean higher wages for the worker). Hence, the value of labour-power "varies with the value of the means of subsistence, i.e., with the quantity of labour-time required to produce them."[19]

When working people sell their labour-power as a commodity, what they receive for it in exchange is a wage, which is the price taken by the value of their labour-power. As Marx emphasises throughout *Capital*, price and value are not the same thing. Value is objective and depends on the productivity of labour, while price is a representation of value in a particular quantity of money. The price of a commodity is generally below its value, although there are cases where it might be above its value. The wage that the worker receives is the price of the commodities that the worker needs to produce his or her labour-power. It is the amount of money they need to purchase food and clothing, and

18 *ibid., p.* 274.

19 *ibid.* p. 276.

pay their bills (i.e., rent, utilities, etc.). Each of these things contain value, and the actual wage may be below or above their value.

A change in the value of labour-power does not mean there will necessarily be an immediate change to the worker's wage. If there is a crisis in production, the capitalists will objectively be in a position to cut wages. They may lay off existing workers and replace them with new workers at a lower wage. However, there are some things that could counteract changes to the worker's wage. If there are strong trade unions, the workers may go on strike to prevent wage-cuts and force the capitalists to maintain the existing wage or even pay a higher wage. Trade unions might also put pressure on the state to subsidise the workers' wages, as was done in the US, Britain, and some EU countries during the 2020 coronavirus outbreak. A strong union is an important weapon that working people can use to protect their wages during a crisis of production. What makes a union strong is its ability to speak on behalf of *all* working people, not just those that are its members. When a trade union speaks on behalf of the working class, it can put pressure on the capitalist state in addition to the employers. Otto Kuusinen points out in the *Fundamentals of Marxism-Leninism* that

> the movement of wages depends essentially on the class struggle waged by the proletariat, its organisational strength and the resistance it offers to the employers. The struggle of the working class for the improvement of labour conditions and its standard of living, without altering the system of private ownership of the means of production, and of political power in the hands of the bourgeoisie, can make its position easier.[20]

The capitalists may themselves view a drastic fall in wages as harmful to their immediate class interests. From an objective standpoint, low wages always help the bourgeoisie and hurt the working class. However, such wage cuts are generally gradual and a sudden cut in wages may cause larger problems that the bourgeoisie is not in a position to address. For example, sudden mass unemployment can create a crisis of effective demand and prevent the realisation of surplus value contained in goods. In such a situation, the capitalist class may appeal to the state for aid to cover the costs of wages. This was the case during the 2008 economic crisis, in which the capitalists of many countries appealed to their government for assistance in covering the wage bill.

---

20 Kuusinen 1963, p. 274–275.

Once the worker has sold their labour-power to the capitalist, they begin their job and start producing goods and services. The capitalist will set up a complex managerial system to ensure that the worker produces commodities within or below the average time required for production. Managers will be present to evaluate the workers performance and ensure they are producing effectively. The management will see to it that the workers do not wastefully use the means of production or raw materials. As Marx says, "the labour-time expended must not exceed what is necessary under the given conditions of social conditions of production".[21] At the end of the working day, workers in a factory, workshop, farm, or other workplace will have produced a certain number of commodities. The textile workers will have produced a few thousand shirts, the farm-labourers produced a certain quantity of food, and the cleaners will have cleaned a few dozen houses. Security guards will have produced a secure space, nurses will have produced medical services, and recording artists will have produced a set of concerts. Marx makes an important observation about this, saying that "the product is the property of the capitalist and not that of the worker, its immediate producer".[22] This is because the capitalist owns the means of production and the use-value of the labour-power, and therefore what the worker produces is the property of the capitalist.

The workers produce a bundle of goods or services but have no legal title to the products of their labour. The construction workers who produce expensive homes for the rich often live in slums that are infested with rats and mould, old rusty radiators that do not provide heating, and do not have clean water. Textile workers who produce thousands of shirts do not have any legal title to the shirts they produce, nor do the farm labourers get to eat the food they have produced. As Andrew Brooks shows in *Clothing Poverty*, garment workers in the Global South often can only afford used clothing, as they are too poor to afford expensive brands.[23] The same is true of cleaning workers: unless they find time to clean within their busy workweek or have a partner that can clean for them, the homes of cleaners will not be as tidy as the homes they clean for Molly Maid.

At the end of the working week, the worker receives a wage that compensates them for the value of their labour-power. As I have already discussed in detail, for Marx this value is equivalent to the value of the goods the worker needs to reproduce their labour-power and come to work the next day. They

21 Marx 1976 [1867], p. 295.

22 *ibid.*, p. 292.

23 Brooks 2019

are not compensated for the equivalent of the value they produce as this far exceeds the value of the means of subsistence. Marx says,

> the value of labour-power, and the value which that labour-power valorises in the labour- process, are two entirely different magnitudes; and this difference was what the capitalist had in mind when he was purchasing the labour-power.[24]

This finally brings us to a clear definition of surplus-value: surplus-value is the difference between the value that the worker is compensated for and the value that the worker produces while engaged in production. It is the difference between their wage, which is a representation of the value of the means of subsistence, and the value of the goods and services they produce. It is the difference between the portion of the working day for which they are paid, and the portion in which they are exploited and unpaid. As Marx puts it,

> surplus-value is the difference between the value of the product and the value of the elements consumed in the formation of the product, in other words the means of production and labour-power.[25]

The surplus value that the workers produced goes to the capitalist who employs them, for he is the only person with a legal title to it. David Harvey emphasises that "surplus-value is a *social* and not a physical, material relation".[26] Although surplus-value is embodied in the products and services produced by working people, it expresses a class relation of exploitation rather than a thing. Because it is not a thing but a social relation, surplus-value can be embodied in both manufactured goods and service commodities. As Alfredo Saad-Filho points out, "wage labour employed by capital in the production of commodities for profit produces value regardless of the form or destination of the product."[27] A coffee farmer who produces coffee beans is just as capable of producing surplus-value as a barista who uses these coffee beans to manufacture a cappuccino. A cleaning worker who works for a commercial cleaning company produces surplus-value just as much as a worker who produces cleaning chemicals. As long as the capital-relation is present in the labour-process, surplus-value will result from the capitalist labour-process. Harvey notes that "the

24 Marx 1976 [1867], p. 300.
25 *ibid.* p. 317.
26 Harvey 2013, p. 23.
27 Saad-Filho 2019, p. 54.

social relation that lies at the root of Marxian value theory is the class relation between labour and capital."[28] The theory of surplus-value reveals the structural dynamics that operate between capital and labour, disclosing the social relations of exploitation that govern the capitalist production process.

What Marx makes clear throughout his writings is that *capitalism is the production and realisation of surplus value*. In the capitalist mode of production, production is organised to maximise surplus value, and circulation is organised to ensure its realisation. Surplus value is not the same thing as profit. Profit is the *realised* form of surplus value, which results only after the commodity has reached its final sale. It is important to distinguish surplus value from profit, as profit is only *one* result of the distribution of surplus value. In addition to profit, banks that have funded a capitalist take a portion of the surplus value in the form of interest, merchant capital takes a portion of surplus value in the form of commercial profit, and landlords derive a portion of the surplus value in the form of rent. Bukharin and Preobrazhensky note this very clearly in *The ABC of Communism*, saying that part of the surplus-value

> goes to the capitalist himself, in the form of entrepreneur's profit; part goes to the landowner; in the form of taxes, part enters the coffers of the capitalist State; other portions accrue to merchants, traders, and shopkeepers. ... Upon surplus value live all the parasites who are bred by the capitalist system.[29]

To equate surplus value with profit is a mistake because it prevents us from seeing the way in which surplus value is distributed between the different sectors of capital. Using a slightly more philosophical vocabulary, we can say that surplus-value is the *content* of the commodity, while profit, rent, taxes, and interest are *forms* in which the surplus-value appears. The job of Marxist value theory is to connect the *content* of surplus-value to its *form* in order to gain knowledge of the social totality.

Something that Marxists sometimes ignore is the process of realisation of surplus value, which is equally important to its production. Significant labour is needed to realise the surplus-value contained in goods and services. Advertising agencies stimulate demand for commodities, but it is retail employees that perform the transformation of commodities into money. A retail employee at H&M, Ikea, or Tesco moves goods from the warehouse to

28 Harvey 2006, p. 24.
29 Bukharin and Preobrazhenky [1923] 1966, p. 36.

the shelves, arranges them so that they are appealing, and works cash registers to complete the sale. A salesperson in a call centre contacts the managers of the large retailers in order to sell cleaning services for outsourcing companies like Bidvest-Noonan. As their job is to provide customer-service, retail workers must perform emotional labour so that their appealing attitude makes the consumer more interested in the commodity. Retailers train their employees to identify with the company so that they are more likely to be excited about the products they sell. The result is that retail employees often feel no immediate solidarity with the producers and are situated in relation to the commodity in a fetishized form.

4 Surplus Value in the Service Industry

The production of surplus value in the service industry is different from industries that produce goods. To illustrate this, I would like to point out that surplus value can exist in two forms: commodities and money. Marx demonstrates this in the second volume of *Capital*, in which he shows that the circuit of industrial capital is not simply M-C-M', but M—C ... P ... C'—M'. On the one hand, there is the surplus value that is crystallised in the commodities produced by the worker. At the end of the working day, a factory, farm, or building site produces a bundle of goods (i.e. shirts, food, houses, etc.). The surplus value is materialised as a definite quantity of unpaid labour in these goods. On the other hand, there is the surplus value that is realised in the money resulting from the sale of the commodity. When a commodity has been sold, the surplus value changes its form and is now realised in the form of money. The capitalist who sells a bundle of shirts, food, and homes to a merchant or consumer realises the surplus value in the form of money. Hence, surplus value can exist in the form of commodities (C') or the form of money (M'). The distinction between surplus value embodied in commodities and money is crucial for grasping the difference between the production of goods and the production of services. Temporally, the circuit of capital in goods-production differs quite significantly from the circuit in the production of services. This difference is connected to a difference in the temporal structure of the forms of surplus value.

With the production of a material commodity, surplus value is *first* embodied in commodities before it is embodied in money. The worker must produce the machinery, equipment, or consumer goods before they can be sold. Their labour is first *materialised* in commodities before it is *realised* in money. The industrial or agrarian capitalist who sells commodities to a merchant *realises* the surplus value and can accumulate more capital as a result of this *realisation*. However, the merchant still has to sell the commodities, either to another manufacturer or to the public as consumer goods. The surplus value is only fully realised when the commodity has reached its final destination in the hands of the consumer. There is generally a lengthy period between the production of a material commodity and its final sale in the hands of the consumer. It usually passes through a multiplicity of suppliers and distributors before it reaches the shops and can be purchased. There are many additional costs, some of which further add value to the commodity, such as transport, storage, testing, marketing, and advertising that are required to *realise* the surplus value. Hence, we might reformulate the circuit of industrial capital from M—C ... P ... C'—M', to M—C ... P ... C'—M1'—M2' ... Mn'. This allows us to see the multiplicity of temporal stages in the process of *realisation* of the surplus value of the physical commodity.

The job of transportation, warehouse, and retail workers is to transform C' is into M' in order to ensure that the process can be repeated. If the commodities containing surplus value (C') are not transformed into more money than when the process began (M'), the capitalist will run into financial problems. The service industry functions as an important market for commodities produced by industrial workers. These commodities contain surplus value, which is realised through their sale to clients in the service industry. Service companies use these commodities as means of production and raw materials in their own business. Because they demand a continuous supply of these commodities, the service industry plays an important role in the social reproduction process.

If a capitalist lacks the money capital needed to continue the process of capitalist production, they will not be able to repeat the process of producing C'. They need the monetary surplus-value from the sale (M'), which they accumulate as capital in order to continue the capitalist production process on an expanded scale. For the big monopolies, occasional problems with the sales-effort can be resolved through the banks, who provide them with credit so that they can continue the production process. The banks will demand interest, which they calculate on the future surplus-value that will be realised when the commodities are sold. On the other hand, the small producer in a developing country such as Bangladesh may find it more difficult to restart the production process if they are unable to find customers as a result of a realisation crisis. In some cases, they will be purchased and acquired by larger local capitalists or the transnational corporations. The comprador bourgeoisie, which controls the state in many developing countries, can arrange a deal with international financial institutions, such as the IMF or the Asian Infrastructure Development Bank. These banks will lend them the capital needed to continue capitalist production in exchange for political compliance and 'structural adjustment' policies.

The circuit of capital in the production of services is quite different from the production of goods. As Fiona Tregenna points out that one-way services are different "is that the production and consumption of services commodities generally cannot viably be separated in time, or, in most cases, in space."[30] When one gets a haircut, has one's home cleaned, or uses public transportation, the service is produced and consumed at the same time. What this indicates is that the circuit of service commodities is different from manufactured goods, which will affect the production and realization of value. Marx himself was aware of this difference, as he states in a passage about transport workers, which is worth quoting in its entirety. Marx says,

> what the transport industry sells is the actual change of place itself. The useful effect produced is inseparably connected with the transport process, i.e. the production process specific to the transport industry. People and commodities travel together with the means of transport, and this journeying, the spatial movement of the means of transport, is precisely the production process accomplished by the transport industry. The useful effect can only be consumed during the production process; it does not exist as a thing of use distinct from this process, a thing which functions as an article of commerce and circulates as a commodity only after its production. However, the exchange value of this useful effect is still determined, like that of any other commodity, by the value of the elements of production used up in it (labour-power and means of production), plus the surplus-value crated by the surplus labour of the workers occupied in the transport industry ... The formula for the transport industry is thus M—C$<^{L}$MP ... P—M', for it is production process itself, and not a product separable from it, that is paid for and consumed.[31]

Marx's formula for the service-circuit is M—C$<^{L}$MP ... P—M', as is demonstrated in the quote above. With the production of services, the surplus-value contained in the service-commodity is materialised in the product of the service but does not assume a physical form apart from this. One major way that the circuit of service-commodities differs from material goods is that the surplus value in the service-commodity is immediately *realised* in the form of

30 Tregenna, 2011, p. 290.
31 Marx 1978 [1885], p. 135.

money after it is produced. Although the service-good takes the form of a commodity after it is produced, it sheds this form and is transformed into money as soon as it exists. The commodity stage is bypassed, and the surplus-value is immediately realised in the form of money. The value the service worker produces is immediately consumed and transformed into money through payment.

At the end of the working week, the capitalist will directly pay the worker a percentage of this monetary surplus value to compensate him or her. Just as with the production of physical goods, the monetary surplus value produced is far greater than the wage that the worker receives. Service workers produce surplus-value, but this surplus-value only assumes the form of money and is immediately realised as soon as it is produced. In the service industry, the possibility that the capitalist cannot sell the commodity *after* its production does not arise. Generally, there is a contract or agreement between the service-provider and the client that payment will be made after the completion of the service. In some cases, the client must pay before the service is performed, especially in the case of expensive services, entertainment, transportation, and tourism. With services that take place on a recurring basis, there is usually a guarantee of payment through a subscription or direct debit system. The *realisation* of the surplus value is thus guaranteed by the legal contract or agreement as soon as the service is produced. In the service industry, there would not be a crisis of overproduction, in which more goods are produced than can be sold. A crisis of surplus-value absorption can only occur *before* the surplus value is produced as a result of a failure to stimulate demand. It is entirely possible that a commercial services company has invested capital into means of production and labour-power but cannot find customers. This would result not in a crisis of overproduction, but rather underconsumption and the inability to stimulate demand for the service.

With service goods, there are still additional costs such as transportation, storing, and marketing, but these costs come *before* the commodity has been produced. There is a significant amount of marketing for the service in order to stimulate demand and find a customer base. A service company invests more of its capital into marketing in order to sell its service, and it can take quite a few months before the service is actually produced. A serious crisis will occur if a service company cannot find new clients or loses clients due to poor management. Just as with material goods, there is a temporal period between marketing and the sale of the commodity. Costs of transportation and storing are generally the costs of transporting and storing equipment used in the service. For example, with a multinational cleaning company like Molly Maid, the costs of transportation are the cars they use to transport cleaning supplies, and the costs of storing is the small facility a Molly Maid franchise owns to store its equipment.

The labour of service workers depends on the ability of their employer to find customers. Although this is not true for all service labour, significant sections of the service workforce are dependent on the stimulation of local demand. It is one reason why some forms of service work tend to be precarious, for they lack the permanency of jobs that produce goods and services necessary for human life. Many service-goods, such as domestic cleaning, tourism, and entertainment are not essential and depend on consumerism. When capitalism is doing well, significant sections of the population have disposable income to spend on these service-goods. However, during a capitalist crisis, incomes are significantly reduced, which directly affects the jobs of many service workers. Unable to find customers, service workers in non-essential industries are in danger of becoming underemployed or losing their jobs. This is one reason why service workers are often put on temporary, zero-hours, or fixed-term contracts. It gives the capitalists in these industries the ability to *flexibly* unemploy their workforce and shift capital elsewhere in times of economic crisis.

Some service work is essential and necessary for human life, such as social care, medical treatment, transportation, and education. Until recently, most essential service work was part of the public sector and managed by the capitalist state. This ensured that it would be accessible to everyone and maintain quality standards. Neoliberalism has caused essential service industries to be privatised, which has resulted in for-profit universities, private bus companies, and profit-seeking hospitals. When essential service industries are organised on a capitalist basis, both the accessibility and quality of the service is reduced. In a for-profit university, teachers are transformed into workers who must prepare students to take standardised tests so that they can get their degree. The teacher entirely loses their autonomy, while the student must learn to regurgitate information on an exam. It is what Paulo Freire called in *Pedagogy of the Oppressed* the 'banking approach', where teachers deposit information that students withdraw without critically engaging with.

In this section, I have argued that both goods-producing and service workers can produce surplus value. Surplus value is not a physical thing but a social relation, and only arises when the capital-relation is present. If the capital-relation is absent, the worker may receive a wage and work under the capitalist form of exploitation, but no surplus value will arise. Therefore, not all service workers produce surplus-value, but only those whose labour is organised on a capitalist basis. In order to make this point clear, I will briefly discuss Marx's important distinction between productive and unproductive labour.

5 Productive and Unproductive Labour

For Marx a worker "is productive and the work he performs is productive if it directly creates surplus value".[32] For a worker to be considered *productive*, they must be employed by a capitalist who consumes their labour power to appropriate surplus value, which is only possible when the capital relation is present (M-C-M'). When a worker does not produce surplus value, they are called by Marx unproductive. Marx says

> The work is consumed for its use-value, not as creating exchange value; it is consumed unproductively, not productively ... the money that he pays for it is *revenue*, not *capital*. Its consumption is to be formulated not as M-C-M, but C-M-C (the last being the *labour* or service itself).[33]

This concept can be somewhat misleading, as an unproductive worker certainly produces something and often contributes to the *realisation* of surplus value. However, they are unproductive because the capital-relation is absent and therefore surplus-value does not result from their labour. The capitalist uses a portion of their capital to cover the costs of advertising, transportation, and storage. Their money here does not function as capital, but as revenue used to compensate services. These services generally do not create surplus value, although in today's capitalism outsourcing has made some of them productive industries.

In some cases, workers can perform both productive and unproductive labour. An example of this are baristas in a coffee chain like Starbucks or Costa. A Starbucks worker creates additional surplus value by manufacturing drinks such as lattes and cappuccinos. Although the majority of the surplus value is materialised in the raw coffee beans, milk, and paper cups, the Starbucks worker uses these things as means of production to produce a new commodity. At the same time, the barista is also employed to sell coffee, using a variety of sales techniques to encourage customers to buy additional products, like food and coffee mugs. They also clean the shop, as Starbucks does not outsource its cleaning labour. Hence, the Starbucks barista is both a productive worker that produces surplus value, and an unproductive labourer that helps to sell commodities. This is a new phenomenon unique to monopoly capitalism and is something I will discuss in more detail in the next chapter.

32 Marx 1976 [1867], p. 1041.
33 *Ibid*, p. 1041.

During Marx's time, most service labour was unproductive and excluded the capital relation. Workers employed in the service industry did work that is necessary for the capitalist system but did not produce surplus value in the process. With the development of monopoly capitalism, forms of labour that were previously unproductive are transformed into productive labour. One reason for this is the emergence of large corporations that sell services such as cleaning, social care, entertainment, and security. Self-employed people often cannot compete with these corporations and gradually disappear. This creates a cheap source of service labour used by corporations to outsource unproductive tasks and reduce labour costs. Fiona Tregenna says that

> with outsourcing, activities previously undertaken in-house are contracted out, typically to another company which either employs workers directly or sub-contracts the work to a third company (or to an individual). An employment relationship with the workers performing the activities is replaced—from the perspective of the original employer—by a commercial relationship with a service provider.[34]

In outsourced industries, such as cleaning, transportation, programming, maintenance, IT, shipping, and teaching, the workers are productive, and their employer is after surplus value. As production and manufacture becomes more automated, the capitalist needs to find new markets in which to get fresh surplus value. The outsourcing of unproductive services creates new outlets for the accumulation of capital, especially in developed countries that have been deindustrialised. Also, neoliberal governments have privatised state enterprises, such as public transportation, health care, and even education. For example, Scotland's train system Scotrail was privatised in 1997, which means that its employees no longer provide a public service. Scotrail is today managed by the Dutch company, Abellio, and its employees are productive labourers that produce the transportation service-commodity.[35] I will discuss outsourcing and privatisation in chapter 8.

Having now discussed Marx's theory of surplus-value, I will discuss the two main ways that capitalists get surplus-value. As I will show, the techniques used to appropriate surplus-value in the service industry is different from in goods-producing industries, although there are some similarities.

34 Tregenna 2010, p. 1431.

35 Wikipedia Article "Scotrail".

6 Increased Surplus-Value

In *Capital,* Marx discusses two ways that the capitalist class can increase the mass of surplus-value. First, there is absolute surplus-value, which is surplus-value that results from the lengthening of the working day. When a worker works longer hours, he produces additional surplus value for the capitalist even when he is paid overtime. The capitalist "would, if it were possible, extend the working day to 24 hours, since the longer the working day, the greater the amount of surplus-value created".[36] If a worker originally worked ten hours and engaged in eight hours of surplus labour, adding an additional two hours will add two additional hours of surplus labour. A capitalist can extend the working day by requiring the workers to work longer hours or pay a bonus as an incentive to make him stay. They can also create competition between the workers by promoting the worker who works overtime. Zero-hour contracts enable capitalists to increase the working day by requiring the worker always to be available for work. Since zero-hour contracts usually result in low-wages, workers are often desperate for money and will work as much as they are asked. If they refuse a job, there is a chance they could be terminated or simply not offered hours in the future. In Britain, zero-hour contracts are very common in-service jobs, being used to employ carers, cleaners, lecturers, taxi drivers, and front-house staff.

Absolute surplus-value can be extracted by getting workers to perform labour while they are on their break, or even off work. The manager might ask him, "could you please help me carry this box, there is no one else around". The worker might only lose four minutes from his thirty-minute break, and on the surface, this seems quite minor. In *Capital,* Marx shows that when we add up all the additional labour attained from workers who are on their break it can add up to over a month of additional labour time for each worker. He quotes a factory inspector who says, "moments are the elements of profit".[37] If there are no rules prohibiting the contact of workers while they are at home, management might also contact the worker to ask them to perform small tasks while they are not working. In today's capitalist society, social media, the internet, unpaid work training, and 'fun' work functions have created a return of absolute surplus value. The managers of contemporary neoliberalism will use the ideology of 'personal development' and 'fun' to make *work* the most important part of the workers' life. They will not just try to make the worker work longer

36 Kuusinen 1963, p. 272.

37 Marx 1976 [1876], p. 352.

hours, but also attend unpaid *work-related* functions such as Christmas parties, cultural events, and workshops. The function of a Christmas party or cultural event is to replace class struggle with *fun* and make the worker think his or her boss is their friend. The capitalist also requires the worker to attend training, which are often unpaid and function to raise the productivity of the worker's labour. Training increases the quality of the workers labour power without compensating them for this improved labour. The capitalist profits when a worker attends a training, while the worker gets nothing in return.

The bourgeoisie uses social media to penetrate into every aspect of the workers life. They may create a Facebook group that is *compulsory* for a worker to join and participate in. The boss may pose a question or create a survey and require the worker to participate. The worker is constantly required to be 'creative' and show how much they care about the corporation. If they aren't participating in the lively discussion about work on Facebook, then they are not being 'creative' and could be terminated. Most corporations give the worker a work-email address and require that they check their email at all times. They may send an email with a training that must be completed before the next working day, or a form that must be filled out electronically. If they do not respond to an email quickly, they could lose their job. If they do not complete the training, they could be temporarily suspended or terminated. As a result, the worker must consider his job while he is on a date, out with friends, or having dinner with his family. The capitalist has penetrated the most intimate spaces of the workers life and is constantly *with* them at all times. Prior to smartphones, email, and Facebook, it would have been impossible for the capitalist to constantly be in communication with his workers. The internet has thus made it possible for the capitalist to get more *absolute* surplus value than ever before. A worker who constantly thinks about work will have no problem staying an extra hour to help his *friend*, the boss. Because social media and the internet has made it possible for the worker to continue work at home, the capitalist can constantly extend the working day indefinitely. Since there are not generally clearly defined rules or policies concerning unpaid work from home, the capitalist can continue the exploitation of the worker when he leaves work.

In some service industries, such as IT, corporate writing jobs, and software programming, the use of email and Facebook makes it possible to get more *absolute surplus* value from the worker than ever before. The capitalist can email the programmer and ask him to make a revision to his software before the next working day. A corporation can email their product-description writer and ask them about some detail in their writing. These workers are not paid while they work from home but must do so on threat of termination. It does not matter if the law prohibits this because most corporations often ignore the laws. If they violate a law or get into a legal dispute, they will employ high paid lawyers to resolve it for them. The high profits they get from breaking the law far exceed the fees they occasionally pay for this. The trade union movement has addressed the problem of unpaid electronic tasks such as work-email accounts, work-Facebook groups, and administrative duties that some workers are required to do from home. In France, a trade union demanded that the workers only be required to access their work email *while* they are at work. They forced management to set up email accounts that would be active *only* while the worker was clocked in, making it impossible for the worker to do unpaid electronic tasks while not clocked in at work.[38] Some unions have also tried to make it illegal for the boss to send a friend request on Facebook and require the worker to participate in a Facebook discussion.

Absolute surplus-value that results from the extension of the working day is only one way of appropriating more surplus-value from the worker. There are often barriers to getting absolute surplus-value, such as labour laws and company policies. Therefore, the capitalist class more frequently seeks what Marx calls relative surplus-value, which is attained through intensifying the exploitation *within* a single day of work. With relative surplus value, the proportion between paid and unpaid labour changes within a single working day. The capitalist gets relative surplus value when the necessary labour time is reduced so that the surplus labour time is raised. When it takes less time to produce the *equivalent* of his own labour-power, the worker has *more* time to produce surplus value for the capitalist in a given working day. The reduction in necessary labour results in more surplus labour and hence more surplus value for the capitalist. The capitalist continues to pay the worker the same wage while getting *more* value from his labour power in a single working day. Relative surplus value is *relative* because it depends on factors directly related to the conditions of production. It is thus the result of increasing the productivity of labour.

In the service industry, relative surplus-value emerges when more services can be produced in a shorter amount of time than before. This often can result from a change to management style, which allows the service to be more effectively planned. For example, a bus company can increase relative surplus-value by creating routes that enable the bus to get from point A to point B faster and thereby allow more customers to use the service. Better systems of traffic management and improved roads also contribute to an increased amount of relative surplus-value. The amount of value in transport services produced by

38 *The Guardian*, 31 December 2016.

the bus driver increases even though he drives the bus for the same number of hours as before. Another example is in the cleaning industry, where strict route and normalisation is applied to ensure that cleaners can produce as many clean spaces as possible. The actual technology is less important in the cleaning industry as the system of management. Cleaners who use an older vacuum cleaner but are managed effectively will be capable of producing significantly more clean spaces than before. The cleaner will experience more exploitation, for they will be under tremendous pressure to work faster and more efficiently.

7 Conclusion

In this chapter, I have shown how the primary categories of Marx's political economy can be expanded to make sense of the labour of service workers. Marx's central category of surplus-value does not only apply to factory workers, but to service employees and retail workers. In the next chapter, I will demonstrate how Marx's theory of the circulation of commodities is helpful for grasping the structure of the retail industry. Just as service labour was generally not productive in Marx's time, there was also not a massive retail industry. However, his theoretical formulations in volume two of *Capital* lay the foundation for an analysis of the retail industry in the era of monopoly capitalism.

CHAPTER 5

Retail and the Circulation of Commodities

As I have indicated throughout this book, there was not a huge retail sector in Marx's time. The primary consumers of luxury commodities were members of the capitalist class and most advertising was directed at them. There did not exist multinational retailers such as WalMart or H&M, although there were some large retail shops such as Harrods and Harding & Co, which sold high-end goods to London's affluent bourgeoisie. These department stores sold expensive clothing and particularly marketed its goods to the wives of capitalists. They also sold goods from the colonies, toys, and early consumer electronics. Because the bourgeoisie had appropriated extravagant wealth from the surplus-value of the proletariat, it was usually capable of purchasing these goods. While small funds went into advertising, the sales effort played a very small role in the sale of commodities.[1]

Retail in the nineteenth century was closely connected to improving communication systems and transportation in order to reduce circulation time. During Marx's time, the bourgeoisie made path breaking discoveries in modern transportation and significant improvements to rail transportation. While Marx was living in London, British industrialists and MPs invested large amounts of capital to improve railway travel. In the 1840's, this resulted in a phenomenon known as railway mania, which was a temporary economic crisis resulting from the overproduction of British railways.[2] The reason for this mania to produce railways stemmed from the fact that improved transportation reduced the time needed to transport commodities from the factory to the shop. If commodities could reach the merchant faster, then the surplus-value contained in them could be realised more quickly. Faster transportation meant that capital could turnover more times per year, which expanded the scale of production and increased the concentration of capital. As most commodities found enthusiastic buyers in the large metropolises—London, Paris, New York, and Berlin—the capitalists did not need to worry about marketing and advertising to sell their products. Their primary goal was getting commodities to consumers as fast as possible in order to sell them quickly.

1 For an excellent documentary on retail in the 19th century, see *Absolute History*. "What Shopping Was Like During the Victorian Era" YouTube. Online: https://www.youtube.com/watch?v=DF4jq_CjQIQ&t=4s.

2 Odlyzko 2010, pp. 22–30.

 | DOI:10.1163/9789004469624_006

Marx analysed the circulation process in great detail in the second volume of *Capital*. Volume Two of *Capital* is essentially a work about retail under capitalism, as its object is the realisation of surplus-value. In the second volume, Marx's primary task was to study the circulation of commodities, the turnover of capital, and social reproduction. Because the text was not completed during Marx's time, it is often neglected and is the least studied volume of *Capital*. Parts of it are very dry and can appear uninteresting and repetitive. As David Harvey notes, Volume 2 is

> a rather boring book (and that may be an understatement). It lacks the literary sparkle and the humor, irony and devastating put-downs that help make Volume I such a readable tome.[3]

When Marxist writers do engage with Volume Two, they often only focus on the final chapters on the social reproduction process. This is unfortunate, as some of Marx's finest theoretical work can be found in the chapters on fixed capital, turnover, and circulation time. For the purposes of this book, Volume Two is seen as the most important part of *Capital*, as it is one of the few places where Marx writes about retail employees, service workers, and the process of surplus-value *realisation*.

In this chapter, I will show how Marx's arguments in Volume Two of *Capital* are helpful in formulating a Marxist approach to the retail and services sector. My goal is to provide a Marxist definition of retail that allows us to see the importance of retail workers and gain an understanding of their place in the division of labour. I will argue that all workers who help to *circulate* commodities are retail employees, and their primary task is to *reduce* circulation time in order to *increase* the turnover of capital. By circulating commodities, retail workers transform commodity capital into money capital so that the surplus-value contained in them is realised. Following Marx in Volume Two, I will argue that some production adding value to commodities can take place in circulation. A Marxist approach to retail shifts attention from sales to circulation, of which sales are a part but not the whole. It will allow us to perceive that logistics workers, transport providers, and retail employees are all part of the *same* circulation process even though they have *different* functions.

Also, I will show how the concept of circulation time is helpful for perceiving the difference between goods production and services. Marx himself was aware of this, as railway transport was a major sector of 19th century

3 Harvey 2013, p. 7.

capitalism. Because productive services in the 19th century were mostly connected to the circulation of commodities, Marx thought that their circulation time was zero. I will argue that this is not the case today, as many services exist that have no connection to the circulation of commodities. Some of them—entertainment, cleaning, education—are themselves commodities, which must be circulated in order to be consumed. In order to make sense of this, I will argue that the distinction between circulation time and working time are reversed in the service industry. The commodity exists as a service but must first be sold before it can be produced, so that its circulation precedes its production. I will begin with a short exposition and discussion of the circulation process as discussed by Marx in Volume Two of *Capital*. I will then introduce his major concepts—circulation time, working time, turnover, and social reproduction—demonstrating how they help us to make sense of the retail and services industry.

1 Circulation of Commodities

In the first volume of *Capital*, Marx discusses the production surplus-value, which is embodied in goods and services. Marx concludes the first volume of *Capital* by demonstrating that the accumulation of capital is only possible through the exploitation of labour-power. Capitalists must constantly expand production and find new ways to exploit labour-power so that they can increase the mass of surplus-value. Production, however, is only one part of the story. Once a commodity has been produced, it must be transported, packaged, marketed, and sold. Its final destination is the consumer, who purchases goods and services to satisfy some social need. Marx divides consumers into two groups that purchase commodities from two different departments.

Some consumers are capitalists that purchase goods and services from other capitalists in order to acquire raw materials, machinery, equipment, software, logistics systems, and financial services needed to engage in capitalist production. Marx calls these producers department one, and they include all industries that produce means of production. Many of the raw materials that are produced in department one are purchased by service industries, such as cleaning companies, restaurants, coffeeshops, and educational institutes. Cleaning supplies, wholesale food, cooking equipment, office materials, and computers are sold to services industries as means of production. These services industries are important corporate clients, as they demand regular shipments so that they can continue production.

The other group of consumers are individuals and groups of people that purchase goods and services for private consumption. This includes things like food, electronics (i.e., iPhones, TV's, laptops, etc.), appliances, cars, and clothing. Marx calls these producers department two, and they include all the capitalists that produce goods for consumption. In contemporary capitalism, the same capitalist who produces means of production can produce consumer goods. If food is produced in large bundles to be sold to restaurants, then it is part of department one because the restaurant is purchasing the food as means of production. However, if the food is sold to merchants to be sold to individual consumers, then it is part of department two. The restaurants themselves belong to department two, as they prepare food for individual consumption.

A central issue of Volume Two of *Capital* is understanding the commodity's circulation, which is the process between its production and its final sale. Marx says

> in commodity form, capital must perform commodity functions ... the articles it consists of, which are produced from the start for the market, must be sold, transformed into money, and pass through the movement C-M.[4]

The circulation process involves the realisation of surplus-value through the transformation of commodities into money. It is the labour of retail workers who stack shelves, use sales techniques, and transfer the commodity to the consumer that enables realisation to take place. Circulation is just as important as production, for without it, consumption would be impossible. As Marx says, "circulation is just as necessary for commodity production as is production itself, and thus the agents of circulation are just as necessary as agents of production."[5] This is an important insight, for it is common for Marxists to privilege production over circulation since the former is where surplus-value arises. Instead of viewing the capitalist system as a totality comprising production, circulation, and distribution, they prefer to only focus on workers at the point of production.[6] Such an analysis is deeply problematic because it misses

4 Marx 1978 [1885], p. 122.

5 *ibid*, p. 205.

6 This position can be seen most clearly in the American Socialist Workers Party 'turn to industry' strategy, in which the party moved all its cadres into industrial jobs. While they played a leading role in the trade union movement, their narrow focus prevented them organizing other sections of the working class. For a very good example of this position, see Barnes (2019), which lays out the central justification for the SWP's strategy.

the key links connecting production to circulation, which is central for the surplus-value to be realised. Politically, it can lead to a narrow understanding the working class that focuses only a section of the working class and neglect the work of organising retail workers. Marx's approach is not to privilege productive workers over retail employees, but to demonstrate their different functions in the capitalist process. Both have the capacity to significantly harm the bourgeoisie if organised properly, although they might need to be organised differently.

Marx says that "the circuit of capital proceeds normally only as long as its various phases pass into each other without delay."[7] Capitalists take significant care to prevent disruptions or delays in the circulation process, for disruptions in the circulation of commodities have an effect on their production. This was clear in the 2020 Coronavirus Outbreak, in which the circulation of many goods entirely stopped. In the European Union, the UK, and other parts of the capitalist world, warehouses and retail shops closed, which severely disrupted the circulation of commodities. Capitalists tried to keep shops open as long as possible, putting the lives of workers at risk. In many places, it took workers going on strike and tremendous trade union pressure to force the state to intervene and close retail shops. Capitalists have a reserve of money in order to deal with such a crisis, as well as the capitalist state. As Marx says, "the money accumulation fund ... serves as a reserve fund to cope with disturbances in the circuit."[8] Circulation is thus taken into account in advance of the production of goods and services. While government aid or a money accumulation fund may temporarily prevent a crisis, long term underconsumption resulting from disruptions to the circuit are devastating to the bourgeoisie. From the capitalist standpoint, circulation is just as important as production, for a disruption to it can cause a systemic crisis to develop. This is again a reason why socialists should take retail workers seriously, for their organisation can put the entire working class in a better position.

2 Circulation Time and Costs of Circulation

Marx constructs a system of concepts for analysing the circulation process: production time, working period, circulation time, and turnover. The working period is the time in which capital is tied directly to commodity production.

7 *ibid*, p. 133.
8 *ibid*, p. 165.

Marx defines it as "the number of interrelated working days that are required, in a particular line of business, to complete a finished product."[9] In the production of physical goods, the working period always defines the period needed to produce a certain quantity of goods in order to meet a production target. For example, if it takes a factory in Bangladesh one week to produce an order of 20,000 t-shirts for H&M, then the working period is seven days. In the service industry, the working period might be defined as the period of days that it takes to produce a certain quantity of monetary surplus-value. Suppose that a franchisee of Molly Maid must get a revenue of £15,000 in order to pay regular fees and get a profit. If it takes two weeks of work to get this money, then the working period is fourteen days.

Capitalists are constantly trying to reduce the working period, for this allows them to expand the scale of production and increase their profits. As Marx shows, decreasing circulation time is important because it encourages a faster working period and the sale of more goods and services. If the shirts produced in Bangladesh can be quickly shipped and sold, this will increase demand and encourage the acceleration of the working period. With service-goods, especially in franchised industries, there is tremendous pressure on managers and franchisees to get more customers. They will strive for good reviews and invest significant capital in marketing in order to decrease the working period for which they can meet their sales targets. With a faster working period, service companies can significantly expand the mass of surplus-value that they can appropriate and thereby increase their profits.

In order to further analyse the temporal structure of the working period, Marx introduces the concept of production time, which is the time that the commodity is being produced. This differs from the working period, as it defines both the time that the commodity lies idle in production, and the time that labour-power is exerted in order to produce the commodity. Once the garment workers at H&M have produced the bundle of shirts, they may need time to be bleached or dyed. Marx includes this as production, for it is part of the period in which the commodity is bound up in the production process. Capitalists are always trying to find ways to reduce these processes in order to accelerate the working period. In service industries, production time includes not just the service, but the labour that goes into preparation and transportation. For example, a cleaner at Molly Maid is engaged in production time while she is driving to a client as much as when she is cleaning a home. Former employees of Molly Maid report on Indeed that there was tremendous pressure on them

9 *ibid*, p. 308.

to drive faster, eat while driving, and take the fastest route in order to get to the next client. Clearly, franchisees are under pressure to reduce non-labour periods of production time in order to meet sales targets and reduce the working period. As Marx says, "the tendency of capitalist production is therefore to shorten as much as possible the excess of production time over working time."[10]

In order to show how capitalism transforms our relationship to time, Marx introduces the term 'circulation time', which is the time needed for the commodity to circulate from the factory to the final consumer (whether this is another capitalist or an individual buyer). For example, if it takes one week for the shirts produced in Bangladesh to reach a warehouse in Britain, then the circulation time is seven days for the Bangladeshi producer. On the side of H&M, the circulation time is the time that it takes to distribute the shirts to the shops and sell them, which can take anywhere from two weeks to six months. Marx's analysis is focused almost entirely on the circulation of physical goods, although he makes a few isolated remarks about the circulation process with transportation. For Marx, transportation sells a 'change of location', and he acknowledges that the circulation process for such service goods differs from the production of goods. However, as most service goods were directly tied to the circulation process, Marx was unable to understand the circulation process of service-commodities, such as domestic cleaning or entertainment.

Service-commodities that are not tied to the production of goods circulate *before* they are produced. For example, in order to provide domestic house cleaning services, a commercial cleaning company must commodify their cleaning package and find customers before it can be produced. This sometimes happens with the production of goods, as multinational corporations gain contracts with suppliers covering extended periods before the goods are produced. However, with physical goods, there will always be a circulation period after the production of goods even if corporate customers have already been acquired. This is not the case with service-goods, as the process comes to an end as soon as the service has been provided. Much more effort goes into keeping customers, which is ensured through direct debit payments and subscriptions.

The concept of circulation time is very helpful for perceiving why capitalists are always trying to improve transportation and communication systems. As Marx points out "the speed with which the product of one process can be transferred to another process as a means of production depends on

10 *ibid*, p. 202–203.

the development of the means of transport and communication".[11] Whenever capitalists find ways to improve transportation, it significantly reduces the circulation time and thereby allows commodities to reach buyers faster. This is why the development of high-speed rail, air transportation, and improved maritime systems is bound up with the accumulation of capital. Every major reduction of circulation time puts pressure on producers to reduce the working period, as it allows them to produce more goods so that more surplus-value can be realised.

In the service industry, reduction in circulation time is usually not the result of improvements to transportation, but rather improved communication systems. I define communications as the process by which the capitalist class communicates with customers and consumers. This could include call centres, in which product representatives communicate with potential buyers in order to secure more customers. It also includes social media operatives, who communicate with potential consumers through advertising on Facebook, YouTube, TikTok, and other platforms. Improvements to social media allow certain sections of the service-industry bourgeoisie to communicate their services and thereby reduce circulation time. One reason why large commercial service company command the market is because they control the means of communication. For example, Uber is able to dominate the market for taxi services because they control the means of circulation. Their app is far more advanced than private taxi firms, which accelerates the accumulation of capital by Uber and the displacement of self-employed taxi drivers.

Marx deduces the concept of 'turnover' from working period, production time, and circulation time. He defines turnover as

> the sum of its circulation time proper and its production time ... it is the period of time that elapses from the moment that capital value is advanced in a particular form until the return of the capital value in process in the same form.[12]

A capital has turned when the capital advanced returns to the capitalist, thereby allowing him to restart the production process. Capitalists are interested in increasing the number of times that capital turns over in order to expand the scale of production. Any stage in the cycle of capital can affect the turnover time of capital. If circulation time is increased, this might reduce the

11 *ibid*, p. 219.
12 *ibid*, p. 233.

scale of production, and thereby reduce the number of times that capital turns over. It could also be the case that production time is increased, resulting in a longer period before a fresh batch of commodities can be put into circulation. Marx shows in Volume 3 of *Capital* that the number of times that capital turns over directly affects the annual rate of surplus-value, which increases with each increase in turnover. This demonstrates how retail workers who do not produce surplus-value nonetheless have a direct effect on the annual rate of surplus-value.

3 Production in Circulation

In Volume 2 of *Capital*, Marx points out that although circulation is the transformation of commodity capital into money capital, production can take place in circulation. Marx says, the "transport industry, storage, and the dispersal of goods in a distributable form should be viewed as production processes that continue within the process of circulation."[13] This is not just unproductive labour to assist with the circulation process, but productive labour that results in additional surplus-value. From the standpoint of the industrial capitalist, the costs of circulation are unproductive in that they do not add any value to his capital. Transport, packaging, and logistics are services that he must purchase with his revenue and are simply costs of circulation. However, from the standpoint of the service and retail companies that provide these services, the workers they employ are productive labourers whose labour results in surplus-value. As Marx says about the transport industry,

> the transport industry forms on the one hand an independent branch of production, and hence a particular sphere of investment of productive capital. On the other hand it is distinguished by its appearance as the continuation of a production process within the circulation process and for the circulation process.[14]

Producers of goods usually do not control transportation networks, and must purchase transport services from railways, multinational shipping firms, and airline companies. Marx points out that what these companies produce is a 'change of location', and that they are consumed as soon they are produced.

13 Marx [1894] 1981., p. 379.
14 Marx [1885] 1978., p. 229.

A transport worker—whether employed to transport goods or people—produces surplus-value through the production of this change of location. They produce far more monetary value in transport services than the wages they receive for their labour-power and are thus productive labourers.

Recall that for Marx, the value of a commodity is determined by the socially-necessary labour-time required for its production. Using the existing technology and scientific resources, one can produce a commodity within an average amount of time. One might raise the question of what constitutes the socially necessary labour time of transport services. Trains, airplanes, and shipping vessels operate according to strict schedules, and there is significant pressure to arrive at one's destination in time. Transport schedules are one determinant of what constitutes the socially necessary labour time to produce a change of location. By stating that the distance between A and B requires X number of hours using existing technology, the schedule says that more labour in normal circumstances would be unnecessary. Of course, there are many conjunctural features that can cause delays, but transport producers take significant care to minimise this as much as possible. If a train, vessel, or airplane arrives later than expected the workers who run these vehicles could be punished. Therefore, the socially necessary labour time regulating the production of transport services is expressed in schedules. Not only does this reduce the socially necessary labour time, but it also reduces circulation time, which allows commodities to arrive faster in the market. When transport is accelerated, the big banks are able to appropriate more surplus value from both the producers of goods and the transport companies that circulate them. The capitalist class as a whole has an interest in reducing travel time in all branches of transportation.

There are other production processes that take place within the circulation of commodities. In the restaurant and hospitality industry, food that has been produced at an earlier stage is manufactured into a cooked meal, which adds additional value to it. Especially in large chain restaurants such as Nando's, large amounts of additional surplus-value are produced through the kitchen staff. By producing a signature Nando's Peri Peri dish, the cooks are transforming the raw chicken into a new commodity. The value created at an earlier stage is transferred to the final product, and additional surplus-value is produced in the process. This additional value is appropriated by Nando's and used to finance the expansion of their stores and thus the accumulation of capital on an expanded scale.

Having now discussed the circulation of commodities, I will turn to their consumption, a topic that has sometimes been neglected by Marxist writers. Although Marx discussed the importance of consumption in the *Grundrisse*, he never provided a systematic account of it. This is understandable, as it was not immediately relevant to his project, nor was there a large consumerist middle class in his time. In the era of monopoly capital, however, consumerism is an integral part of life, and must be taken into account if we are to adequately understand the relationship between production, circulation, and consumption.

4 Consumption Time and Consumption Period

The primary temporal categories of Marx's *Capital* are socially necessary labour time, production time, working period, circulation time, and turnover. These concepts allow Marx to analyse the structures that regulate the production and circulation of commodities, and the accumulation of capital. Marx does not account for the temporal structure of consumption itself, as it is not immediately relevant to his analysis. However, in contemporary monopoly capitalism, it is necessary and important to account for the consumption process.

Once a bundle of commodities has been sold, the capitalist has turned over his capital and can start a new cycle. It is very important that the capitalist finds a stable, permanent customer basis in order to ensure the continual purchase of their goods and services. Capitalists do not just seek permanent customers but anticipate the time that it takes for them to consume their products. I will call *consumption time* the time that it takes for a consumer to fully consume a commodity, and a *consumption period* the period in which a commodity is being consumed. Consumption time accounts for the lifespan of a particular commodity and consumption period is the entire period that the consumer is enjoying their commodity. The consumption period comes to an end when the consumer returns to the market and repurchases the same good or service. This concept is helpful because it allows us to perceive forms of production that are directly connected to the consumption of commodities.

Consumption time is not a natural process, resulting from the properties of the commodity, but is anticipated with its production. In the era of monopoly capital, capitalists try to reduce the consumption time for many different groups of commodities. Some high-end goods, such as laptops and smartphones, are planned to break down and require replacement in the future. This can be done by introducing an update that makes a particular phone or computer dysfunctional, as is frequently the case with Apple products. It could also be done by discontinuing a particular electronic and making its parts unattainable, as is frequently done in the video game industry. For example, when Nintendo introduces a new console, such as a Switch, it gradually discontinues previous models such as the Wii and 3DS. Not only do they stop selling the games and parts of these software, but they take down servers to run online games. If one wants to play Splatoon online, one must buy a Switch and purchase Splatoon 2.[15] The purpose of this is not simply improvement, but the discouragement of the continued consumption of the previous system and pressure to purchase the new model. Nintendo's goal is to keep the consumption time for a particular console to a certain period in order to ensure new purchases of their consoles and games. The consumption time is entirely planned and is an integral part of their business model. Another interesting aspect of consumption time is that it can be artificially extended. For example, Nintendo could extend the consumption time of a particular game such as Zelda by introducing an expansion pack. Nintendo will usually release an expansion pack a year after it has been released, and spend prior months anticipating the launch. This way, when a gamer has completed the game, Nintendo can continue the consumption period by stimulating the user with new features.

Concerning the consumption of commodities, a concept that is analogous to turnover is *replacement*. Whereas turnover measures how many times the capital is reinvested in a year, replacement measures how many times a commodity is replaced per year. Monopoly capitalism tries to increase the number of replacements each year by decreasing consumption time. This is further aided by decreased production and circulation time, as it ensures that there will always be a stable supply of commodities in the shop. With every increase in the replacement of a commodity, capitalists increase the number of times they can turnover their capital in a single year. Hence, decreasing consumption time increases the turnover of capital, and can increase the rate of surplus-value if there is a corresponding wage decrease.

In the same way that Marx visualises the turnover of capital and its effect on the rate of profit, we can visualise consumption time and the replacement of commodities (Table 1). Let us suppose that the commodity in question is a t-shirt, whose price is £5 per shirt, which is purchased by H&M for £1/per shirt that is produced by a worker who makes 10p per shirt.

What this table shows is that by decreasing the consumption time and thereby increasing the annual replacement, the retailers are able to realise more surplus value. An interesting fact about this table, however, is that the rate of exploitation does not change, remaining at 400% with each increase. Capitalists must therefore find ways to further cheapen the labour costs, despite already being extremely low. Unless they do this, they will not benefit

15 Webster, Andrew. "Nintendo is Slowly Erasing the WiiU From Existence" The Verge, 1 May 2018.

TABLE 1 Consumption time and rate of surplus value

Consumption time	Replacement	Revenue	Realised surplus- value (£1/H&M shirt)	Wages of producer, 10p per shirt	Rate of surplus value
4 months	3 times	£15	£12	30p	400%
3 months	4 times	£20	£16	40p	400%
2 months	6 times	£30	£24	60p	400%

from the decrease of consumption time. Because they occupy a monopoly position, multinational corporations put tremendous pressure on their suppliers to further decrease wage costs in order to increase the rate of surplus-value.

A corollary of consumption time is the concept of consumption period, which is the entire period that the commodity is being consumed. The consumption period ends when the user no longer uses it and sells it. A Nintendo Switch console, for example, is in the consumption period during the entire period that it is being used. Once it has become obsolete or broken down, thereby requiring replacement, its consumption period ends. The reason why I have introduced the concept of consumption period is because it allows us to perceive production processes that take place to service the consumption of many goods. For many goods, consumption requires additional labour, and cannot exist without the aid of specialist workers. The same process that is a consumption period for the consumer is a production process for service workers. Marx was aware of this, as he points out in Volume 2 of *Capital* that service goods such as transportation are consumed as they are produced. The consumption period therefore does not exist once the commodity has been attained but must constantly be produced.

By the *production* of the consumption period, I mean the process of *servicing* the consumption of goods through the use of service workers. Some goods require a complex labour process for their consumption, such as computer gaming, and electronic communications. In order to play an online game, whether on a computer or a Nintendo console, significant labour is needed to run servers and update the system.[16] Without computer programmers,

16 For a discussion of gaming workers, see Woodcock (2019)

it would be impossible to run these servers and the consumption of online gaming would stop. For a Nintendo Switch, the consumption period must be produced by computer programmers, customer service representatives, and IT specialists. The console, controllers, and games must be constantly updated, which is a continual process. If this labour were to stop, most Switch owners would be unable to play many of their games and for some, the consumption period would come to a halt. Therefore, in the same way that the capitalists try to prevent disturbances in production and circulation, significant effort is applied to ensuring that there are no disturbances during the consumption period. Using social media also requires IT specialists to ensure that these communication systems function at all times. YouTube, Twitter, Facebook, and Google are always on demand, and depend on communication workers for their consumption. Were these workers to stage a political action, such as a strike or even slow-down, it would have catastrophic effects on the consumption process. Not only would it disrupt the consumption of social media, but also the sales effort that results from online advertising. Some electronics, such as phones and gaming consoles, would not be consumable were it not for the labour of communications workers.

It was for this reason that Ernest Mandel correctly viewed consumerism as a major cause of the expansion of the services industry.[17] As the production of goods increases, it becomes necessary not just to sell them, but to continue production within the consumption period. This process of producing consumption contributes to the realisation of surplus-value rather than just making commodities consumable. For example, the labour of Nintendo programmers makes it possible to realise the surplus-value contained in Nintendo games by constantly expanding the possibilities of their consumption. Online capabilities, such as player-to-player competition, makes the commodity more appealing and increases the number of buyers. These commodities are unique in that they are not necessarily completed when they are released, but can continue to be produced, improved, and further developed. Business decisions about whether to further develop a game and extend consumption time are directly related to the demand element. Nintendo is able to assess whether a game will turnover desired profits, and create an add-on package a year after it has been released.

The concept of consumption period is helpful because it allows us to perceive the production process that takes place within consumption. Workers who produce services in the consumption period sometimes produce surplus-value

17 Mandel 1978

and can therefore be productive labourers. For example, Nintendo sells a yearly subscription service so that gamers can access its online features; nearly all of its signature games require Nintendo Online. Surplus-value is here the difference between the cost of labour for the programmers, and the revenue that Nintendo gets from the sale of Nintendo Online subscriptions. The revenue that Nintendo gets from the sale of Nintendo Online subscriptions is far greater than the amount of money made by the programmers who maintain the online service. For most electronics and complex goods, the consumption period contains a production process. However, simple goods also contain a production process, although less labour is required as the consumption period is shorter. For example, while one visits a restaurant, the consumption period is the entire time that one spends in a restaurant. The hospitality workers produce an *experience* in order to aid the consumption that occurs during the customer's visit. Customer service is precisely the service labour that is needed to make the consumption of food and drink pleasant. This labour does not produce surplus-value, but rather ensures that the customers will return frequently.

These concepts are helpful in conceptualising consumerism and ways to overcome its negative effects. Consumerism may be defined as *the decrease of consumption time and an increase of productive labour during the consumption period.* In a consumerist society, commodities have a short life span, and some require exorbitant labour to service their consumption. For products made of low-quality material, as in fast fashion, the consumption time can be as low as three weeks and require constant replacement. Even higher quality clothing is made obsolete faster through advertising and the creation of new fashion. A video game console or phone today will have a consumption period of one to three years and require massive additional labour to allow their consumption. Consumerism ensures that at the end of every few turnover periods, a consumer will return to the shop to replace their commodities. Decreased consumption time thus causes capital to turn over more times, which increases the rate of profit and further concentrates capital.

Using these concepts, we can also define an anti-consumerist strategy for a socialist society. As Bettelheim points out, a defining feature of socialism is the plan. In a socialist social formation, production is planned and surplus-value production stops. Although the state may appropriate a surplus and invest it in socialist infrastructure, the goal of production is satisfying people's needs in a planned way. A socialist state has the ability to plan both consumption time and the period of consumption. An anti-consumerist strategy may then be defined as follows: an *increase* in consumption time and a *socialisation* of labour to service consumption.

A socialist society discourages consumerism by increasing the lifespan of commodities. Instead of planning their obsolescence or producing goods of such low quality as to require continual replacement, a socialist society makes high quality goods designed to last a long time. Furthermore, labour required to service consumption is socialised so that service workers become state employees. In a socialist society, programmers will work for a publicly owned video game company and collectively manage production. They will gain skills to do not just one type of gaming labour, but many of them. By eliminating capitalist monopolies through their amalgamation into a single entity, it will be possible to make all video games accessible on a single server and create a super console. Socialism will create entirely new gaming experiences that are unthinkable under capitalism. I will discuss in more detail how socialism will liberate service workers in chapter eleven.

Now that I have discussed the circulation and consumption process, I will shift my attention to monopoly capitalism and imperialism. Because most retail workers are employed for multinational corporations, it is vital to have an understanding of imperialism. The next two chapters will view retail workers as part of a larger value chain in order to demonstrate their relationship to workers in the developing world. Chapter seven will attempt to visualise this process by dividing production and circulation into two stages that are linked by monopoly capital.

CHAPTER 6

Monopoly Capital and the Sales Effort

In their masterpiece of Marxist scholarship *Monopoly Capital*, Sweezy and Baran argue that the sales effort occupies a far more important place in the twentieth century than it did in Marx's time. The primary reason for this is that capital is highly concentrated and centralised in large, multinational corporations. A result of monopoly capital is a considerable growth of production and the necessity to realise significantly more surplus value than before. These corporations are the product of a shift from competitive to monopoly capitalism that began at the end of the nineteenth century and was fully completed during the 1980's.

Sweezy and Baran began serious theoretical work on monopoly capitalism in the 1960's, and were followed by Braverman, Samir Amin, John Bellamy Foster, and John Smith. Their work is helpful for grasping the centrality of the sales effort in the era of monopoly capital and the significance of retail employees. Before turning to their work, I will briefly discuss Marx's analysis of commercial capital in volume three of *Capital*, which is extremely important for understanding large retailers such as WalMart and H&M. Sweezy, Baran, and some of their followers often contend that Marx could not have understood monopoly capital because capitalism had not yet reached that stage. I think this is incorrect, as Marx was distinctly aware that capital tends to become centralised in the hands of monopolies as capitalism develops. He offers a very helpful analysis with his concept of commercial capital, which is more dominant today than in Marx's time. While Marx did not live to experience monopoly capitalism, he was very perceptive of some of the tendencies that came to define it.

1 Marx on Commercial Capital

In the previous chapter, I discussed the circulation process, in which commodities are packaged, transported, distributed to shops, and sold. I left the question as to *who* purchases these goods unanswered, as it was not immediately relevant to grasping the circulation process. Generally, goods are not directly purchased by the consumer, but by merchants that sell the product in shops. Marx points out, "as the capitalist mode of production presupposes production on a large scale, so it also necessarily presupposes large-scale sale; sale to

 | DOI:10.1163/9789004469624_007

the merchant, not to the individual consumer."[1] A commercial capitalist possesses a large reserve of money capital and is further assisted in purchasing commodities by bank loans. Banks often invest significant funds in merchant capital in order to appropriate a portion of the surplus-value in the form of interest. Sometimes, large retailers are funded exclusively by banks, who have significant power to influence business decisions. The capitalist merchant uses this capital to purchase goods from the industrial capitalist and makes a profit from the sale of the commodities. From the standpoint of commercial capital, the profit *appears* to arise from buying goods at their production price and selling them at a higher price. For example, to the clothing merchant who buys a bundle of shirts for £1000 and sells them for £3000, a profit of £2000 appears to arise from the difference between production and sales price. Marx argues that this is an illusion created by the assumption that the commercial capitalist purchases goods from the industrialist at their production price. As he says, "it is a mere semblance that commercial profit is just a supplement, a nominal increase in the price of commodities above their value."[2]

If the commercial capitalist does not make a profit from such a 'nominal increase', where does commercial profit come from? In Volume 3 of *Capital*, Marx analyses commercial profit in relation to the average rate of profit, which is determined by the competition between industrial capitalists. The commercial capitalist purchases goods from the merchant at a price not determined by their production price, but by the average rate of profit. Suppose that the value of the industrialist's capital (c+v) is £1000, and that he derives a surplus-value of £100, leaving a total value of £1100. Furthermore, suppose that the average rate of profit is 10%, which means that with the given investment of £1000, an average profit rate of 10 percent can be acquired. Marx's argument is that if the commercial capitalist uses £100 to purchase goods from the industrialist, he will take 10 percent of the surplus-value of £100, as this is the average general rate of profit. The actual purchase price for the merchant is therefore not £1100, but £1000+£100-£10= £1,090, which allows him to acquire 10 percent of the surplus-value on an average rate of profit of 10 percent. Hence, Marx says that "if he still does not sell the commodities above their value or price of production, this is precisely because he got them from the industrial capitalists below their value or price of production."[3] I will not engage here with the voluminous literature of the average profit rate and its tendency to fall, for it is not relevant to the discussion here. The basic point of Marx's analysis is that the purchase

1 Marx [1885] 1976, p. 190.
2 Marx [1894] 1981. p. 395.
3 *Ibid.* p. 398.

price of commercial capital is below the production price of the industrialist. Because of this, the commercial capitalist is able to capture a percentage of the surplus-value contained in the commodities and realise it through their sale on the market. In contemporary monopoly capitalism, large retailers continue doing this through purchasing commodities not at their production price, but their market price. As I will show later, they do this by exploiting the dynamics of unequal exchange by purchasing these goods from developing nations where production costs are far lower than in the imperialist centres.

While the merchant must pay for some of the costs of circulation—transport, storing, etc.—his primary function is to buy and sell in order to transform commodity capital into money capital. Commercial capital conducts these functions by employing buying-specialists, marketing and advertising experts, asset managers, and investment consultants. These merchants sell the commodities through shops, for which they hire retail employees, skilled salespeople, store managers, and sometimes franchisees. Marx argues that commercial employees do not produce surplus-value but allow the commercial capitalist to realise surplus-value. As they are wage-labourers with little control over the labour-process, they work under relations of exploitation. A portion of their labour is unpaid, which does not result in new surplus-value, but allows the capitalist to appropriate surplus-value from the industrialist. Hence, Marx points out that

> their unpaid labour, even though it does not create surplus-value, does create his ability to appropriate surplus-value, which, as far as this capital is concerned, gives exactly the same result, i.e., it is its source of profit.[4]

The more unpaid labour the commercial employee performs in relation to waged labour, the greater the amount of surplus-value the commercial capitalist can realise. Therefore, commercial employees are not simply unproductive workers that perform commercial function, but tools the capitalist uses to make a profit.

A commercial employee is paid for the costs of their reproduction, which Marx acknowledges could be higher for some skilled labourers such as clerks and marketing specialists. Their labour requires special training, which is incorporated into the costs of their reproduction. Because of this, the commercial capitalist will try to find ways to deskill administrative, clerical, and other forms of office labour, as this reduces the cost of their labour-power. This is a phenomenon that was not generalised until the twentieth century and

4 *Ibid.* p. 407.

was first systematically theorised by Harry Braverman in *Labor and Monopoly Capital*. The primary reason for this is that the need for commercial employees and clerical workers remained relatively low during the time of Marx, for the scale of production was not large enough to necessitate their existence. Marx recognises this, saying that

> the capitalist increases the number of these workers, if he has more value and profit to realize. The increase in this labour is always an effect of the increase in surplus-value and never a cause of it.[5]

As Braverman points out, the growth of office work and commercial labour in the twentieth century is directly tied to the growth of monopoly capitalism. He notes that monopoly capitalism brought about "those types of enterprises which, entirely separated from the process of production, carry on their activities either chiefly or entirely through clerical labor."[6] With the concentration of capital and its centralisation in the hands of large corporations, production grew on an astronomical scale. This required the creation of massive offices with departments for every aspect of commercial activity, such as accounting, investment, product design, and advertising. Although the workers in these offices are part of management, Braverman points out that their labour process is similar to factory workers. They face long working hours, high stress levels, management bullying, and repetitive alienating labour. While they are often paid a higher wage, their labour is used solely to allow large corporations to appropriate surplus-value from workers and peasants in the developing world.[7] The organisation of office employees is of tremendous importance, as they have the power to disrupt the entire supply chain. If commercial employees such as clerks, accountants, and administrators organise themselves in a large corporation, they have the power to obstruct the entire control mechanism that capitalists rely on to conduct their business operations. By threatening to organise themselves, commercial employees have a strong position from which to collectively bargain with the bourgeoisie. One of the primary challenges is that because they work in a management office, they are more likely to be won over to the company. Even if they feel rage against its policies, there is a real challenge that is primarily ideological.

Office employees and retail workers are important not just for the commercial capitalist, but for the entire circulation process. In Volume 2 of *Capital*,

5 *Ibid.* p. 415.
6 Braverman 1974, p. 207.
7 *Ibid*, p. 224–225.

Marx discusses how commercial capital reduces the circulation time of commodities. Marx points out that

> one section of circulation time—and relatively the most decisive one—consists of selling time, the period in which the capital exists in the state of commodity capital. According to the relative extent of this interval, the circulation time in general, and hence also the turnover period, is lengthened or shortened.[8]

Workers in logistics and retail thus play an important role in reducing the circulation time of commodities. Sales associates receive training on how to awaken the desire to buy in the customer. In *Commodity Aesthetics*, W.F. Haug points out that in the eighties, capitalists tried to make shopping an experience rather than just the acquisition of goods. Significant attention was given by management to the physical appearance of the sales employee and the shop itself was often envisioned as a theatre. Haug notes that

> the exhibition of commodities, their inspection, the act of purchase, and all the associated moments, are integrated into the concept of one theatrical total work of art which plays upon the public's willingness to buy. Thus the salesroom is designed as a stage, purpose-built to convey entertainment to its audience that will stimulate a heightened desire to spend.[9]

One example of this is Hamley's, the toy shop in London which has a variety of attractions and entertainers to get customers in the door. Families that visit Hamleys get to see clowns, magic, and performances while they shop. The entertainment is carefully designed to encourage children to beg their parents for toys, often resulting in purchasing commodities on credit. During Christmas, Hamleys has an entire holiday performance that has been created by psychologists and marketing specialists to ensure increased spending. Retail employees at Hamleys are subjected to daily corporate propaganda, which is designed to win them over to the company they work for. They might receive special bonuses during holidays, such as an expensive Christmas gift or extra money. They are under tremendous pressure to be happy, friendly, and constantly smile in order to sell the goods. Hamleys thus not only tries to make the

8 Marx 1978 [1885], p. 326.

9 Haug 1986, p. 69.

shopping experience fun, but to transform the labour process into a creative activity.[10] Haug notes that retail employees must therefore "become automata of selling, of selling for its own sake."[11] The result is that shop employees often enjoy their job while feeling contradictory feelings of frustration, which is explained away by their corporate managers.[12]

Retail employees in shops such as Hamleys are important in reducing the circulation time of commodities and aiding the realisation of surplus-value. Although they do not produce surplus-value themselves, each successful sale of a bundle of goods allows the capitalists to expand production and appropriate more surplus-value. In this way, sales associates play an important role in the accumulation process, and indirectly contribute to expanded reproduction through their labour. Organising them is very difficult, as their job training ideologically prepares them to identify with the company that they work for. Even if they feel stressed and do not feel excited about their job, their material practices prevent them from taking a rebellious attitude towards their labour. Yet, if they were organised, they could disrupt the circulation time and put the entire working class in a better position.

2 The Emergence of Monopoly Capital

Now that I have discussed the main elements of commercial capital, I will turn to Sweezy and Baran's path-breaking analysis of monopoly capitalism.[13] With the development of capitalism, capital becomes more centralised and capitalists form large corporations, resulting in the emergence of monopoly capitalism. One major feature of monopoly capitalism is the dominance of commercial and finance capital, which orchestrate the entire capitalist system. Whereas in competitive capitalism, the dominant fraction was industrial capital, in monopoly capitalism the dominant fraction is finance capital. Monopoly capital commands the entire process of production, circulation, distribution, marketing, and consumption from the beginning to end. In Marx's time, these processes were largely fragmented and conducted by distinct fractions of capital—industrial, circulation, commercial, rentier, and finance. A defining feature of monopoly capitalism is the integration of these fractions through their incorporation into capitalist monopolies.

---

10 *Inside Hamleys at Christmas* (2005), Channel 5.
11 Haug 1986, p. 66.
12 Kearsey 2020, p. 507.
13 Sweezy and Baran 1966

Sweezy and Baran note an important change that occurs with the concentration and centralisation of capital. Competitive capitalism, which characterised the nineteenth century, came to an end when capital became centralised in the hands of massive corporations. Instead of many small and medium firms competing for market hegemony, there are only a few corporations that are dominant. In competitive capitalism, each capitalist sought to increase the productivity of labour in order to sell commodities below their value and thereby reduce prices. Sweezy and Baran point out that this process comes to an end with monopoly capitalism, for the giant corporations generally do not reduce prices. If one corporation reduces its prices, then it will initiate a price war and all the others will also reduce their prices in an attempt to secure their position in the market. As a result, corporations tend to increase their prices, which affects the form of competition between them.[14] Sweezy and Baran show how the giant oligopolies avoid reducing prices through cheapening the costs of production. Monopoly capitalism drives the search for cheaper labour and low-cost raw materials that tend to be of lower quality and often synthetic. If a company fails to reduce its costs, there is a good chance it will not be able to compete with the oligopolies that dominate the social formation. Even though production costs drop rapidly under monopoly capitalism, prices tend to go up and rarely drop except in rare circumstances.

The result of this process is that the big oligopolies are able to capture more surplus-value than before, for they command massive value chains and are able to exploit labour on a scale unknown to competitive capitalism. Sweezy and Baran therefore conclude that the monopolies make super profits from the new social relations generated through the concentration and centralisation of capital. As they say, "the monopolistic structure of markets enables the corporations to appropriate the lion's share of the fruits of increasing productivity directly in the form of higher profits."[15] They argue that an important effect of monopoly capitalism is that the economic surplus compromising total output and investable capital tends to rise. Because the corporations are able to appropriate more surplus-value and reduce costs significantly, they have massive amounts of accumulated capital to invest in new machinery and thereby expand production.

A major problem is that it becomes more difficult to realise the surplus-value, thereby reducing the outlets for the absorption of the economic surplus. The growth of the economic surplus means that the total amount of

14 Sweezy and Baran, pp. 57–59.
15 Sweezy and Baran 1966, p. 71.

commodities to be sold is far greater than it was in the era of competitive capitalism. Sweezy and Baran point out that the primary problem of monopoly capitalism is that it cannot find adequate outlets to absorb the economic surplus. As they point out, monopoly capitalism "generates ever more surplus, yet it fails to provide the consumption and investment outlets required for the absorption of a rising surplus and hence the smooth working of the system."[16] In the era of monopoly capital, there is more surplus-value than ever before, but it cannot be realised and lacks an outlet for absorption as a result of low demand. There is a huge surplus of capital available for investment, but not enough outlets in which to invest it productively. Often, the monopolies fail to stimulate demand for the large amount of goods and services that they produce. Sweezy and Baran argue that this causes a rise in irrational, wasteful production, such as creating new models of the same commodity each year in order to stimulate demand for it. Most importantly, however, they show how the era of monopoly capitalism puts more importance on the sales effort than ever before. This gives rise to a massive advertising industry, which employs thousands of people in jobs to specialise in what Fritz Haug calls 'commodity aesthetics', as well as a huge retail sector dominated by commercial capital.

Unless wages increase or credit becomes available, the working class will lack the funds needed to purchase the goods and services produced by the oligopolies. The ever-increasing costs of housing, energy, food, and other necessities tend to reduce the demand for the products of the monopolies. Sweezy and Baran point out that a tendency develops to continue using old equipment long after it has expired even after new technology is discovered. This is because it is pointless to use newer, more productive technology when the existing equipment already produces more goods than can be sold. The effect of a growing surplus that cannot be absorbed is that in the long-term, monopoly capitalism will stagnate, and it will become harder and harder for it to function in a profitable way. As Sweezy and Baran point out, "since surplus which cannot be absorbed will not be produced, it follows that the normal state of monopoly capitalism is stagnation."[17]

In much the same way that Marx identified ways that the tendency for the rate of profit to fall is prevented by counteracting forces, Sweezy and Baran identify ways that stagnation arising from the growing surplus can be prevented. It is here that Sweezy and Baran are very helpful for analysing the retail, sales, and services industry. They point out that one of the defining elements of

16 *ibid*, p. 108.
17 *ibid*, p. 108.

monopoly capitalism is the sales effort, which is conducted through marketing agencies and retail employees. Corporations invest significant funds into packaging, product design, flavouring in foods, and advertising to ensure that they can sell their goods. Through these large investments, the oligopolies are able to stimulate short-term demand to absorb the surplus of goods and services on the market. With the emergence of capitalist monopolies, the sales effort becomes more important because demand must be stimulated to absorb the rising economic surplus of consumer goods.

Sweezy and Baran point out how a significant portion of the goods and services that we consume on a daily basis contain unnecessary elements that are designed to sell the product. They argue that significant amounts of use-value are lost to wasteful expenditures designed to make commodities more desirable. Many of the products that we consume on a daily basis contain elements that are purely aesthetic and add no intrinsic use-value to the product. Product design and packaging make the commodity more appealing, but do not contribute any use-value to our consumption. Their function is to stimulate the desire of the consumer so that they purchase the commodity, resulting in the realisation of surplus value for the corporation that sold it to them. Monopolies encourage the massive consumption of unnecessary goods so that they can continue to meet their profit margins and pay their shareholders.

The result of inscribing the sales-effort into the production of commodities is a massive loss of use-value. Working people must spend their wages not just to pay for goods, but also to cover the costs of marketing that stimulated the desire for the commodity in the first place. One of the examples Sweezy and Baran give is the design of cars, which often does not contribute to the quality of the vehicle and is purely aesthetic. As the car manufacturers have to constantly stimulate demand for their cars, they will change the design yearly while retaining nearly identical internal features. As discussed earlier, their goal is to reduce the consumption period for a car by encouraging faster replacement. A car's design is only partially relevant to its performance, yet tremendous capital is invested to create a vehicle that is pleasant to look at. When we buy a car, we are not just paying for the parts that make it useful for transportation, but aesthetic elements such as its colour, design, the shape of its rims, and its interior features. While there is nothing wrong with adding these things after one has purchased it, we are rarely given the option of just purchasing a simple car that provides basic transportation needs. Instead, unnecessary elements are added to the price, which make it appear more appealing but provide no additional use-value. Car manufacturers also constantly try to sell us cars in places where public transportation is already decent and could even be improved if less people drove cars. These corporations have no interest in protecting the environment, but only ensuring that they realise the surplus-value in the cars that they sell.

Sweezy and Baran point out that corporations take into account the needs of social reproduction in the production of goods. As already discussed in the last chapter, they engage in planned obsolescence by giving the product a lifespan. Instead of creating a car, phone, TV, or computer that is designed to last for a long time, they design the product so that it breaks down in the future. The commodities lifespan is planned to ensure that the customer comes back in the future to purchase new goods. Cars are designed not to last for a lifetime, but to break down and require frequent maintenance in order to ensure that they are replaced every few years. In addition to this, the parts (i.e., the brakes, tires, etc.) need constant maintenance, as they are intentionally made with lower quality materials to cheapen costs and ensure continual repurchase. Phone systems require frequent updates, and phone companies such as Apple have the ability to 'kill' a model in order to force customers to purchase the latest model. A new model of a car or phone comes out each year in order to create a constant differentiation and show how the newer model is better.

The fashion industry does not make aesthetically pleasing clothing in order to allow people to express themselves through their garments. Rather, fashion companies like H&M and Primark use low quality materials that require constant replacement. Instead of buying a sweater or shirt that lasts many years, one can buy a cheap shirt to get immediate clothing needs but require replacement in the near future. All these unnecessary features of commodities that make them desirable cause them to break down early or become obsolete or make us unhealthy, creating massive profits for the corporations while encouraging an obsession with the satisfaction of immediate needs. Consumerism is the result of the domination of the imperialist centres by transnational corporations, and a very significant reduction in the quality of life for the many.

Sweezy and Baran point out that from the standpoint of a socialist society, such consumerism represents a tremendous loss of economic surplus. They argue that unnecessary expenditures on the sales effort is part of the potential economic surplus, which is reduced because it is utilised for non-productive purposes. Baran develops this idea further in *the Political Economy of Growth*,[18] where he shows that in a rationally planned socialist economy, the potential economic surplus could be fully utilised in meaningful ways that contribute to human development. Under capitalism, the potential surplus is lost by being invested into the sales effort, which results in thousands of people being

18 Baran 1957

employed to help realise the surplus-value in commodities so that the capitalist system can reproduce itself.

Historically, socialism has been shown to be the best alternative to capitalism. A socialist society, in which the majority of society's working people run the government, plan production, and control their workplaces is the only solution to the contradictions of monopoly capitalism. Socialism removes the sales-effort from production and allows the state to direct all of its resources to the satisfaction of people's needs. A socialist government can invest a portion of the economic surplus to finance the expansion of socialism, gradually abolishing the class structure and improving the material conditions of all. As a result, the quality of life in a socialist society can only improve in order to ensure a happy life for its people. In a socialist society, the government creates economic plans to ensure the production of high-quality goods that last for a long time and provide optimal use-value. As prices are set to allow all to purchase these goods, there is no longer a need to inscribe the sales-effort into the production of goods. Some state funds may still be used to create advertisements, but their function is simply to make people aware of the goods available. As a result of this, electronics, food, and clothing may not be as shiny and aesthetically beautiful, but the quality and use-value they provide is far superior to capitalist commodities. Visitors to socialist Cuba have often been surprised to see that Cubans have continued driving the same cars for decades. The automobile magazine *News Wheel* reports that

> Cuba is literally a rolling car museum. Everywhere you look is an old-school American brand vehicle ... These are all vehicles that the majority of American car lovers would spend hundreds of thousands of dollars on—and they are used as Cubans' everyday vehicles.[19]

Because cars built in socialist Cuba are designed to meet the transportation needs of the Cuban people, they make their automobiles so that they last for a very long time. Every car owner in Cuba is educated on how to look after their car, and they are encouraged to do regular maintenance to avoid having to replace it. Instead of buying a new car each time it breaks down, Cuban car owners produce new parts, often made from recycled materials, and use them to keep their cars running without having to get a new car.[20] The quality of life under socialism is significantly better because it generalises the consumption

19 *The News Wheel*, July 20, 2015.

20 *Ibid.*

of high-quality use-value. By not encouraging consumerism, socialism offers people the opportunity to enjoy their lives by dedicating their time to activities, such as sports, art, theoretical work, and community groups. I will discuss this in more detail in the final chapter of this book, which will demonstrate the benefits of socialism in all its elements.

A high quality of life for all of society is impossible in the era of monopoly capitalism. The imaginary nightmare that apparently existed in the former socialist countries, still promoted by the capitalist media and bourgeois politicians, should really be applied to monopoly capitalism. It is under capitalism that people are constantly managed, watched, and live in miserable conditions. Because there is tremendous pressure to constantly shop, many people end up with huge debts that they will never be able to repay. Once they are in debt, they will be harassed by banks and forced to accept low-wage jobs to pay off the debt. This has resulted in high levels of depression for millions of people in the capitalist world, which allows the pharmaceutical companies to profit from the prescription of antidepressants. Instead of addressing the source of their unhappiness, the capitalist state and its experts prefer to put people in prisons or get them hooked on pharmaceutical drugs. As Sweezy, Baran, and Lenin all note, at a certain stage every capitalist social formation will enter its monopoly stage, resulting in a rising economic surplus. It then becomes compulsory to add unnecessary elements to the commodity to stimulate demand for the product. Monopoly capitalism enables banks to take advantage of the consumer, who it provides with high-level credit caps to ensure continual borrowing and the resulting situation of debt. The conclusion of monopoly capitalism is a society where people are unhappy, unhealthy, in poorly paid uncreative jobs, and indebted to the banks.

The necessity of the sales-effort in the era of monopoly capitalism creates a workforce of salespeople, marketing specialists, and advertising employees that did not exist in Marx's time. Capitalists invest large portions of their capital into hiring product designers, who use modern psychological techniques to make commodities more appealing. This significantly reduces the quality of life in the core capitalist countries, transforming large sections of society into salespeople whose job it is to sell commodities. In addition to this, the growth of monopoly capitalism results in imperialism and globalisation, which transforms the people of the global South into producers of commodities. As imperialism is central to the dynamics of monopoly capitalism, I would like to briefly discuss here how it functions and the main recent debates about imperialist political economy.

3 Imperialism and Monopoly Capitalism[21]

A major effect of the growth of the economic surplus is the rise of imperialism, which is important for understanding the relationship between the production of goods and their sale. A Marxist analysis of retail and sales is incomplete without a brief discussion of the dynamics of imperialism. In order to properly formulate the politics of service and retail workers, it is essential to gain an understanding of imperialism. The term 'imperialism' was first used in the work of Hobson and Hilferding and popularised by Lenin in his *Imperialism: the Highest Stage of Capitalism*. While Marx wrote about how the emergence of a world market affects the international composition of the working class, he did not have a theory of imperialism. Colonial domination by the dominant capitalist countries—Great Britain, Portugal, Spain, France, Italy, the Netherlands, Germany, and Russia—was the primary form taken by the bourgeoisie on the international stage during Marx's time. Colonialism was an integral part of the primitive accumulation of capital and the development of the bourgeoisie as a class. Through direct colonial occupation, the bourgeoisie gained access to inexpensive raw materials, cheap labour and a market to export goods. Often, the colonial powers would directly enslave the colonised population and steal their natural resources (i.e., gold, minerals, etc.). Colonialism transformed colonised peoples into producers of food, tea, tobacco, and sugar, which was exported to Great Britain, America, and other colonial powers. During the colonial period, the bourgeoisie would dominate the colonies and exploit its resources, while maintaining non-capitalist forms of production. Most of these pre-capitalist social formations in Africa and Asia were characterised by feudalism, traditional handicraft production, and a large peasantry. The colonisers utilised the feudal landlords and local oligarchs to appropriate the products of agrarian labourers and maintain a system of slavery. Walter Rodney and Andre Gunder Frank pointed out in the seventies that colonialism underdeveloped Africa, Latin, America, and other parts of what was then called the 'Third World'.[22] By draining countries of their natural resources—such as Angola, Algeria, and Tanzania—and super-exploiting the labour of Third World peoples, the colonialists prevented its colonies from developing their productive forces.

---

21 As I do not assume that every reader possesses detailed knowledge of Marxism, this section will be somewhat introductory. Those who are familiar with the debates in the Marxist theory of imperialism may skip this section or return to it later.

22 Frank (1967); Rodney [1972] 2018.

Although colonialism laid the foundation for imperialism, it was not identical to it. During the colonial period, the bourgeoisies of the dominant capitalist powers kept their major productive forces within the borders of their nations and conducted the manufacturing of goods within their own social formation. In Marx's time, capitalism was still in its competitive stage, which was characterised by the existence of multiple small and medium firms that competed for market hegemony. One way they did this was by finding ways to increase the productivity of labour and thereby reduce the price of commodities. The local market was sufficient to realise the surplus-value and allow for the accumulation of capital. Marx noted in Volume 3 of *Capital* that the development of capitalism causes the number of capitalists to be reduced, thereby causing capital to become more concentrated and centralised in the hands of a few capitalists. A major cause of this was the first major crisis of capitalism in the 1870's, which drove many capitalists to merge with others, resulting in joint-stock companies, trusts, and cartels. These early forms of the modern corporation, which would become the dominant organisation of the bourgeoisie in the twentieth century, was first called by Lenin 'monopoly capitalism'.

An effect of the concentration and centralisation of capital was a massive increase in the productivity of labour. In all the major capitalist countries, more capital was accumulated than could be productively invested in the domestic market. Furthermore, the surplus value produced was far too large to be realized on the domestic market, resulting in a crisis of social reproduction. As John Smith explains,

> the accumulated wealth of the imperialist ruling families has reached such proportions that the gigantic mass of surplus value necessary to convert their wealth into capital … far outstrips the amount of surplus value that can be extracted from its domestic workforce.[23]

Imperialism emerged in the late 19th century as a political response to the new contradictions created by monopoly capitalism. The capitalists had to find new geographical locations in which to appropriate surplus-value and create a market for realising it. The newly emerging imperialist nations fought for new colonies, resulting in a series of destructive wars of redivision. In the late nineteenth century, the European capitalists divided Africa, resulting in the emergence of dozens of new capitalist social formations. Other parts of the world, such as Cuba and the Philippines, came under the domination of the United

23 Smith 2016, p. 232.

States, which would later play a leading role in the consolidation of imperialism globally.

Paul Sweezy, following Lenin, points out that the primary feature of imperialism that distinguishes it from colonialism is the export of capital to the colonies. As he says,

> the contradictions of the accumulation process have reached such maturity that capital export is an outstanding feature of world economic relations.[24]

In the imperialist stage, the capitalist class began exporting capital to the colonies, which resulted in the emergence of capitalist social relations, a local bourgeoisie, and a domestic working class. Although the export of capital occasionally took place on a small-scale in the colonial era, it was not a dominant tendency and therefore the capitalist mode of production only existed in its nucleus. With the emergence of imperialism, the export of capital became generalised, and the capitalist mode of production began appearing in the Third World.

The imperialists continued to exercise the same colonial relationship to the colonies, but important changes could be seen that distinguished imperialism significantly from colonialism. In order to facilitate the growth of a productive working class, the imperialists ended slavery and established some constitutional rights for working people. This did not make them progressive, as the imperialists continued treating newly liberated workers in a way similar to slaves. They used brutal methods to extract surplus value from cheap colonised labour and set up dictatorial regimes around the colonial world to maximise the rate of profit. Lenin points out that a driving force of imperialism was the lower level of working-class organisation in the colonies, and the extremely cheap labour that they could get from colonised workers.

4 Imperialism and the Split in the Bourgeoisie

Imperialism also caused an important split to occur in the local bourgeoisies in the colonies. This split is very important for understanding how the dynamics of class struggle operates in developing nations. A small section of the bourgeoisie—called 'comprador'- aligns themselves with the imperialists in

24 Sweezy [1942] 1970, p. 307.

exchange for special privileges. Poulantzas defines the comprador bourgeoisie as

> that fraction of the class whose interests are constitutively linked to foreign imperialist capital (capital belonging to the principle imperialist power) and which is thus completely bound politically and ideologically to foreign capital.[25]

The comprador bourgeoisie is dependent on the imperialists for capital, technology, and international contacts. This section of the local capitalist class is composed of former landlords, warlords, and oligarchs that had already collaborated with the colonisers. These dependent comprador bourgeoisies are often extremely reactionary, and in recent times, have formed the bulwark of support for using death squads in Latin America to suppress socialist movements.[26] Although the comprador bourgeoisie can be hegemonic—especially in Colombia and Brazil—they represent a small section of the capitalist class.

A larger section of the bourgeoisie in the developing world—called the national bourgeoisie—tended to be negatively affected by colonialism and does not benefit from imperialist domination. Poualntzas defines the national bourgeoisie as

> that fraction of the bourgeoisie whose interests are linked to the nation's economic development and which comes into relative contradiction with the interests of big foreign capital.[27]

The national bourgeoisie attempted to create their own firms but were unable to accumulate enough capital in order to effectively act as capitalists. Large amounts of the surplus value that they appropriated is expropriated by the imperialists, sometimes in the form of what Samir Amin calls a monopoly rent. Furthermore, they have often been the target of racist discrimination, and excluded from international capitalist organisations. In order to safeguard its interests, the national bourgeoisie uses nationalism and demands independence from imperialism.

Social formations in the developing world are generally characterised by a constant struggle between the national and comprador bourgeoisie. One fraction will tend to be hegemonic and will mobilise other classes to solidify

25 Poulantzas 2008, p. 200.
26 For a very good discussion of this, see Hristov (2014).
27 *The Poulantzas Reader*, p. 200.

its hegemonic position in society. For example, if the comprador bourgeoisie becomes hegemonic, it will seek the support of sections of the petty-bourgeoisie, the informal working class, and lumpen-proletariat. It can do this through directly funding its organisations or by giving them positions of power within the state. Each fraction will have its own political party and will also try to win influence in the parties on which its organisational base depends. Once the hegemony of a fraction of the bourgeoisie is solidified, it becomes tremendously difficult to change this. Generally speaking, only during moments of intense political, economic, and ideological crisis will a fractional hegemony break and be replaced another fraction.

Because both the working class and the national bourgeoisie are oppressed by imperialism, there is a material basis for an alliance between them. In his book about the history of Trotskyism, Kostas Mavrakis points out that the contradiction between the national bourgeoisie and the working class in the colonies is sometimes a non-antagonist one.[28] In so far as they are both oppressed by the imperialists, the national bourgeoisie is able to enter into an alliance with colonised workers and sections of the petty-bourgeoisie. This resulted in many independence movements, with important struggles erupting over what class would lead the fight for national liberation. In April 1955, many newly independent nations met in Bandung, Indonesia and developed what came to be known as the non-aligned movement. Samir Amin sums up the primary ideological line of Bandung:

> the fight against imperialism brings together, at the world level, the social and political forces whose victories are decisive in opening up possible socialist advances in the contemporary world.[29]

The anti-imperialist national bourgeoisie demands import-substitution policies to develop local industry and create a foundation on which it can accumulate capital. In many postcolonial states, such as Nasser's Egypt, Boumedienne's Algeria, and Allende's Chile, the national bourgeoisie supported a strong social democratic welfare state to improve the material-being of the population and anti-imperialist nationalism. While they supported some land reforms, this was mostly in the form of farmer cooperatives, with profit in command. The experience of these countries has shown that only a socialist approach to national economic development allowed colonised

28 Mavrakis 1976. p. 36.
29 Amin 2018, p. 123.

peoples to break free from underdevelopment.[30] When postcolonial states such as Kenya and Jamaica were led by the national bourgeoisie and took the capitalist road, they found themselves pressured into a neo-colonial relationship to the former colonial masters and were unable to create a social system that benefited their people. Only countries that made a total break with colonialism, such as Cuba and Vietnam, were able to become modern independent nations entirely free from foreign domination.[31] For a national liberation movement to take a socialist road, it is necessary for them to be led by the working class. This is because a socialist state with a planned economy and alignment with the Soviet Union is not in the interests of the bourgeoisie. As Vijay Prashad showed in the *Darker Nations*, it was often difficult to win proletarian leadership of the national liberation movements. Even when the proletariat took control of the state, such as in Angola and Mozambique, the absence of a mass-line of the MPLA and Frelimo in its later years negated the socialist content of these governments. While they instituted popular land reforms, socialist education policies, and strong trade unions, they were overly dependent on the Soviet Union. In the nineties, after the end of socialism in the USSR, the national bourgeoisie was able to take command of these parties and formally abandon Marxism-Leninism, replacing it with social democracy. As a result, the proletarian power in Angola, Mozambique, and Namibia was overthrown, and these states began instituting neoliberal reforms.[32]

Anti-imperialism came to occupy a central position in the analyses of many Marxist writers with the emergence of the non-aligned movement and dozens of new postcolonial states. In the writings of Sweezy, Baran, Emmanual, Samir Amin, Frank, Walter Rodney, and Clive Thomas, one can perceive a new theoretical horizon that places the struggle of working people in the Third World as central figures in the global struggle against capitalism. I will discuss some of the conceptual breakthroughs that emerged from the writings of Third World and anti-imperialist Marxism: unequal exchange, value transfer, centre/periphery, and neocolonialism. These concepts are foundational to how I understand capitalism and are helpful for theorising the retail and service sector.

30 See Thomas (1974) for a socialist theory to combat underdevelopment.
31 For a good discussion of the non-aligned movement, see Prashad (2014).
32 Saul 2014

5 Dependency Theory: Centre and Periphery

As Lenin shows in his writings, a major result of imperialism is that the world becomes divided into oppressor and oppressed nations. Even when the oppressed nations have become independent, they often remain dependent on the imperialist countries for capital, knowledge, technology, and markets to sell their products. In order to conceptualise this division, writers from dependency theory (i.e., Frank, Baran, Amin, and Wallerstein) developed the notions of *imperialist centre* and *periphery*. The imperialist nations—collectively forming a triad of North America, Europe, and Japan—are the *centre* of the world capitalist system. They dominate global capitalist institutions, produce the dominant systems of accumulation (i.e., neoliberalism), and exploit the labour-power of people in the developing world. In these nations, one can also see an upward tendency of wages and significantly better material conditions, for "at the center, real wages have risen gradually for the past century, parallel with the development of the productive forces".[33] On the other hand, the former colonies and developing nations are part of the periphery, for they are excluded from the commanding heights of global decision making. While it is true that people from peripheral nations sometimes occupy positions of power in the IMF and the World Bank, it is the leaders from the imperialist centre that dominate these institutions. Peripheral nations receive capital from the institutions of the imperialist centre, which puts them in a dependent relationship to them. In the periphery, wages tend to be extremely low and there is a gradual worsening of the material conditions of production. As Samir Amin points out, "in the periphery the absolute pauperization of the producers exploited by capital has revealed itself in all its brutal reality."[34] The metaphor of centre and periphery is helpful because it helps us to see the dialectical connection between the two. Peripheral nations are the *product* of domination by the imperialist centre, which forms the horizon of their modern history, politics, and institutions. Amin points out that th periphery "adjusts 'unilaterally' to the dominant tendencies on the scale of the world system in which it is integrated, these tendencies being the very ones governed by the demand of accumulation at the center."[35] Geographically, the imperialist centre has been conceptualised as the global North, while the peripheral nations are part of the global South.

33 Amin 2018, p. 48.
34 *Ibid.* p. 48.
35 *Ibid.* p. 89.

Recently, some writers have posed the concept of semi-periphery.[36] These are countries such as Brazil and South Africa, which exercise an exploitative relationship to other peripheral nations, but are themselves exploited by the imperialist centre. Their semi-peripheral nature gives them some leverage to negotiate with the imperialist centre, but this remains limited because of their peripheral nature. Semi-peripheral nations can form alliances through institutions such as BRICS and the Asian Infrastructure Development Bank, which strengthen their collective confrontation with imperialism. However, because semi-peripheral nations are dominated by the national bourgeoisie, they are often unable to fully delink from imperialism and continue to formulate their development policies within the horizon of capitalism. There are also semi-peripheral regions within the capitalist centres. These are geographic regions in the core capitalist countries that have historically been underdeveloped and contain oppressed nations. One example is the US South, which is semi-peripheral because it developed through the dynamics of slavery, Jim Crow segregation, and sharecropping. During Jim Crow segregation, most of the cotton-producing plantations were owned by absentee landlords with funding from Northern banks. Harry Haywood—an important American communist—argues that dominant nation within the US South are the African-American people, who never saw land reforms during the period of Reconstruction, and continue to live under the domination of the Anglo-imperialist centre. The semi-peripheral nature of the US South explains why it contains some of the poorest areas in the United States, with high levels of police brutality, racism, and inequality.[37]

The concepts of centre and periphery are helpful to conceptualise the class forces on the international stage. They allow us to see the specificity of contradictions within each nation and articulate them through their historical relationship to imperialism. One major strength of dependency theory is that it allows us to perceive the way that capitalism operates within peripheral nations, which is often quite different from the imperialist centres. Also, dependency theory allows us to conceptualise the geography of production, distribution, and circulation. The majority of raw materials, manufactured products, and electronics are produced in peripheral nations dominated by the comprador bourgeoisie. By collaborating with imperialism and instituting neoliberal economic policies, the comprador bourgeoisie organises production so that goods are mainly exported to the imperialist centres. On the other

36 Garcia et al. 2015

37 Haywood 1978.

hand, most retail services, advertising, marketing, product design, and scientific research is conducted by the imperialist centres. Although multinational retailers like Starbucks operate in peripheral nations such as Indonesia, they are controlled by the dominant imperialist nations. The primary consumption of Starbucks coffee takes place in the imperialist centres, which is facilitated by baristas in its coffee shops.

The imperialist bourgeoisie tries to obscure the super exploitation of Southern workers through the ideology of 'fair trade', corporate philanthropy, and the promotion of consumerism. Unless Northern workers unite with working people in the peripheries, they will usually go no further than social democratic policies, which make life easier but in no way address the central contradictions of capitalism. As Zak Cope points out,

> the global hegemony of imperialist institutions (financial, monetary, corporate, military, and communications), especially those of the United States is at least tacitly accepted and often enthusiastically championed by the working class of the imperialist countries.[38]

Often, trade unions and many well-meaning socialists support pro-imperialist policies, such as the invasion of Syria by the United States. Believing that US intervention in Syria would make it more democratic, many socialists ended up backing the most reactionary forces in the Middle East. It takes tremendous ideological effort to combat these reactionary ideas and win working people in the imperialist centres over to the position of Southern workers.

Samir Amin points out that "the principle contradiction … is the one that counterposes the peoples of the periphery (the proletariat and the exploited peasantry) to imperialist capital, and not, of course, the periphery as a whole to the center as a whole."[39] What this means is that workers in the imperialist centres are not enemies of Southern peripheral workers, as Third Worldists like Zak Cope would have it. Rather, Northern workers must be organised to unite with working people in the Global South in order to form a united front against the imperialist bourgeoisie. This means waging a protracted ideological struggle against pro-imperialist ideas in the centre, and campaigns against the comprador bourgeoisie in the periphery. An anti-imperialist consciousness can only emerge through material bonds of solidarity between Northern and Southern workers. Retail employees can be organised so that they see through

38 Cope 2019, p. 9.

39 Amin 2018, p. 93.

corporate propaganda and dedicate their lives to the struggles of the people in the developing world. This requires a transnational organising model, where delegations of retail employees are organised to visit the factories in the developing world that produce the goods they sell. Only then can real relationships emerge between Northern and Southern workers, and a shared struggle against the imperialists. Such a transnational organising model will be explored in chapter ten.

6 Unequal Exchange

A concept that is important for grasping the structure of the retail industry is *unequal exchange*. This concept—first coined by Arghiri Emmanuel in his *Unequal Exchange*—demonstrates how inequalities in the system of trade allow large multinationals to make superprofits. Retailers such as H&M, Ikea, and Nike realize large masses of surplus-value through exploiting the system of unequal exchange. Unequal exchange is the product of trade between Southern producers and transnational corporations. The TNC's exploit the lower level of the productive forces and access to cheap labour to get a lower price for commodities than they would in the imperialist centre. Because they are able to set prices, the multinational corporations are able to sell the commodities for a much higher price than they acquired them. The beneficiaries of this are the imperialist monopolies, not the people of the global South. The latter are unable to develop their productive forces because the imperialist monopolies dominate their economy.

Multinational corporations are controlled by monopoly capitalists located in the core imperialist countries. In the early stages of imperialism, foreign direct investment (FDI) was the primary way that imperialists exercised domination over peripheral nations. Through access to cheap land, capitalists would open a factory in the Third World and purchase labour at a much lower rate than in the imperialist centres.[40] This cheap labour allowed for super-exploitation and a massive transfer of value from the South to the North. As Samir Amin points out, "the underdeveloped countries are so because they are superexploited and not because they are backward".[41] FDI is a form of neo-colonialism that aided the accumulation of capital by the imperialist centre and continued the underdevelopment of peripheral nations. Often, these

40 Smith 2016, chapters 2–3.

41 Amin 2018, p. 89.

countries had recently attained independence, but failed to implement policies that effectively transformed social relations and improved the material lives of the working class. Led by the national bourgeoisie, they attempted to become independent solely by changing flags, but made no effort to change the relations of production. With little access to capital goods, they were forced to use inferior machinery, but sell their products on the international market. Once a crisis of capitalism caused high inflation, unemployment, and debt, the comprador bourgeoisie ascended to power with close alignment to the United States.[42] Postcolonial governments, such as Jomo Kenyatta's Kenya and Mobutu's Zaire adopted development strategies that discouraged the development of the productive forces and made them highly dependent on imperialism. In the 1980's, many peripheral nations adopted export-oriented industrialization policies and organised export-processing zones (EPZs). John Smith explains that "EPZ's provide governments in low- wage countries with a way to attract inward FDI and connect to global value chains."[43] Large retailers are able to purchase goods from producers at a much lower cost in the periphery than the centre because of the significantly cheaper labour costs. Although Southern workers in Bangladesh and India have organised against imperialist exploitation, comprador bourgeois governments in these countries have succeeded in maintaining labour conditions favourable to imperialism. Only in countries where socialist revolutions have succeeded in delinking Third World peoples from imperialism has the comprador bourgeoisie been eradicated from the state, and has unequal exchange been made impossible.

In their writings, Arrighiri Emmanuel and Samir Amin showed how a structure of unequal exchange characterises the relationship between the imperialist centre and the peripheral nations. Unequal exchange emerges because the cost of labour-power is much cheaper than in the periphery than in the core capitalist nations. In her recent book on unequal exchange, Intan Suwandi points out,

> the much higher rates of exploitation of workers in the Global South has to do not simply with low wages but also with the fact that the difference in wages between the North and South is greater than the difference in productivity.[44]

42 See Clive (1974) for a discussion of the inability of the national bourgeoisie to combat underdevelopment.

43 Smith 2016, p. 56.

44 Suwandi 2019, p. 59.

Multinational corporations and large retailers are able to use their monopoly position to dictate prices for goods produced by Southern workers for extremely low wages. Because these corporations are often permanent corporate clients, Southern producers will prioritize production of export for multinationals over local clients. This only ensures that they will remain peripheral and prevents them from ever being in a position to compete with the capitalist monopolies.

John Smith points out in *Imperialism in the Twenty-First Century* that FDI is no longer the dominant form of imperialist penetration of peripheral nations. Rather than directly controlling the production process through FDI, transnational corporations prefer arms-length outsourcing. In such an outsourcing relationship, a transnational corporation (TNC) does not directly command the production process in a developing nation, nor do they have ownership of the production facility in which goods are produced. Rather, a TNC uses its monopoly position to get clients in the developing nation, who fiercely compete with other local capitalists to gain contracts with the TNC. This is made possible through export-oriented economics in developing countries such as Bangladesh and India, which encourages low-wage labour in order to compete for corporate clients. The result is that the TNC is in a better position than the Southern producer, and less vulnerable to disruptions in the periphery. As John Smith explains, "arm's-length relationships also allow TNCs to offload many of the costs and risks associated with cyclical fluctuations in demand and with much larger disruptions in world markets."[45] If there is a large strike, a political crisis, or an unfavourable peripheral government, the TNC can simply change its supplier. This puts tremendous pressure on Southern producers to unite with politicians favourable to the imperialists, and to use repressive means to crush campaigns demanding higher wages. Although members of the national bourgeoisie in the South exploit the working class, they themselves are exploited by the transnational corporations from the imperialist centre. This puts tremendous pressure on them to utilise all possible means to maximise the rate of surplus-value. The result is one where Southern proletarians work in sweatshops, often under managerial terror, while also facing repression from the capitalist state whenever they take measures to improve their material conditions.

As capitalism grows into its monopoly stage, large corporations command the entire production process by controlling social reproduction. Thus, while Southern producers of raw materials, machinery, and consumer goods may

---

45 Smith, 2016, p. 82.

find buyers on the local domestic market, it is the transnational corporations situated in the North that are their main customers. These transnational corporations use their capital to purchase commodities produced by Southern workers at a price below their value in order to appropriate a large portion of the surplus-value. Suwandi points out that "the financial headquarters of a multinational retains monopolies over information technology and markets and appropriates the larger portion of the value added in each link in the chain."[46] The goods produced mostly by Southern workers (which includes parts of Eastern Europe in addition to East Asia, Latin America, and many African nations) are purchased by the monopolies. They are then sold in shops in the imperialist centre, as well as in semi-peripheral nations like Brazil, South Africa, and China. In the next chapter, I will provide a visual model that allows us to conceptualise the process of unequal exchange, and how retail workers can join the anti-imperialist front to liberate the peoples of the developing world. I hope to show that retail workers are not just sales associates but occupy a position in the division of labour that enables them to assist working people in the peripheral nations.

46 Suwandi, 2019, p. 52.

CHAPTER 7

Two Stages of Production and Realisation

In the previous chapters, I discussed the process by which surplus-value is produced and realized. This is a process that passes through many stages and is dependent on a multiplicity of factors. Capitalism, which is the production and realization of surplus-value, can only function if each stage operates smoothly. If there is a disruption in any of the stages, it will have an effect on the entire process of social reproduction and effect the profits of the capitalist class. Working people—whether they produce goods in a factory, distribute them to the shops, or help to sell them—have the power to end capitalism and end the exploitation on which the capitalist's profits are founded. In order to conceptualise the effects workers in each stage can have on the social reproduction process, I will develop a two-stage framework that articulates the production, circulation, and realisation of surplus-value. This two-stage framework, which is already present in Marx's writings, is helpful for formulating a transnational organising strategy, which seeks to unite Northern and Southern workers.

1 Stage One: Production of Goods

The first stage is where the surplus-value is produced, which is materialised in commodities. During the first stage of production, workers gather raw materials, manufacture goods, and produce machinery. In stage one, mine workers extract metals and minerals that are necessary to produce many components that are used in plastic, electronics, cars, airplanes, and other complex goods. During this stage, coffee and tea are grown by farmers in Kenya, Colombia, and other developing nations, as well as refined and packaged in factories located in cities like Houston, Texas. The first stage also includes the gathering of materials used in textiles, such as cotton in countries like Zambia, and their transformation into clothing in garment factories in Bangladesh, India, and China. In his path-breaking book, *Imperialism in the Twenty-First Century*, John Smith shows that most physical-goods are produced in the developing countries of the global South and the peripheries of the North (i.e., Eastern Europe, the US South, and some Mediterranean countries like Greece). As I discussed in the previous chapter, transnational corporations often do not own the factories in which the first stage of production takes place. The TNC's will outsource production to locally owned factories in the developing countries because it is

 | DOI:10.1163/9789004469624_008

more profitable and allows them to capture more surplus-value. Exploiting the system of unequal exchange, TNC's take advantage of the cheap cost of labour and the fact that they can often dictate the price for the goods.[1]

In some cases, the Southern capitalists who own these factories get capital loans from state-owned banks, which appropriate a portion of the surplus-value in the form of interest. What happens to the surplus-value that has been appropriated by the state depends on what section of the bourgeoisie is dominant, and the strength of the working-class movement. If the internal or national bourgeoisie is dominant and there is a strong trade union movement, the state-appropriated surplus-value could be used to improve the material conditions of the people. An example of this is Brazil during the Lula years, in which the Brazilian national bourgeoisie was dominant, and the trade unions aligned with PT held positions of state-power. The surplus-value appropriated by the state from the sale of commodities was transformed into the welfare programme known as Bolsa Familia, which was a massive cash-transfer programme to the poorest sections of Brazilian society. Although Brazil was still a capitalist country in the Lula years, the dominance of the national bourgeoisie combined with a strong workers movement allowed the working class to capture portions of the economic surplus. Also, it gave the Brazilian state a position from which to bargain with the TNC's rather than being entirely dominated by them.[2] A similar situation existed in the early 21st century in Russia, India, Indonesia, South Africa, and China, which are collectively known as the BRIICS countries.

The imperialists and the TNC's often try to weaken the domestic capitalist class of a peripheral nation by aligning itself with the comprador bourgeoisie. They will provide material support to politicians such as Jair Bolsonaro, who want to put the comprador bourgeoisie in command of the state and destroy the political organisation of the working class. When the comprador bourgeoisie takes control, the surplus-value that is captured by the state is appropriated by comprador capitalists to create more export processing facilities and militarize society in order to weaken the working class. If the comprador bourgeoisie becomes dominant, Southern workers have fewer rights than in the imperialist countries, work extremely long hours, and receive a very small wage. Often, they work for criminally corrupt capitalists that use terror to punish militant workers and weaken trade unions. Because the TNC's do not exercise direct control, they can absolve themselves of any responsibility for

1 Smith 2016, chapters 2–3.
2 Saad-Filho and Morais 2018

the crimes committed against these workers. In countries such as Bangladesh, Colombia, India, and China, workers produce much of our clothing, food, and electronics, often under extremely repressive conditions. While the TNC's appropriate massive amounts of surplus value, the Southern worker does not benefit from foreign domination of their economic life.

A good example of this process can be found in the coffee industry. James Brittain shows how coffee-farmers are exploited by transnational corporations in his *Revolutionary Social Change in Colombia.* An important fact is that the workers in Colombia who produce coffee do not actually get to drink Colombian coffee but must import lower quality coffee from elsewhere. This is because the massive coffee plantations in Colombia are owned by the Colombian landowners, who have contracts with big American companies like Starbucks. The plantation owner employs extremely cheap farm-labour, exploiting workers that must toil long days to produce massive quantities of raw coffee. As Brittain explains,

> from a US $4 cup of coffee bought in North America, 'around one cent will go back to the farmer'. In 1997, Colombian-based coffee farmers were reportedly paid US$3.80 for every pound of coffee they produced, while in 2004, the producers received about 0.70¢.[3]

At the end of each cycle, the owner has a large quantity of coffee-beans, which they will then sell directly to coffee-shops like Starbucks and transport to the imperialist countries. The ideology of fair-trade mystifies this process, for commercial coffee companies only gives the plantation owner a 'fairer' price, while it remains up to them on how much to pay their workers. Unless the workers are exceptionally well organised, the plantation owner will pay them as little as they can in order to appropriate as much surplus-value as possible. They will make every attempt to use violence to rule over the workers and repress attempts to organise for better wages.[4]

Once the first stage of production ends, the coffee is shipped to refining plants in order to be processed, packaged, and distributed. Starbucks is able to appropriate a portion of the surplus-value contained in the raw coffee beans by purchasing them at a commercial price. This price exploits the unequal exchange between the North and the South and allows retailers to purchase the coffee at a price below their value. For the owner of the plantation, this is

3 Brittain 2010, p. 85.
4 Hristov 2014.

often a good deal, but for the farm labourers, it means an extremely low wage and long working hours. The peasants of Colombia produce thousands of kilos of coffee each year, but more than four fifths of it is appropriated by transnational monopoly capital. This drives the peasants into poverty, and in the case of Colombia, has encouraged them to produce coca plants and forced them into the drug market. Although companies like Starbucks do not directly own the plantations where the coffee beans are produced, they are able to determine the prices for the coffee beans by offering the owner a corporate contract. Companies like Starbucks are what Marx called Merchant Capital, for they use their capital to purchase goods produced by industrial proletarians, and then sell it in order to obtain a commercial profit. Leech explains,

> the international market price for coffee—Colombia's leading legal export for most of the 20th century—plummeted in the post Cold War era, forcing many farmers to seek alternative means of survival. Consequently, increasing numbers of farmers began replacing their coffee plants with coca plants.[5]

As Brittain and Leech demonstrate, the US-backed Colombian government spends millions of dollars each year funding paramilitaries who terrorise the Colombian people. The Colombian state is a quasi-fascist dictatorship hidden behind the facade of 'free' elections. It has only been the Revolutionary Armed Forces of Colombia (FARC) that have defended the peasants by pressuring the government to create protectionist policies that favour the peasant and encourage crop diversification. The Colombian state, with the assistance of US imperialism, has waged a relentless war on the FARC in an effort to force the peasantry to cooperate with the dictates of transnational corporations.

In this section, I have argued that the majority of physical goods from the first stage are produced in the global South and in some of the peripheries of the North. First-stage production is a very important part of the production process, as the entire capitalist process depends on it. Most of what Marx analysed in the first volume of *Capital* examined the structure of the first stage of production. To conclude this section, I would like to provide a visual representation of the first stage of the capitalist accumulation process (Figure 1). This visual representation comes directly from Marx's *Capital*, but will be expanded significantly at the end of this chapter to include the other stages.

5 Qtd in Brittain 2010, p. 84.

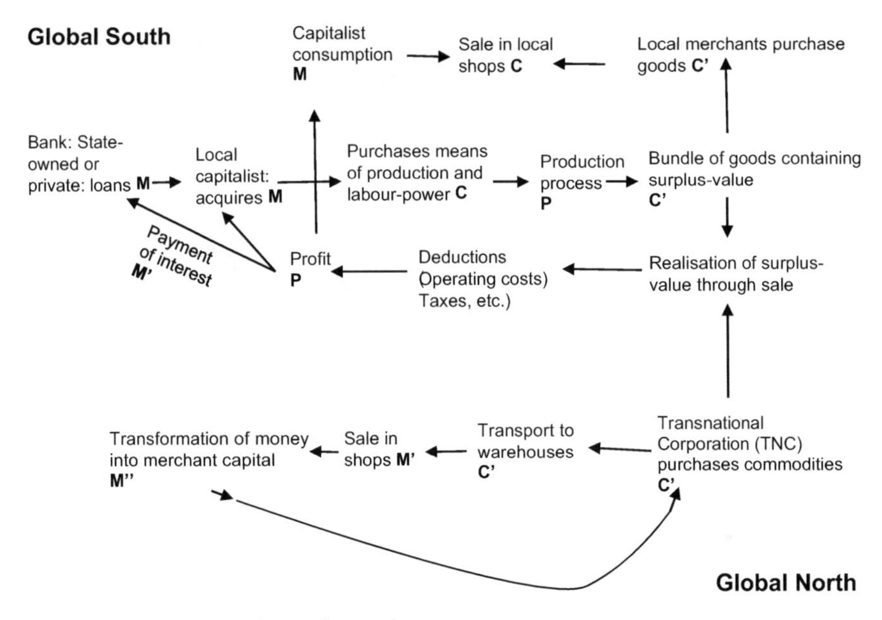

FIGURE 1 Stage One of capitalist production

Figure 1 allows us to visualise the structure of production, which is located mainly in the global South. It articulates the process of arms-length outsourcing, in which multinational corporations purchase commodities from Southern producers at a low cost. The starting point is with the banks, which are sometimes owned by the state depending on the social formation. For example, in China, most large banks are controlled by the state, which allows the Chinese government to exercise control over finance capital. By doing this, the Chinese state is able to give capital loans to companies that are performing well while restricting credit to those that are not.[6] In others, the bank providing the funds are privately owned, and often tied to the international finance capital (i.e., HSBC, Chase, etc.). Although the Southern capitalist may get his capital from other sources, such as investments and profits, finance capital often plays an important role. Their motivation for providing a loan is to appropriate a significant portion of the surplus-value that will result from their capital loan. For this reason, in my visualisation of the production of surplus-value, the bank is the starting point.

Once the local capitalist has acquired money capital, he or she will purchase means of production and labour-power. There is a strong tendency for the cost

6 Hart-Landsberg and Burkett 2005, pp. 55–57.

of labour-power to be significantly lower in the global South, often being close to the equivalent of the costs of reproduction. Southern capitalists are under significant pressure to keep wages as low as possible, as they will not retain large amounts of the surplus-value produced by their workers.[7] Those capitalists who are closely aligned with imperialism will receive special benefits for keeping wages low, such as permanent customers, access to knowledge, invitation to international imperialist meetings, and material privileges.[8] Capitalists who refuse to align themselves with imperialism often are denied access to technology, and must rely on older, inferior equipment. They will find it hard to compete with the comprador bourgeoisie, which has access to the best technology because it has aligned itself with imperialism. This is one reason why the national bourgeoisie, despite being part of the capitalist class, will sometimes adopt anti-imperialist political views. An anti-imperialist state can give the national bourgeoisie access to the machinery, equipment, and knowledge that the imperialists have denied them. The state is able to do this by appropriating a portion of the surplus-value and investing it into better technology.

In Figure 1, the Southern capitalist begins the process of production once he or she has acquired labour-power and the means of production. In the developing countries, workers often face more abuse from management than they do in the imperialist centres. They are under pressure to produce as much as possible and complete an order before the due date. Sometimes managers in Southern nations use violence, terror, and bullying to increase the productivity of labour. The result of the production process is a bundle of commodities that contain surplus-value and must be transformed into money. Although Southern producers sell some of their products to local suppliers, the majority of it is sold to transnational corporations. Their monopoly nature gives them the ability to dictate the prices for these commodities, which is often far lower than the price they would pay in the imperialist centres. As Intan Suwandi explains,

> Unequal exchange, or the exchange of more labor for less, is closely related to the value capture made possible by the formation of monopolies, which enables the capitalist centers to appropriate large shares of the surplus generated elsewhere.[9]

7 Amin 2018, p. 84.

8 Suwandi 2019, pp. 102–111.

9 Suwandi 2019, p. 156.

There is thus a massive transfer of value from peripheral Southern nations to the imperialist centres in the global North. Suwandi shows that Southern producers are under intense pressure to fulfil orders within the time frame set by the multinational corporations. If they do not meet the target, then they might lose their corporate customer and face the threat of bankruptcy.[10] The imperialist monopolies will support politicians that reduce tariffs and make it easier for them to gain access to Southern markets. The local market usually does not allow for the same level of capital accumulation as does trade with multinational corporations. Local shops that purchase goods from Southern producers generally sell their goods at a high cost and are only affordable by domestic capitalists. In *Clothing Poverty*, Andrew Brooks shows that working people in the developing world often shop at second-hand clothing markets, as these provide designer clothing that is higher quality than locally made products.[11] The result is that local producers are often unable to accumulate capital by their own means and are highly dependent on the imperialist centre for access to capital goods.

In Figure 1, once the Southern producer has sold their commodities, they must make deductions from the surplus-value. This includes operating costs, such as rent, dividend-payments to investors, taxes, and debts. Also, they will pay a portion of the surplus-value to the bank, which will use their payment to decide whether their company will receive future investments. What this means is that even though the Southern capitalist exploits the labour of the working class, they are left with very little profit once all the deductions have been made. Imperialism prevents them from accumulating significant capital, leaving them with monetary wealth, but little capital in order to become independent. As I have indicated above, this situation puts pressure on Southern capitalists to betray their own people and become agents of imperialism. This involves supporting the militarisation of society by using the economic surplus to build the repressive apparatuses of the state, as well as clandestine payments to death squads. Increased repression is always felt chiefly by the working class, who are disorganised through police terror and the criminalisation of their organisations. This gives the comprador bourgeoisie access to the wealth of the imperialists, even if they accumulate very little capital in the process of supplying goods to multinational retailers.

What Figure 1 demonstrates is the process of social reproduction in the first stage of production. Its geographical location is the global South and the

10 *Ibid.* pp. 134–145.

11 Brooks 2019

peripheries of the North, and its social agents are the imperialist bourgeoisie, the Southern proletariat, the peasantry, and merchant capital. Although there are production relationships in contemporary capitalism that are different from the one described above, this is the one that is most common. The poverty and oppression that Third World peoples face is a direct product of their domination by generalised monopoly-finance capital. As Samir Amin argues throughout his writings, countries that successfully delink from the imperialist world system—Venezuela, Cuba, Vietnam—can secure a decent future of their people and create a situation in which transnational corporations can no longer dominate them. At the same time, every revolution in the advanced capitalist centres enables peripheral nations to become freer of imperialist domination and thereby gain access to equipment needed to the develop the productive forces. Now that I have discussed the first stage, in which commodities are produced, I will examine the second stage, in which commodities are distributed.

2 Stage Two: Realisation of Surplus-Value

The second stage production begins once the *physical* commodity has been produced. In the second stage, retail workers add additional labour in order to transport, store, refine, and sell the commodity. While retail and service workers exist in large numbers in both developing and imperialist nations, it is in the imperialist centres that most service labour is found. One reason for this is that the service industry exists as a direct result of consumerism. Although poverty exists in the peripheries of the imperialist countries, it is in the centre that commodities are primarily consumed. As Sweezy, Baran, and Foster note, in contemporary monopoly capitalism, there is a persistent necessity to realise the surplus-value contained in commodities. A unique feature of the sales-effort is that some retail employees do not just sell commodities, but also produce new ones. Working people who are employed to help absorb the economic surplus are sometimes themselves productive employees, who produce additional surplus-value through their labour. Those who work in restaurants, coffeeshops, bakeries, and cafes, for example, add additional value by producing meals, coffee-drinks, and deserts. A worker at Starbucks, for example, helps to sell coffee *and* produces surplus-value by manufacturing coffee drinks such as Frappuccino's and Lattes. They are not simply employed to help sell commodities, but themselves produce surplus value through their labour. This does not apply to all retail employees, such as shop employees and salespeople. For example, a worker at Ikea who stacks shelves and helps customers provides labour that is necessary to the realisation of the surplus-value contained in Ikea's furniture. Without their labour, the shelves would be empty and there would be no way to arrange the commodities so that they evoke the desire of the customer. While some retail labour might be automated, such as self-checkout cashiers, labour such as stacking shelves will always be necessary to ensure the realisation of surplus-value. The only conceivable situation in which retail labour largely disappears is in the case of a total shift to digital web shops, which is what happened in many parts of the capitalist world during the 2020–2021 coronavirus pandemic. In this case, the retail employee is shifted from a sales function to a logistics one, packing orders and getting it to the customer.

Regardless of its geographical location, the primary function of stage two is to realise the surplus-value contained in products from stage-one. The second stage is integral to ensuring a stable market for goods produced in stage one and allowing for the regular reproduction of the production process. Returning to our example of Starbucks, once the coffee beans have been refined and arrive at the coffeeshops, they can be transformed into new products that contain additional surplus-value. The barista takes the coffee-beans and transforms them into filtered coffee, cappuccinos, lattes, and espressos. Their labour, though far less intensive than the picking of raw coffee beans, is integral to completing the final product. Without the barista, it would be impossible to have filtered coffee, cappuccinos, lattes, and espressos. The main difference is that the coffee drink produced by the barista is immediately purchased and consumed as soon as it is produced. In a single working day, the barista adds a large amount of value to the raw beans by producing coffee drinks.

In the United Kingdom and most other places they operate, Starbucks pays the minimum wage. Let us suppose that a group of four baristas each make 80 GBP/day for a ten-hour day, leaving a wage bill of 320 GBP. Suppose that during that ten hours, the workers produce 8000 GBP of coffee. This means that they produce a total of 7,680 GBP of surplus-value. Suppose that the individual shop must spend 800 GBP daily for the raw materials: coffee beans, flavouring, milk, sugar, and other ingredients. If we deduct this 800 GBP from the surplus-value, it leaves 6,880 GBP. In addition to this, the daily operating costs of heating, electricity, water, etc. cost 150 GBP, leaving 6,730. Finally, we must deduce the daily rent of 1000 GBP (if it is prime real estate), leaving 5,730 GBP. If we deduct the remaining 730 GBP for additional expenses, we are left with 5000 GBP in profits. Even if the numbers in the above example are different in actual practice, it is clear that the primary source of Starbucks profits are from the low-wage labour of both the coffee farmers and the baristas. It is the unequal exchange relationship between Starbucks, located in the global North, and the coffee farmers, located in the global South that allows Starbucks to purchase the coffee beans for a very low price. Furthermore, the exploitation of the baristas in the local shops allows Starbucks to appropriate additional surplus value. One should notice how other sections of capital also profit from the commercial exploitation of workers in both the North and South. First, energy companies appropriate a small portion of the surplus-value by receiving payment for daily operating costs of their corporate clients. Second, real estate company's appropriate surplus value by collecting monthly rent from Starbucks shop owners. In big cities such as Glasgow and London, most land in the city centres is owned by a few large real estate companies. They make extraordinary profits from renting their land to companies like Starbucks and appropriating surplus-value produced by their workers.

The second stage of the capitalist process (Figure 2) thus involves the selling, marketing, and realisation of surplus value of goods produced in the first stage. I will now introduce a second figure, which brings out some of the complexities of the second stage and shows the importance of retail and service workers.

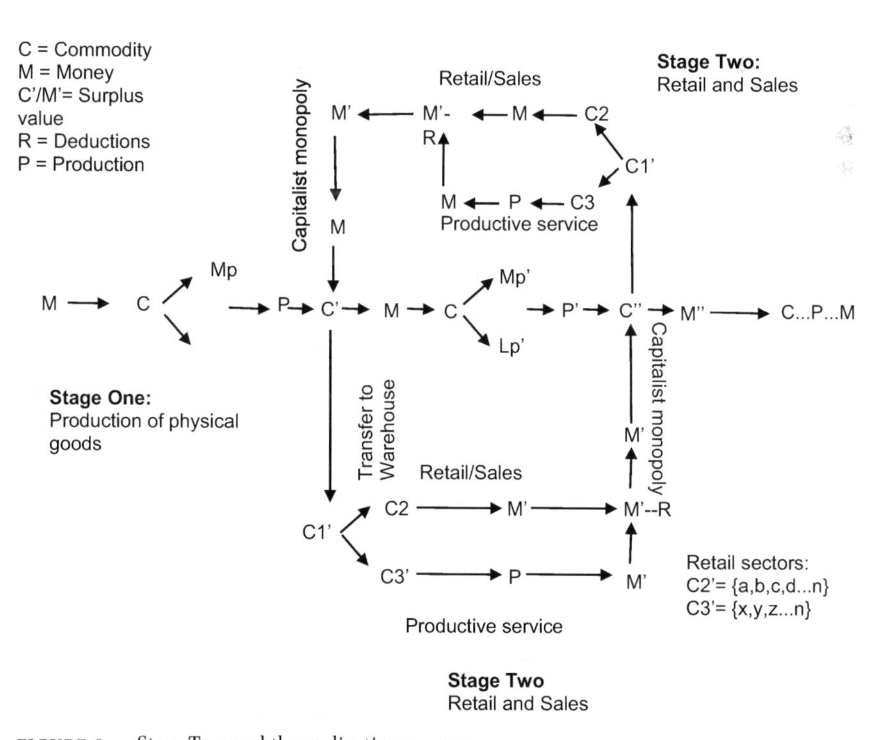

FIGURE 2 Stage Two and the realization process

Figure 2 assumes the content of Figure 1, which articulated the process by which surplus-value is produced. Here, the focus is on the process by which surplus-value is realised through the sale of commodities, as well as the production of new value by retail employees. Once a multinational corporation has acquired a bundle of commodities, they must employ workers to transform it into money. Figure 2 is a visual representation of the process of retail in the era of monopoly capitalism.

I will begin here by dealing with C2' in its entirety before turning to C3'. A portion of C1 will be transported to local shops, which is a set of shops equal to C2={a,b,c...n}, where each variable represents a shop. Depending on the size of investment, there could be a few shops or hundreds of them. Each local shop will sell their portion of the C2', ensuring that C' is transformed into M'. It is in this stage that retail employees perform a variety of sales tasks, from stacking shelves to persuading customers to purchase the goods. Their labour does not add value to C2' but ensures that the surplus-value is realised to allow for the absorption of the economic surplus. What Figure 2 demonstrates is the dependence of the entire process of social reproduction on the work of retail employees, who ensure that the surplus-value is realised. Without their labour, some of which is hard to automate, the capitalists in both stage one and two would run into serious problems, as it would disrupt both the continued production of goods, as well as the realisation of the value in them.

Once the surplus-value of the commodities has been realised by being transformed into M', the retail process in C2' does not come to an end. I have included here an additional stage, in which the shop owner must first make a series of deductions (R) from the M'. This includes operating costs, such as heating and electricity, rent, taxes, licensing fees, and wages, which must be subtracted (M'-R) before the process can continue. Once the shop owner has made deductions, they then pay a sizable portion of the remaining M' in the form of a fee to the capitalist monopoly. As can be seen, the store owner only keeps a small portion of the surplus-value, while the rest of it is appropriated by the large corporation that supplies them with the goods. The large corporation then purchases new goods from the capitalists in stage one, which then allows the process of social reproduction to take place on an expanded scale.

As a result of realising the surplus-value of both C1 and C2, both capitalists in stage one and stage two have accumulated capital and grown so that their operations take place on a larger scale. For the capitalists in stage one, this might result in the purchase of new machinery and the creation of new factories. They might also be able to invest a portion of their funds into improved management and logistics. The result is that the productivity of labour in stage one will increase with each *successful* cycle so long as nothing happens that disrupts the process. However, as Marx shows in *Capital 3*, there will be a tendency for the rate of profit to fall, eventually resulting in a crisis. In the second stage of C2', represented by the first upward arrow, the monopolies now have adequate funds to open new shops, as well as expand their market influence by investing funds into more advertising. This means that the surplus-value in the stage of expanded reproduction will be greater than before, meaning that the economic surplus will rise. The monopolies will have to find new ways to stimulate demand in order to ensure that the larger bundle of goods can be sold. They may change the layout of their shops, in order to make shopping a more exciting experience and attract new customers.

As C2' is a set of many shops {a,b,c,d … n}, there will always be money coming in to allow the monopolies to accumulate capital. Because of this, the workers employed in all the shops must be organised into a single trade union, in order to allow them to combat the monopolies rather than individual shop owners. If they organise a strike that shuts down the entire set of shops, it will prevent the monopolies from accumulating capital-funds needed to reproduce the process. The capitalists in stage one can continue the process of capitalist production once the capitalist monopolies have purchased their goods. They anticipate that they will sell the goods and purchase a fresh batch of them at the end of the business cycle. It is this anticipation, founded on the basis of dependable corporate clients, that allows them to continue the process of capitalist production indefinitely. If the retail employees in C2, organised across shops a,b,c,d…n, go on strike for a single day, it will cause a disruption in the first stage, as there is a chance that the goods produced there will not be sold within the target timeframe. This would reduce the turnover time of capital and cause a crisis for both the first and second stage capitalists. What Figure 2 would seem to suggest is that the workers involved in the sale of C2' could benefit by organising a relationship with the workers who produced these commodities (C1') in stage one. Doing so would allow them to coordinate an action, which would put them both in a better position against the capitalists that exploit them. Instead of just organising the workers in stage one or stage two, the entire value chain must be organised in order to give the workers a weapon for combatting the monopolies. This would also include logistics and transport workers, who I will not analyse here but are just as vital to the process.[12] If we were to expand the graph to include the labour of transport and warehouse workers, we could produce a geography of anti-imperialist action and a map to help articulate the process of creating international working-class solidarity.

12 For a fantastic discussion of logistic workers, see Wilson and Ness (2018).

In addition to C2', which distributes the commodities to shops to be sold, a portion of the goods are distributed to service providers, C3', which is a set of restaurants, coffeeshops, and cleaning companies {x,y,z...n}. The workers in x,y,z...n transform C3' into M' by producing new goods and services. These could include baristas at a cafe, who transform the coffee (C) into a latte or cappuccino, thereby adding surplus value to it and at the same time selling the coffee. At the end of work week, the productive sales employees will have transformed C3 into M', which itself exceeds the value of the elements of production. Once the franchise owner has made all deductions from M', such as rent and operating costs, they will pay the larger corporation a portion of the surplus-value, leaving them with a small profit at the end of the business cycle. In the case of productive services, the process of social reproduction differs from the direct sale of commodities (C2'). Whereas in C2' no new value is created, in C3' additional surplus-value is produced. This additional surplus-value is used to fund the expansion of production, enabling franchise owners to open new shops, acquire more territories, and command a larger share of the market.

3 Possibilities for Resistance to Monopoly Capitalism

Workers in stage two possess the power to bring the entire commodity chain to a halt, and thereby empower workers in the first stage to take action. This is only possible if retail workers are organised transnationally, with direct links to the workers in the developing world who produce the goods that they sell. If retail employees organise a strike only to advance their own interests, it may have an effect on capitalism in the global South. However, this effect will not directly benefit the Southern proletariat, as the local bourgeoisie will simply produce goods for another corporation. For example, if H&M workers across Britain go on strike without forming links with Bangladeshi garment workers, capitalists in Bangladesh will just produce shirts for a different retailer such as Primark. By creating transnational organisational links between workers in stage one and two, it becomes possible to coordinate an action directly with the garment workers union. They could agree to go on strike at the same time, thereby hurting both the Bangladeshi capitalists and the imperialist monopolies. If the garment workers go on strike, the H&M retail employees could promote their strike to their co-workers in order to expose the super-exploitation behind a t-shirt. What the above model makes clear is that retail employees, not just Southern producers, possess significant power when they are organised on transnational lines.

In chapter ten, I will discuss a campaign by German trade unionists to organise retail employees to unite with garment workers in the developing world. Before turning to this, I will explore how outsourcing has transformed significant sections of the workforce into low-wage service employees. As I will show, outsourcing does not just happen between multinationals and Southern producers, but within multinational corporations themselves. In order to cut costs and appropriate more surplus-value, multinational corporations outsource unproductive service tasks to corporations such as Bidvest-Noonan. This process destroys the stability of employment and reduces millions of workers into low-wage, temporary employees with no prospects of a better future.

CHAPTER 8

A Marxist Analysis of Outsourcing

A prominent feature of the contemporary services industry is the widespread use of outsourcing. A large percentage of productive service employees work for private companies who employ them in order to get surplus value. In some cases, these companies specialise in outsourced services, operating through the acquisition of contracts with retail shops, corporate offices, entertainment venues, schools and universities, hotels, and other workplaces.[1] Outsourced workers often work on temporary or zero-hour contracts for little pay and with high levels of stress. They must be ready for work at all times and can be penalised if they do not accept a job when it is available. If they do not perform according to the strict standards set by the outsourcing firm, they can be terminated.

Although the working class does not benefit from outsourcing, the capitalists reap massive profits from it. Outsourcing allows a company to reduce its labour-costs on service tasks that do not result in the production or realisation of surplus-value. By outsourcing unproductive tasks, jobs are transferred from "high-wage firms with strong promotional systems to lower-wage firms with less secure employment".[2] For example, although cleaning is necessary for workers to continue working, it does not add any value to commodities, nor does it help to sell commodities. The more a capitalist has to spend on unproductive tasks such as cleaning, the less profit he will get at the end of the business cycle. Traditionally, cleaners in a factory would have belonged to the same union as the productive shop workers and participated in industrial actions. When workers took this approach, organising an entire shop irrespective of occupation, it strengthened the position of all the workers. Their large numbers and collective unity gave them a powerful weapon to combat the capitalist class and advance their interests. The result of this was that unionised cleaning workers enjoyed higher wages and secure employment conditions, as well as unity with the other workers in the same shop. Outsourcing stems from the capitalist need to break up unions and weaken the power of working people to fight for their interests.

1 Davis-Blake & Brochak (2009), p. 322.

2 *Ibid.* p. 322.

 | DOI:10.1163/9789004469624_009

Capitalists have used multiple strategies to attack *organised* service workers. One strategy used by big companies is to recognise *multiple* trade unions in a single shop, and encourage separate unions based on occupation.[3] For example, in a pipe-fitting factory, the management might encourage divisions in the workers by recognising a welder's union *and* a 'support staff' union. The argument is that these workers have *occupation-specific* needs, and they can advance their interests best if they are organised along occupational lines. The result of this is that the ability of the workers to go on strike depends on the agreement of two separate unions. Although this strategy makes it harder to organise workers, a trade union is still harmful to the bourgeoisie, for it puts the cleaners in a better position than if they were totally unorganised. They can demand higher wages, a secure employment contract, and engage in industrial actions against their employer. This is not in the interests of the capitalist, who must try to reduce costs of unproductive labour as much as possible in order to get as much profit as possible. The best solution to the capitalists' dilemma is to outsource the cleaning workers. What this means is that they will no longer directly employ the cleaners, but instead gain a contract from an outsourcing company like Noonan or WGC. These outsourcers will charge a significantly lower cost for unproductive cleaning tasks, which results in capital being freed up for productive investment. Furthermore, the outsourcers will utilise 'flexible' employment patterns in order to reduce the cleaner's ability to take industrial action to improve their material conditions. Instead of having set hours and a single employer, they will work on a 'zero-hours' contract, in which their employment depends on whether work is available. Of course, work is always available, but the outsourcers decide when and where the cleaning worker will work. The cleaner loses the solidarity that she or he previously held, and instead is atomised into an individual who must be available for work at all times. Although some may develop stable employment in a single place even in this outsourced relationship, others will work in multiple locations each week. Two major reasons why capitalists use outsourcing is thus the reduction of labour costs and the weakening of labour organisation.

Before proceeding further, I would like to now define outsourcing, as this will reveal more reasons why capitalists resort to it. *Outsourcing is the transformation of unproductive tasks into productive labour that results in surplus-value.* An outsourcing company employs workers to do services in order to appropriate the surplus-value created by them. When this happens, they lose their unproductive nature and become productive functions that are profitable. In the era

3 See Machin et al. (1993) for the capitalist strategy of recognising multiple trade unions.

of monopoly capitalism, it is not always profitable to invest in capital intensive industries because the rate of profit tends to be low. As Sweezy, Baran, and Steindl have shown in their works, monopoly capitalism is characterised by stagnation and the inability to fully utilise capacity. Foster and McChesney, in *the Endless Crisis* show that significant amounts of surplus capital are invested in financial products designed to stimulate speculation and debt-trading.[4] As Samir Amin explains, financialization "provides not only the sole possible outlet for surplus capital, it also provides the sole stimulus to the slack growth observed, since the 1970s in the United States, Europe, and Japan."[5] In addition to investments in financial products, significant amounts of excess capital is invested into outsourcing, which creates new outlets in which to appropriate surplus-value. When the bourgeoisie can no longer get a profit from manufacturing and industrial production, it will need to find new sources of surplus-value, which the outsourcing of service tasks enables.

Cleaning, security, front-house staff, administration, logistics, transportation, entertainment, and education are all forms of labour that can be outsourced and reorganised on a capitalist basis. Some of these tasks may have historically been part of the public sector, particularly public administration and education. Neoliberalism has resulted in major tax cuts, particularly to capital assets of corporations, which have discovered many ways to avoid paying taxes. This means that local governments in the United States, the UK, and the EU often have less funds available to directly finance public services. Just as corporations, they resort to outsourcing in order to get lower labour costs. Some public services are privatised and taken over by private companies, such as for-profit universities or private security firms. In the care sector in the UK, local councils sometimes gain contracts from outsourcing firms to provide services such as home-visits for disabled people.[6] People who were formerly employed by the state are now employed by private companies. Outsourcing is therefore a major result of the neoliberal system of accumulation, which integrates private capital more closely with the state and transforms employment patterns.

This brings us to another reason why capitalists use outsourcing, which is that it changes the management structure of unproductive tasks. An outsourced worker will be managed by the outsourcer, which will employ

---

4 Foster and McChesney 2012

5 Amin 2018, p. 65.

6 See White (2017) for an overview of how the British capitalist class has outsourced public services. The United Voices of the World Union has produced significant work on outsourcing in the NHS, which is available on their website.

techniques to maximise the productivity of their labour. The outsourcer wants to get as much labour out of the outsourced worker while paying them as little as possible. They will employ capitalist management techniques such as Taylorism, which reduces the time between tasks as much as possible. For cleaning work, they will develop an organisational structure that results in an increase in cleaned spaces. Public care workers will be given as many clients as possible, resulting in extreme stress levels and overwork.

In outsourced industries, the law of value exercises a regulating function over the labour process. The value of a service-commodity is determined by the socially necessary labour time required for its production. Workers will be under pressure to produce services in the time that it takes on average to produce them. Management will take care to eliminate time between tasks and organise groups of service-workers into a production line. Each worker will be responsible for a task and will become a specialist in that particular task. The goal of production will be to turn out as many service-commodities in as little time as possible. Workers that sit around and do nothing will be punished, as they are being idle when they could be producing value. In the cleaning industry, a standardised approach to cleaning a home will be developed, which ensures that the job can be done as quickly and efficiently as possible. The standardisation of cleaning brings the production of a clean space in line with its value. Some cleaning workers will receive piece wages, in which they are paid per job rather than hourly. As I will show in the next chapter, this allows for extremely high levels of exploitation and heavy pressure on the cleaning worker to work more. If they clean more houses than usual, their income will only rise by a small amount in proportion to the value that they have created.

Some might find it difficult to see how the law of value operates in some labour-processes, such as transportation. How does a public transport worker who works for a private company such as Firstbus increase the productivity of labour? How is the socially necessary labour time for transport goods determined? Bus drivers operate on a strict bus schedule, and the bus schedule measures the average time it takes to drive between stops. The price, which is divided into zones, is regulated by this socially necessary labour time. Even if there is traffic and it takes longer than usual, Firstbus operates according to the socially necessary labour time to produce a bus ride rather than the actual time spent driving. Bus drivers are not under pressure to arrive at the stops on time, something which they cannot always control. It is not the bus drivers who determine the productivity of labour, but the bus-schedule planners. If they want to increase the number of bus-rides produced, they can put more buses on the road, or find routes that reduce the amount of time of the journey. Operational researchers use a Taylorised method, which measures the speed of the bus at different times of day and compare the journey with different modes of transport (i.e., walking, cycling, train, etc.).[7] Also, bus-schedule planners use algorithms that can reduce empty trips in order to optimise the amount of revenue and reduce operational costs.[8] The drivers are under significant pressure to work longer hours, as this is necessary when more bus routes are added. Instead of hiring more workers, a bus company would make more profits by finding ways to get its drivers to work longer hours in order to allow the expansion of services. This is a major reason why publicly owned transportation is often privatised and sold off to companies like Firstbus, Abellio, etc. Instead of providing more funding to the state through taxing corporate assets, which would allow for improved transport services, they prefer to keep taxes low and privatise transportation. The result is not more efficient public transportation, but more expensive fares, greater pressure on workers to be productive, and reduced quality.

Most workers in outsourced industries are thus productive labourers, and they are subjected to the same tendencies as workers who produce physical goods. Unproductive workers who provide tasks necessary to capitalist production will face exploitation and experience some of the pressures of management. However, their work will be regulated not by the law of value, but rather targets and goals. For example, a group of janitors in a Halliburton office who are not outsourced will be given a set of goals and will be required to meet these targets within their work hours. A manager will plan their production so that they meet these targets, but they will be able to work at a reduced pace and there will be far less pressure. In outsourced industries, this is not the case, as the cleaning worker must clean a space in the time that is socially necessary and face pressure to clean as many spaces as possible. The manager will organise production not to meet the goals, but rather to maximise the productivity of labour.

An important function of outsourced industries is that it creates a large market in which to absorb the economic surplus. Outsourced workers use goods produced by workers in stage one as means of production and raw materials. For example, cleaning workers use vacuum cleaners, cleaning liquid, and brooms produced by first stage workers. This is the same dynamic as exists between stage one and stage two production, with one important difference. In the two-stage model, surplus-value produced in stage one finds its realisation in stage two, which then allows for social reproduction. Outsourced industries help to

7 See Koblar and Mladenovic (2020) for an interesting example of such a case study.

8 For some accounts of bus-planning, see Wren (1972)

absorb some of the surplus-value produced in stage one but are themselves not related to it in the same way as stage two. This is because outsourced labour is itself a first stage of production and is part of the capitalist production process. Although some of the tasks performed by outsourced workers helps to circulate commodities, their labour is part of the first stage in which surplus-value is produced. However, because they are producing service-goods, which are paid for at the point of production, there is no temporal period needed to realise the surplus-value. Their clients are mostly corporations and small businesses, who provide them with a stable supply of customers. They pay them a monthly fee for their services, which makes it highly profitable because there is no need to worry about demand once a contract has been attained.

So far, we have been considering how outsourcing transforms unproductive tasks necessary to capitalist production into productive ones. There is another form of outsourcing, which is largely related to the digitalisation of life under capitalism. This is the emergence of companies that operate through apps: Uber, Airbnb, Withlocals, Task Rabbit, and JustEat. They are a form of outsourcing, but they operate in a very different way than companies like Noonan or WGC. Instead of hiring a worker on a zero-hour contract, they hire them as freelancers. What this means is that no actual employment contract exists between the company and the employee, and therefore the worker loses any kind of employment rights. Instead, they are required to meet a set of criteria, sometimes undergo an interview, and are then allowed to rent the service in order to get clients. For example, an Uber driver must own a car, have a clean driving record, and have the right to work. Uber helps the driver to get clients, but sets the prices and takes a percentage of the fare, which is essentially a rent charged to the driver in exchange for use of their app. The driver must pay for all expenses, such as gas, car maintenance, insurance, etc. Once all these operating expenses are deducted, the Uber driver will barely make the minimum wage. If they receive a few bad reviews or even a single complaint, they can be indefinitely shut out of the app and be left without work. Adam Booth notes that

> the companies at the centre of the 'sharing' economy derive their profits from taking a proportion of the rents, which in turn are a share of the surplus value generated in real production.[9]

9 Booth (2015).

Instead of directly appropriating surplus-value, Uber exploits its workers by collecting a rent in exchange for the use of its app. However, this rent is just a masked form of surplus-value, as it is created through the Uber worker who does not profit from using the app. A company like Uber is driven by the same needs as other capitalists, which is to reduce costs as much as possible. The only cost that Uber has are those needed to run an app (i.e., programmers, marketing specialists, etc.), but they need not hire a management team or open offices in the cities where they operate. Instead, the nature of the app forces the Uber driver to manage themselves. They must be disciplined, work long hours, and accept as many jobs as are available. If they do not do this, they will not be able to make a living as Uber drivers. Uber does not have to worry about trade unions, as its drivers are not employees, although there have been some attempts to organise them. Companies like Uber emerge because there are large amounts of excess capital, which cannot be profitably invested in developing the productive forces.[10] The stagnation of monopoly capitalism, identified by Sweezy, Baran, and Steindl creates the gig economy, driving millions of people into extremely insecure jobs with no employment rights.

So far, I have shown how outsourcing is a unique component of the service industry. The process of outsourcing can take many forms, but its function is the same: to transform unproductive tasks into productive labour resulting in surplus-value. Neoliberalism, which involves the massive privatisation of public assets, accelerates outsourcing and encourages corporations to outsource unproductive tasks. In order to further demonstrate how this process takes place concretely, I have included a case study of Bidvest-Noonan, one of the UK's largest outsourcing firms.

1 Bidvest-Noonan: A Case Study in Outsourcing

One of the largest outsourcers in the UK and Ireland is a South African company Bidvest-Noonan, which provides cleaning, security, mailroom, and hospitality services to corporate clients. Some of the clients of Bidvest-Noonan include universities, hospitals, retails stores (i.e., Ikea), shopping centres, and airports.[11] Noonan started in 1977 as an Irish cleaning company, and has had multiple owners since being acquired by Bidvest in 2017 for €175m. The business strategy of Bidvest-Noonan is to purchase smaller service companies

10 For an excellent Marxist analysis of Uber, see Perez (2016).

11 Bidvest-Noonan Website.

and then add them to their profile of outsourced services. For example, in November 2017, it acquired Ultimate Security Services, a medium sized firm that employs more than 2,100 workers that provide security to businesses across Ireland and the UK. Noonan also acquired the Northern Ireland outsourcing company Resource Group in 2016, the Shield Guarding Company in 2016, and Federal Security in 2009, which allows it to play a dominant role in outsourced security labour.[12] Bidvest-Noonan currently commands a labour force of over 15,000 workers and made over €230 in profits in 2019. Although it currently only operates in the UK and Ireland, it is seeking to expand to other parts of Europe in order to dominate the outsourcing industry.[13]

An interesting fact about Bidvest is that one of its former CEO's is Cyril Ramaphosa, a well-known trade unionist and ANC leader who is the current president of South Africa. He was instrumental in the anti-Apartheid struggle and has spoken at congresses of the South African Communist Party.[14] Bidvest is an example of the BRICS economic strategy, which seeks to elevate the domestic bourgeoisie of a peripheral nation in order to develop capitalist relations of production. In South Africa, the Bidvest Group is a very large company, and has its own bank and insurance company. Instead of challenging neoliberalism, which destroys stable employment patterns for working people and forces them into low-wage, outsourced jobs, the domestic bourgeoisie accepts capitalism and will do whatever is necessary to create a functioning, capitalist state.[15] By acquiring Noonan, Bidvest has enabled the South African domestic bourgeoisie to take advantage of the most vulnerable, low-paid workers in Ireland and Britain in order to make super profits. It shows how a developing nation is capable of becoming an imperialist nation when the productive forces reach a certain level of development.

Bidvest-Noonan makes its profits by appropriating the surplus-value produced by its cleaners, security guards, reception staff, and logistic workers. Its workers are usually given zero-hour contracts for extremely low pay. A zero-hours contract is an employment agreement used in the UK and the EU, which requires the employee to always be available for work, but not to be guaranteed any hours. It is designed to give the employer absolute control over the workers' life, who must always be ready for work, but does not have the security of set hours. If a worker does not respect his manager or refuses to do what is asked of him, he could find himself without any hours of work. Zero-hour

12 Brennan 2017a
13 Brennan 2017b
14 Wikipedia "Cyril Ramaphosa".
15 Bidvest Website.

contracts are widely used in outsourced industries, as it allows companies to pay them a low wage, discourage trade union activity, and enforce discipline.[16]

For most of its jobs, Bidvest-Noonan pays its workers £8.21, which is the lowest legal wage in the UK. In their 2019 Companies House financial report, Bidvest-Noonan states that one of its primary economic risks is "unrealistic increase in wages or infrastructural costs impacting adversely on competitiveness of the company."[17] This explains why they use zero-hour contracts, as it weakens trade union power and puts the workers in a more difficult position to collectively bargain for higher wages. It also creates a situation where the company that has outsourced its service labour sometimes pays its workers much higher and gives them permanent contracts. For example, at Ikea, retail staff are paid £9.30, given holiday pay, and a contract with set working hours.[18] This is also the case at the London School of Economics, where Noonan cleaners "have significantly worse pensions, derisory sick pay and much worse annual leave than their in-house counterparts".[19] By paying its employees as little as possible and giving them zero-hour contracts, Bidvest-Noonan is able to appropriate large amounts of surplus-value from its workers. From its standpoint, a wage increases to £9.30 would be 'unrealistic' because it would result in lower profits for Bidvest-Noonan, and the possibility that the workers might demand the abolition of zero-hour contracts. The result of these low wages are extremely high profits for Noonan's investors.

One can get a good sense of what it is like to work at Bidvest-Noonan from the reviews on Indeed and from the trade union, United Voices of the World. A major complaint of nearly all the workers is that they are paid very little and given very unstable working hours. A worker reports that "the pay is terrible and needs looking at, most of the staff employed have separate incomes to balance the salary those that don't do not earn enough to have a life."[20] Some were almost always required to work, while others struggled to find enough hours to survive. One worker on Indeed amusingly reports, "when I got this job I was put on a rota that made me think to take a bed to work".[21] Not all the workers gave Noonan a negative review, but most of them reported that it was difficult to acquire new skills through training, and employees received little support from management. One worker reported that his experience was

16 United Voices of the World Union, 2017.
17 Bidvest-Noonan Financial Statement 2020.
18 This information was supplied to me by a former Ikea worker.
19 United Voices of the World Union, 2017.
20 Indeed Review, 2019.
21 Indeed Review, 2019.

decent, but "if you are looking to progress or at least learn new skills, it will be very difficult as there is a lack of initiative."[22] This is an example of what Harry Braverman calls the 'degradation of labour', which systematically reduces the worker by simplifying their labour without offering them any new training of career advancement. As Braverman says, the purpose of modern management structures is to "cheapen the worker by decreasing his training and enlarging his output."[23] By depriving the worker of training, workplace knowledge, and autonomy, outsourcers like Noonan reduce the worker to a provider of inexpensive manual labour.

Besides low pay and zero-hour contracts, most workers at Bidvest-Noonan reported that they received a lot of bullying from management. In the absence of a strong trade union, workers are powerless to stand up against their boss and are vulnerable to management bullying. One of their only representatives, the United Voices of the World says that Noonan workers "are constantly monitored while at work … and are often subjected to harsh disciplinary action for the smallest of supposed infractions."[24] Some examples of management bullying at Noonan include homophobic discrimination, ageism against its elderly cleaners, and overwork resulting in extreme physical strain. They are constantly monitored, subjected to unnecessary discipline, and timed to ensure that they complete their job as quickly as possible. Outsourced workers at Noonan thus work in a heavily Taylorised work-space, in which "production units operate like a hand, watched, corrected, and controlled by a distant brain."[25]

Bidvest-Noonan's primary capital funds come from investment firms that expect a return at the end of business cycle. Before Bidvest acquired Noonan in 2017, it was controlled by the private equity company, Alchemy. The United Voices of the World union reports that during its first years, "Alchemy was reported to have made a return of £1bn for investors, including Goldman Sachs Asset Management and British Aerospace investment fund."[26] While Bidvest provides the capital, Noonan is in charge of its primary operations and management. The constant capital is used to purchase means of production, such as cleaning equipment, office space, vehicles, computers, and storage space. A portion of their constant capital also compromises marketing, advertising, and branding. Their variable capital is used to pay cleaners, security guards, reception staff, and other workers. Although some wages may vary,

22 Indeed Review, 2019.
23 Braverman 1974, p. 81.
24 United Voices of the World Union, 2017.
25 Braverman 1974, p.86.
26 United Voices of the World 2017.

Bidvest-Noonan generally pays £8.21 and hires young workers when possible in order to pay them even less. In addition to labour costs, additional capital is used to pay managers and administrative staff, whose job it is to extract surplus-value from the workers by controlling their labour process.

To get a sense of the value of their total capital, it is interesting to examine their accounts on Companies House.[27] In their 2019 report, Bidvest Noonan reports that the monetary value of their intangible assets ('goodwill') are £25mn, while their property and plant equipment was only £1.6mn. One can deduct from this that Bidvest-Noonan invests significant capital into the sales effort in order to advertise its brand and get new clients. In their company accounts, the total revenue that they received from all services in 2019 was £174mn, while their total labour costs were £148mn. The surplus-value appropriated by Bidvest-Noonan is roughly £23mn, which does not appear in the company accounts, but can be deduced by subtracting labour costs from total revenue. Because company accounts generally combine management and labour costs, it is unknown how much of the £148mn went to workers and to managers. However, the company accounts state that it only employed 140 people for management and administration. Multiple adverts on Indeed state that managers make £11.71 on full time contracts, which means their annual salary is around £22,530. If we suppose that this is true, then we can subtract roughly £3mn from the £26mn to account for management and administration costs—unproductive tasks that do not create surplus value. This means that the total surplus-value produced by workers at Bidvest-Noonan in 2019 was £23mn. After it paid all of its additional expenses, this left them with a gross profit of £17.3mn, a massive amount acquired by the super exploitation of its cleaners, security guards, and other service personnel. As the United Voices of the World puts it,

> Noonan's profits represent millions of pounds being taken out of the pockets of low paid workers, who are often women and from migrant backgrounds, and put into the hands of Noonan's exclusively white and male executive board.[28]

The structure of capitalist exploitation at Noonan can be visualised in Table 2.

Table 2 lays out the primary elements that Marx uses to calculate the rate of surplus-value and the rate of profit. A few simple deductions can be made

27 Bidvest-Noonan Financial Statement 2020.

28 United Voices of the World 2017.

TABLE 2 Exploitation of Noonan workers

Constant capital	Variable capital	Surplus-value	Rate of surplus-value	Rate of profit
£26mn	£145mn	£23mn	15%	13%

here. First, the rate of profit is only slightly less than the rate of surplus-value, which is due to the fact that the labour costs at Bidvest-Noonan are significantly higher than the costs of means of production. The reason for this is that the primary source of their profit comes directly from the *service* that their workers provide. Their means of production—vacuum cleaners, cleaning supplies (i.e., brooms, liquids, etc.), software, security systems, and vehicles—are not very expensive. Because labour is the primary expense of Bidvest-Noonan, it is unsurprising that they use heavily Tayorised managerial practices. They must get as much labour out of a single worker as possible in order to reduce labour costs and increase the output of production. Service work, because it is not capital intensive, is less vulnerable to the falling rate of profit, which results when "the constant capital is increased in such a way that the total capital increases more sharply than the variable capital."[29] It is unlikely that fixed capital costs of equipment and tools needed for cleaning, security, reception, and administration will rise significantly. While a slightly larger amount of equipment will be needed when the business expands, it will remain relatively constant in proportion to variable capital. Even if cleaning supplies and security software becomes more expensive, or there is high inflation on motor vehicles, a company like Bidvest-Noonan will always find a way to keep the costs of constant capital relatively low.

It is unsurprising that the main concern of Bidvest-Noonan is a rise in wages. Recall the quote from the beginning of this section, in which they state that their main worry is "unrealistic increase in wages or infrastructural costs impacting adversely on competitiveness of the company."[30] Marx is aware of this in volume three of *Capital*, in which he states that "a rise in wages, with circumstances remaining the same, would reduce the rate of surplus-value".[31] Let us imagine a situation in which the workers at Bidvest-Noonan win a

29 Marx 1981 [1894], p. 153.

30 Bidvest-Noonan Financial Report, 2019.

31 Marx 1981 [1894], p. 144.

TABLE 3 Exploitation of Noonan workers (increase variable capital)

Constant capital	Variable capital	Surplus-value	Rate of surplus-value	Rate of profit
£26mn	£180mn	£27mn	15%	13%

successful campaign for higher wages with only a slight increase in the surplus-value (Table 3).

The result of such a situation would not be favourable to Bidvest-Noonan, for both the rate of profit and surplus-value do not increase. While the workers improve their material conditions and slightly increase their output, the company does not profit from this. Rather, they have higher labour costs while getting the same amount of profit at the end of the business cycle. A successful trade union campaign to force the company to pay higher wages would also put the workers in a strengthened position. They will be less likely to accept management bullying, and correctly view management as their class enemy. Also, a successful campaign could force Bidvest-Noonan to recognise a trade union, which would mean that workers would be able to file grievances to further prevent management harassment. Management would be powerless to force the workers to increase their output as a result of their increased class consciousness. They might also challenge zero-hour contracts, rejecting the ideology of 'flexibility' and demanding fixed hours. For the above reasons, Bidvest-Noonan will do everything to prevent their workers from unionising. A higher wage through industrial action means a lot more than simply higher pay. It means that the company will lose the ability to bully workers while paying them as little as possible. Instead of collective bargaining with trade unions, Bidvest-Noonan would prefer to keep wages fixed and prevent workers from holding meetings.

2 Conclusion

In this chapter, I have developed a Marxist approach to thinking about the outsourcing of service labour. I have argued that outsourcing involves the transformation of unproductive labour into sites of profitable investment. In outsourced service firms, tasks that formerly contributed only to social reproduction now result in surplus-value. This organises them on a capitalist basis and transforms the labour-process. I examined Bidvest-Noonan, as it is a good example of an outsourced service firm, and how these tendencies operate at a concrete level. Outsourced cleaners, security guards, and administrators who work at Bidvest-Noonan work for a much lower wage than if they were insourced by the company purchasing the services. Furthermore, their employment is generally insecure, and workers have a much more difficult time organising themselves because of the nature of their work. As I will show, the historically unique nature of outsourcing requires an equally unique approach to organising outsourced workers. Because their labour process differs significantly from insourced workers, traditional organising models and campaigns might not always be effective. Before I examine how service and retail workers can organise themselves, I would like to examine an additional category of service employee. These are not outsourced workers, but service workers who work for companies that exclusively sell a service. As the clearest example of this is domestic cleaning, the next chapter will focus on workers in the firm Molly Maid.

CHAPTER 9

Cleaning Workers and Surplus Value

A major source of employment in today's capitalism is the cleaning industry, which employs millions of people worldwide to clean homes, workplaces, hotels, and offices. Companies such as Molly Maid and WGC specialise in the production of cleaning-services that turn out massive profits. Cleaners—many of whom are women and immigrants—are some of the lowest paid and unsecure workers. They are often given zero-hour contracts, only get part-time work, and generally find it difficult to get enough hours to pay their bills. Most cleaners are not unionised, although there have been few successful strikes by cleaning workers.

With the development of capitalism and the dissolution of non-capitalist social relations, cleaning was gradually transformed into a value producing labour process. In the eighties, large commercial cleaning companies began emerging, which specialised in cleaning and sold nothing else than clean spaces. Commercial cleaning companies are capitalist firms that employ cleaning workers to get surplus value. In some cases, corporations that produce cleaning products created commercial cleaning companies in order to generate an outlet to absorb their economic surplus. Once commercial cleaning companies became hegemonic, almost all capitalist enterprises outsourced their cleaning work. Offices, factories, hotels, and other workplaces stopped directly hiring their own cleaners, but outsourced their cleaning labour to companies such as WGC and Bidvest Noonan (as already discussed in the previous chapter). The development of capitalism therefore transformed cleaning from an unproductive activity related to social reproduction, to a productive one that results in surplus-value.

An important change also occurred in personal cleaning services, which also came under pressure to reorganise itself on a capitalist basis. Traditionally, personal cleaning services were conducted by small independent cleaners that owned their own equipment and had some stable clients. These small-business owners were members of the petty-bourgeoisie, who made a living cleaning houses with their own cleaning supplies, vacuum cleaners, and brooms. If they had the funds, they may have hired one or two workers, but they were not able to operate on a capitalist basis. Their lack of capital may make them difficult people to work for, and a relationship of exploitation certainly can still exist between an independent cleaner and their few employees. However, their workers are not paid from *capital*, but with *money* to compensate them

 | DOI:10.1163/9789004469624_010

for their services. The small-business owner's lack of capital makes them unable to expand beyond a certain point, as capital is necessary for this. Small independent cleaning companies thus acquire their wealth through cleaning homes themselves, and also managing their own business. In order to examine the transformation of non-capitalist cleaning tasks into capitalist enterprises, I will here provide a case study of Molly Maid, which is one of the largest multinational cleaning firms.

1 Molly Maid: A Case Study

One of the largest service sectors in the global capitalist economy is the commercial cleaning industry, which turn out large profits through the super-exploitation of cleaning workers. In the United States in 2016, the commercial cleaning company Molly Maid turned over $20 million in profits resulting from surplus value of cleaning workers.[1] Molly Maid operates as a franchise, which means the company essentially decentralises its operations to individual franchise owners in exchange for fees. As one Molly Maid franchise owner put it,

> This franchise is interesting because it's a microcosm of a large company. Our business involves everything a big corporation deals with in complete miniature.[2]

In order to become a franchisee, the franchise owner must have an initial capital of $30,000, of which $14,900 is a start-up fee, $8,500 for supplies and equipment, and additional $30,000-$50,000 for the first three months of operations. Molly Maid will require the franchise owner to have about $100,000 for its initial investment. This money will cover the costs of office space and office equipment, the leasing of vehicles, insurance, and permits & licences.[3] Molly Maid then "trains the franchisee how to recruit, train, motivate, and manage employees to do the actual cleaning."[4] It provides the franchisee with its brand name, marketing service, and continuous training, overseeing its operations and closing franchises that do not meet its profit margin. Molly Maid requires that the franchise owner pay regular fees, which is essentially a portion of the surplus value in the form of rent. In the franchise, the fees that the franchisee

1 Daszkowski 2018
2 Daley 2011
3 Molly Maid Franchise Information.
4 Daszkowski 2018

pays to the larger corporation is a portion of the surplus value produced by their workers. Since rent in Marx's time was mainly ground-rent, Marx would not have been able to analyse it. However, franchise fees are clearly a form of rent, as it is a payment in order to use the intellectual property of a corporation for a defined period of time. Molly Maid is able to accumulate more capital and expand its operations by appropriating massive amounts of surplus value in the form of fees. If they are successful, the franchise owner will be offered expansion with added territories in which they can operate. On the other hand, if they fall behind on fees, receive regular complaints, or fail to meet targets, then they can be closed by Molly Maid.

Molly Maid has a strict selection process and generally only franchises itself to people who have experience in business.[5] The franchise owner begins as a member of the petty-bourgeoisie, which is the class of people who own their own means of production but do not derive their profit from the capitalist exploitation of the working class. The small businessperson or high-salaried professional who becomes a franchise owner generally has some savings derived from their income. If they do not have savings, they can apply for a small business loan or seek investors to fund their franchise. They invest this money as *capital* into a franchise, but do not thereby become members of the bourgeoisie. While they do have to use their own capital to make an initial investment and start-up, their class position has not significantly changed. Franchisees can make more money because they are working for a large corporation and operating on a capitalist basis, but they do not have the capital to appropriate large amounts of surplus-value. It might be helpful to class franchise owners as members of the upper-strata of the petty-bourgeoisie who are in transition to becoming part of the capitalist class. They are not quite capitalists yet, as they are managed by the bourgeoisie who owns the capital and allocates it to them in exchange for regular payments. At the same time, they could become capitalists and move into a corporate job at Molly Maid if they prove themselves worthy of doing so. Indeed, there is tremendous pressure on them to manage their cleaners productively, get as much profit as possible, and be 'successful'. Yet, their lack of large capital funds means that they will permanently exist in a dependent relationship to the larger company that uses them to exploit the labour of cleaners and appropriate as much surplus-value as possible. The commercialisation of personal cleaning services is an example of the ways that non-capitalist businesses are transformed into ones conducted on a capitalist basis. The franchise owner, though operating on a capitalist basis,

5 Molly Maid Franchise Information.

remains a member of the petty-bourgeoisie. In some ways, they are similar to managers in a large company, who manage the work of others and have hiring and firing power, but do not themselves directly appropriate the surplus-value of others. The franchise owner helps the larger Molly Maid company to exploit the labour-power of cleaning workers and is directly paid out of this surplus-value. However, they must pay the majority of it directly to Molly Maid in the form of fees and are themselves closely supervised by the larger corporation.

The emergence of commercial cleaning companies has caused the dissolution of non-capitalist forms of cleaning labour. Even those who remain in business as small independent cleaners must try to maximise profits, for otherwise they will not be able to compete with commercial cleaning companies. While they are not part of the same large business networks as the large cleaning companies, they can still get clients who prefer the greater quality that some devoted private cleaners might provide. However, they are dependent on a smaller number of clients who have the ability to pay higher costs for cleaning services. Most people who need their home cleaned once or twice a month would probably rather use Molly Maid, as it is much cheaper and more efficient. As a result, the small independent cleaner faces a high level of competition from the larger cleaning company and is under tremendous pressure to maximise profits. The result of this is that they may find it difficult to compete, and eventually become a franchise of Molly Maid rather than continue as an independent company.

Once the franchise owner is in business, he or she will go to the labour-market and purchase labour-power. Because Molly Maid is not a publicly traded company, it is quite difficult to find exact information about the wages it pays, but the workers themselves have given very insightful information on Indeed and Glassdoor. These websites are interesting because they reflect the *spontaneous* experience of the labour-process discussed by Lenin in *What is to be Done?* and are a goldmine of information about any type of work. Two former Molly Maid workers report on Indeed that,

> This place advertises a $500–600 a week pay, but neglects to inform you that this is your gross pay. When you start you work a full week at a very low hourly and barely any hours. They withhold a week so you then have worked two weeks for less than $300.[6]
>
> Was told that I would be making around $500 a week but that wasn't the case- very underpaid for the work that was done. The work itself is ok

6 Indeed Job Reviews. 29 July, 2018.

> I guess but not worth it, only made about $200-$300 a week and considering that my team would do 3–5 houses a day it was honestly insulting.[7]

Another worker reports that "average wages will be slightly above minimum at $8.50 an hour".[8] They do not have fixed working hours for each week but work on the basis of jobs determined by the clients. Molly Maid does not pay the worker hourly, but rather piece-wages that are calculated as a small percentage of what the worker produces. As one worker says, "Molly Maid pay at a percentage they do not have an hourly pay."[9] Another worker explains that

> you got a percentage from each house you cleaned (18–21%), but houses were severely undercharged. You spent half of the time traveling to houses, spend two or more hours cleaning only to charge that house 100$.[10]

On the basis of the information provided by the workers, let us suppose that the average Molly Maid worker works 30–35 hours a week, receiving an average wage of $200-$300 per week on the basis of 20% of the cost of the job. The average cost of a Molly Maid job is $100 per clean, with the labour of two maids per house. Most workers who worked full-time at Molly Maid claim they cleaned between 2–5 houses a day depending on the size of the job. Let us suppose that the average houses cleaned for a full-time Molly Maid worker per week is 10–20, and that the average weekly monetary value produced by the workers is $1,000-$2,000. We can derive the following table (Table 4), which gives a general picture of exploitation at Molly Maid.[11]

There are a few *general* conclusions that we can derive from this table. First, since the cleaners are not paid hourly, they are constantly under pressure to increase their productivity. Their wage does not necessarily increase if they work longer hours, but only if they produce more clean houses. This means that the workers must intensify their labour by driving faster to each house, cleaning homes as quickly as possible, and reducing all non-productive activities while at work (i.e., lunch, breaks, etc.). One way that they can slightly increase

---

7 Indeed Job Reviews. 18 July, 2018.
8 Indeed Job Reviews. 23 July, 2018.
9 Indeed Job Reviews, 24 May, 2018.
10 Indeed Job Reviews. 23 April, 2018.
11 The *actual* figures may differ quantitatively, but this basic structure will be operative at Molly Maid; this is simply an *abstraction* to illustrate a structural feature of employment at Molly Maid.

TABLE 4 Exploitation of Molly Maid worker

Wages (Variable capital- V)	Total value	Houses cleaned ($100/job)	Surplus value (S)	Rate of surplus value (S/V)
$200/week	$1,000	10	$800	400%
$250/week	$1,500	15	$1,250	500%
$300/week	$2,000	20	$1,700	560%

their income is if to flatter their customer into tipping them, which involves additional *emotional* labour. Although the company reports that it employs men, most of the workers at Molly Maid are women. Molly Maid uses highly gendered imagery of female maids to sell its product. We see this reflected in how the consumers themselves experience the consumption of their cleaning services, as many of the customer reviews referred to the workers as 'lovely ladies', 'pleasant girls', and 'beautiful cleaning women'. One customer reports: "I am very pleased the two girls are very pleasant"[12] and another that "the ladies are lovely and so efficient."[13] This means that the women who work at Molly Maid are under constant pressure not just to increase production, but to be pleasant to the customer. This allows them not only to get a higher wage through tips, but to impress their managers and get promoted in the company.

Many workers at Molly Maid in the United States and the United Kingdom report that managers use bullying, gossiping, and threats to coerce the cleaners to be more productive. They work on a zero-hour contract without a trade-union, and with the constant threat of being fired. One worker says that the "franchise owner is a money grabbing coward of a man who would always lie to you."[14] Another worker refers to her boss as a dictator, saying "attitude from management who think they are a mini dictator. Impossible deadlines and ridiculous routing schedules and complete lack of organisation."[15] This managerial coercion allows Molly Maid to capture a higher amount of *relative* surplus value, which arises through the intensification of labour-process.

An interesting pattern in the reviews of Molly Maid is that its managers also use favouritism in order to divide the workers. The workers who gave the

12 Molly Maid Website, Customer Reviews.
13 Molly Maid Website, Customer Reviews.
14 Glassdoor Job Reviews. 6 May, 2016.
15 Indeed Job Reviews. 4 January, 2017.

company a favourable review generally worked there for many years, received special privileges and bonuses, and were promoted to managerial positions. Even they admitted that the work was difficult but felt stable because of the material privileges they enjoyed. One worker who has been with Molly Maid for many years says,

> I have worked for Molly Maid for many years. The job isn't easy but very rewarding when knowing you've provided a good service to people who need it. There's a lovely bunch of girls and each morning we all sit over coffee and a crumpet for a catch up before we start our days. We are a strong unit, even when challenges arise such as staff members not showing up for their shift, we all muddle in and make sure all the customers are getting the service they're promised.[16]

This narrative reveal that the worker has identified not with her own proletarian class interests, but with the interests of the company. As a result of her loyalty, she was promoted to route manager and given some autonomy at work. Using gossip and favouritism, the franchise owner can consolidate this worker and use her as a tool to manage the other workers. This favouritism creates an environment of terror and anxiety that coerces the other workers to compete with each other for the same material privileges. It makes it very difficult to unite the cleaning workers against the franchise owner so that they organise themselves into a union and improve their material conditions.

When they increase production, the worker only gains a slightly higher wage, while Molly Maid captures a much higher amount of surplus-value. Once the franchise owner pays its fees to the larger company, it can invest the remaining surplus value to get more constant capital and expand its territory. Intangible assets such as a brand are sometimes part of constant capital in the service industry. Whenever a franchise owner expands its territory, it is essentially investing in *more* access to the brand. The territory expansion fee is $35,000,[17] which allows the franchise owner to expand its operations into new areas and thereby get new customers. A portion of this $35,000 is used for marketing in the new territory in order to stimulate demand in the new area. This expansion gives the franchise owner the ability to purchase more labour-power and increase the rate of surplus-value. I now produce a new table (Table 5), similar to Table 4, which demonstrates the rate of profit for the business owner and

16 Indeed Job Reviews, 18 April, 2018.

17 Daszkowski 2018

TABLE 5 Exploitation of Molly Maid worker (increased constant capital)

Constant capital- C	Variable capital- V (Total wages)	Workers employed	Total value	Monthly houses cleaned ($100/job)	Surplus value (S)	Rate of surplus value (S/V)	Rate of profit (S/C)
$60,000	$15,000	30	$25,000	250	$10,000	66.67%	13.3%
$80,000	$15,000	30	$25,000	250	$10,000	66.67%	10.53%
$100,000	$15,000	30	$25,000	250	$10,000	66.67%	8.70%

how it tends to fall as the organic composition of capital grows. Let us suppose that this is the value composition of a typical franchise owner of Molly Maid for a single month. It is again a general picture of Molly Maid and expresses certain tendencies operative in it.

What Table 5 shows is that the tendency for the rate of profit to fall is operative in the commercial cleaning industry. Whenever a franchise owner expands their operations, the rate of profit will fall if the wages of the workers remain the same. As any other capitalist, they must increase the amount of the constant capital employed, thereby increasing the organic composition of capital. Reducing their workforce while capturing the *same* amount of surplus value will increase the rate of surplus value, but it will cause the rate of profit to continue falling. Table 6 makes this point clear.

The only way that the franchise owner can counteract the tendency for the rate of profit to fall is by combining a cut in the workforce with an increase

TABLE 6 Exploitation of Molly Maid worker (reduced variable capital)

Constant capital- C	Variable capital- V (Total wages)	Workers employed	Total value	Monthly houses cleaned ($100/job)	Surplus value (S)	Rate of surplus value (S/V)	Rate of profit (S/C)
$60,000	$15,000	30	$25,000	250	$10,000	66.67%	13.3%
$80,000	$12,000	25	$25,000	250	$10,000	83.33%	10.87%
$100,000	$10,000	20	$25,000	250	$10,000	100%	9.09%

in the *mass* of surplus value. Simply increasing their geographical expansion, while not at the same increasing the mass of surplus value, will only result in a falling rate of profit. The remaining workforce must not only intensify their labour but increase the amount of surplus value they produce. This is the only way that an expansion of territory can allow a franchise owner at Molly Maid to capture a larger portion of surplus-value. Table 7 makes this clear.

Perhaps the investment in more constant capital allows the franchise owner to make the workers more productive in a single day. They may use their increased investment to introduce better management practices, which Taylorise the labour process and allow them to increase the mass of surplus value. This may result from more standardised cleaning practices, better scheduling, and quicker transportation. At the same time, it means the workers will ever more be transformed into 'cleaning machines' who are under tremendous pressure to produce as much as possible. Thus, as with every capitalist industry, the franchise owner must find ways to increase the productivity of labour or else they will witness a fall in their rate of profit. At a certain point, they will not be able to increase productivity beyond a certain level, and every increase in constant capital will result in a falling rate of profit. This is one reason why franchises like Molly Maid are structurally hostile to unions, as a union would give the cleaners the ability to challenge managerial terror, demand breaks, and bargain for a higher wage. Without the unchecked rule of the managers, Molly Maid would find it difficult to extract a high amount of surplus value from the workers. Employment security would make it harder for managers to use the threat of termination to coerce cleaners into being more productive. Any rise in the variable capital

TABLE 7 Exploitation of Molly Maid worker (increased surplus value)

Increased C, Reduced V, Increased S							
Constant capital- C	**Variable capital- V (Total wages)**	**Workers employed**	**Total value**	**Monthly houses cleaned ($100/job)**	**Surplus value (S)**	**Rate of surplus value (S/V)**	**Rate of profit (S/C)**
$60,000	$15,000	30	$25,000	250	$10,000	66.67%	13.3%
$80,000	$12,000	25	$30,000	300	$18,000	150.00%	19.57%
$100,000	$10,000	20	$35,000	350	$25,000	250.00%	22.73%

through increased wages would make it more difficult to expand with higher amounts of constant capital. The reduction of variable capital, made possible through the absence of a union, is one of the ways that companies like Molly Maid counteract the falling rate of profit.

The franchise form of organisation can itself be a factor that counteracts the tendency for the rate of profit to fall. By franchising itself to *multiple* franchise owners in a single city, each franchise owner can productively dominate a single geographical area without increasing the constant capital beyond a certain extent. Whenever a franchise owner experiences a falling rate of profit, Molly Maid can shut down the franchise or simply open a new franchise. Because the risk is transferred to the franchise owner, not the Molly Maid corporation, the franchise-form of organisation can counteract the tendency for the rate of profit to fall. Molly Maid plays a very strong supervisory role over its individual franchisees and will only allow a franchisee to expand its territory if it has demonstrated a high level of productivity.[18] Although some franchise owners employ a very large staff of 80–90 cleaning workers, with an annual profit of $4 million, most of them do not. It requires tremendous management skill and a high rate of productivity to employ that many cleaning workers with a high mass of profit. In most cases, a Molly Maid franchise is a small capitalist business that works under the domination of a much larger monopoly corporation.

2 Conclusion

The above discussion clearly demonstrates that cleaning workers can be hired to produce surplus value and are under tremendous pressure to increase their productivity. Although I have only focused on the cleaning industry, the same tendencies could be observed in numerous service industries, such as haircutting, fast-food restaurants, programming, and transportation. Cleaning workers are therefore an important sector of the working class, especially in today's capitalism. Just as outsourced employees, domestic cleaning represents a major form of employment for many working people. These workers produce surplus-value and thereby create huge profits for the companies that exploit them. In the next chapter, I will discuss campaigns by retail employees, cleaners, and outsourced workers. What I will demonstrate is that being attentive to the form of labour is tremendously important when organising workers. Those

18 Molly Maid Franchise Information.

who operate with a simplistic, fit-all method of organising workers are unlikely to get far in the retail and service industry. Contrary to popular belief, I will argue that service workers can be organised and that doing so is integral to strengthening the unity of the whole working class.

CHAPTER 10

Organising Retail and Service Workers

One of the defining features of the service sector is that it is notoriously difficult to organise. Although some service workers might have a trade union, there is a much smaller percentage of them engaged in organised resistance. Those who do take action face a danger of retaliation, whether this is a political campaign such as the Fight for 15 in the United States, or an organised strike at an Amazon warehouse. Retaliation could take the form of extreme bullying from management, or simply termination of employment. Often, service workers experience alienation from workers in the first stage of production and hold the mistaken belief that they are not part of the working class. In this chapter, I will discuss the primary difficulties of organising service workers and examine strategies for transforming them into an active social force.

I will begin by examining a campaign of H&M workers in Germany that sought to organise international solidarity with textile workers in Bangladesh. One of the powerful lessons of this campaign is that retail employees can break through corporate propaganda by directly engaging with the workers that produce the goods they sell. After examining this, I will turn to a campaign of fast-food workers, which was organised by the Fight for 15 campaign. I will discuss the organisational innovation developed by this campaign and what can be learned from it. Once I have looked at these two concrete examples, I will deduce some organisational principles from the foregoing analysis. I will argue that anti-imperialism should be an important component in the organisation of retail workers. This anti-imperialist approach involves uniting workers in stage two with stage one workers and the organisation of international solidarity. In addition to this, I will argue that socialists in the retail sector should produce anti-consumerist propaganda in order to win the popular masses to their side. Anti-consumerism is important in all sections of the service industry, as it is directly related to the growth of consumerist behaviour. Doing this involves organising consumers to unite with retail and service workers in a worker-consumer alliance. When the popular masses break free of consumerist propaganda, they are less likely to be hostile to organised efforts of service and retail workers.

 | DOI:10.1163/9789004469624_011

1 Retail: H&M Workers in Germany

Many of us have probably visited an H&M at some point in our lives. The Swedish retailer can be found across Europe, the United States, Canada, and some developing nations such as China. H&M likes to present itself as a defender of workers' rights, using only suppliers that pay a living wage, and safe working conditions. However, as Athit Kong, a representative of the Cambodian Apparel Workers Democratic Union has noted:

> H&M's PR rings hollow to workers who are struggling everyday to feed their families. A sustainability model that is put forth and wholly controlled by H&M but is not founded on genuine respect for organized workers and trade unions on the ground is never going to result in real change for H&M production workers. Instead, it serves as a public relations facade to cover up systemic abuse.[1]

The primary way that H&M makes its profits is through arms-length outsourcing. By outsourcing production to workers in Bangladesh, Cambodia, Vietnam, and India, H&M is able to purchase t-shirts, denim, socks, and other clothing at an extremely low price. John Smith discusses H&M in his *Imperialism in the Twenty-First Century*, and it is worth quoting here at length so that we may easily perceive the exploitation of garment workers. Smith says,

> H&M pays the Bangladeshi manufacturer €1.35 for each T-shirt, 28 percent of the final sale price, 40¢ of which covers the cost of 400g of cotton raw material imported from the United States; shipping to Hamburg adds another 6¢ per shirt. Thus €0.95 of the final sale price remains in Bangladesh, to be shared between the factory owner, the workers, the suppliers of inputs and services and the Bangladeshi government, expanding Bangladesh's GDP by this amount. The remaining €3.54 counts toward the GDP of Germany, the country where the T-shirt is consumed, and is broken down as follows: €2.05 provides for the costs and profits of German transporters, wholesalers, retailers, advertisers, etc. (some of which will revert to the state through various taxes); H&M makes 60¢ per T Shirt; the German state captures 79¢ of the sale price through VAT at 19 percent; 16¢ covers other items … a worker at the factory earns €1.36

1 Asia Floor Alliance 2019, p. 4.

> per day, for 10–12 hours, producing 250 T-shirts per hour, or 18 T-shirts for each euro cent paid in wages.[2]

The shirts produced by Bangladeshi workers are appropriated by H&M, a dozen transporters and retailers, advertising companies, and the state. This is because the giant corporations that outsource their production to Bangladesh have a legal title to the product of their labour, not the working people of Bangladesh or even the Bangladeshi national bourgeoisie. In addition to Bangladesh, significant number of H&M factories are located in Cambodia. The Asia Floor Alliance shows that 95% of the 700,000 workers employed in Cambodia's garment industry are women, and often faced sex-based violence. Many of them are young women in their twenties and are from rural parts of Cambodia. They migrate to the cities and are often thereby cut off from their families and traditional networks of support. Besides their friends and their trade union, young female garment workers are extremely vulnerable and often the subject of sexual exploitation. Because many of them do not have access to legal representatives, they are often powerless to take action against sexual abuse. As they are low-waged, they have less money for food and consume less calories, resulting in serious malnourishment. Although the International Labour Organisation has created guidelines to enforce compliance with international regulations, in practice the Cambodian government has created an environment that is friendly to the internal bourgeoisie.[3] While H&M shop employees may be marginally aware of the workers who produce the shirts they sell, they are generally alienated from them. H&M makes a conscious effort to conceal this process of exploitation by filtering it through their own propaganda. From the day they hired, H&M workers are required to watch 'training' videos displaying the 'fair' nature of labour in H&M dominated factories.[4] Workers are organised to develop a strong identification with the company and a feeling that they belong to a family. What H&M fears most is that their retail employees will organise solidarity with the textile workers in Bangladesh that sell their products.[5]

Such an international solidarity campaign was successfully organised by a group in Germany called the Transnational Information Exchange (TIE). The TIE points out that a patriarchal image dominates the way that we think of retail workers, which are perceived as largely female employees on precarious

2 Smith 2016, p. 13.

3 Asia Floor Alliance 2019, pp. 3–7.

4 These training videos can be viewed on the YouTube channel of H&M.

5 Asia Floor Alliance 2019, pp. 4–6.

contracts who are dependent on their union representative for support and are therefore unable to take independent industrial action. Retail workers sometimes belong to trade unions, such as USDAW in the UK or the AFL-CIO in the USA. While these unions will advocate on behalf of the retail workers, they usually do not have an active self-conscious membership. Their union reps will do most of the organising but make little effort to make their membership active in the union. This bureaucratic approach to union organising—systematised in the so-called 'organising model'—prevents the union from empowering retail workers to take action. The Transnational Information Exchange points out that it is

> very difficult for unions not only to organize fashion retail workers but also to develop a self-organized union work at the shop floor level which improves working conditions and strengthens the workers in their struggles for a decent life.[6]

Between 2010 and 2015, a group of trade unionists in Germany (which later became the TIE) organised over 400 H&M workers, creating work councils, improving workplace safety, and fighting against precarious work contracts. They took a class struggle approach to organising, which empowered the workers to build an organisation that they could use to improve their material conditions. The TIE argues that the reason they succeeded was not because they strove solely for bread-and-butter demands, but because they "developed an international worker-to-worker network with garment unions which organize workers who produce for H&M and other retailers."[7] It was an anti-imperialist approach to organising, which sought to organise international solidarity, that successfully overcame the drawbacks of organising retail workers. Instead of focusing solely on the particular stage in which they were located, they developed a long-term strategy for uniting workers across the supply chain in multiple stages of the production process.

The TIE has identified some major challenges when organising in the retail sector. First, large retailers like H&M, Gap, Primark, and Next compete for low labour costs, which is achieved through precarious contracts, decreasing the number of workers on the shop floor and giving them larger workloads. As a result of this,

6 Transnational Information Exchange 2017
7 *ibid.*

> the workers often neither know in advance when they work during the week nor how many hours they work and therefore do not know how much money they earn in a month. If you want to make ends meet, a second job is often vital but it is difficult to accept one because retail workers only know week by week when they will work.[8]

The precarity of retail workers who often are on zero-hour contracts can make it difficult to arrange a meeting. Many of them have the legitimate worry that they will not receive work hours that they are caught organising a union. Instead of firing them, the company can punish them by significantly reducing their hours. The German trade unionists that later became TIE identified precarity as one of the primary challenges to organising retail workers. Instead of allowing precarity to prevent union organisation, the TIE made it one of their central concerns and used it to win retail workers to their campaign.

The second major difficulty of organising retail workers identified by the TIE is that many of the workers have been indoctrinated to accept a corporate form of ideology. At Ikea, workers spend hours watching videos about the company's founder Ingvar Kamprad, and how he made Ikea into a successful global enterprise. Retailers like Ikea overcome the resistance of their workers by creating the appearance of an easy work environment where there is less hierarchy and in which the worker is part of a family rather than exploited by the company. As the TIE notes,

> The retailers create an atmosphere in which hierarchies are allegedly low, individual promotions and gratifications are possible and problems can be solved on the individual level. The company promotes a culture which claims the workers and the company have the same interests.[9]

Althusser once pointed out that ideology is largely sustained through everyday material practices embodied in rituals.[10] In the retail industry, these rituals are the daily team meetings, which can be full of laughter and humour, as well as reports about the company's internal business. The purpose of this is to gain the workers support for the company, which they are organised to identify with so that they don't struggle against it. The retailers try to individualise problems while allowing workers to speak about them in meetings in which a manager

8 *ibid.*

9 *ibid.*

10 Althusser 2014, Appendix 2.

is present. If they perform exceptionally well, then they can get promoted and gain access to special privileges. The TIE points out that this ideological indoctrination makes union organising very difficult. As the company already provides a venue for workers to voice their concerns, those who try to organise a union are viewed as outsiders and often harshly repressed by management. As a result, one of the key tasks of unions in retail is to break through the company culture and organise the workers so that they view the company as their exploiter rather than their friend.

In an article on hospitality workers, Joe Kearsey discusses the ideological barriers to organising workers in the food and restaurant industry. First, he points out that managers actively try to make work enjoyable and create a craft-based identity. Managers will encourage bartenders to learn cocktail recipes on their time off and give them the opportunity to show off their skills at work. Furthermore, they try to create a feeling of camaraderie between workers, which ensures a smooth functioning of the labour process. Taking each other's shifts, venting about abusive customers, and discussing sales tactics enable management to control the relationships between workers. Kearsey concludes that the feeling of camaraderie in the hospitality sector "ensures the smooth running of shifts, can create a friendly atmosphere even under considerable strain and can drive enthusiasm in the product."[11] An effective organising campaign in the retail and hospitality sector must build on existing bonds of solidarity that already exist between workers. Whereas management uses this camaraderie to increase exploitation, socialists must find ways to turn it against management.

The Transnational Information Exchange has developed a unique strategy for organising retail workers, which overcomes the drawbacks of precarity and ideological indoctrination. The TIE's approach was to begin with a work council composed of those who wanted to organise a union despite the company culture. These committees were brought together and were a space where workers could discuss the problems they encountered at H&M—management bullying, heavy workloads, extreme pressure from executives. By doing this, they united a committee from multiple stores, which would lead the organising effort. These committees would then organise meetings with H&M workers, in which they could speak freely and in the absence of management. TIE points out that

11 Kearsey 2020, p. 507.

> once the workers understood that they share common problems which are caused by H&M, this offered the possibility to develop solutions and break the isolation of the few works council activists.[12]

The union organisers would visit unorganised H&M shops, in order to hold meetings with the workers and expand their organisation. Their central task was to identify collective problems shared by all the workers—precarious contracts, heavy workloads, low wages—and to isolate them from management ideology. The workers councils created a space in which the workers could speak about their experience at work. The union organisers consciously connected the precarious working contracts to company policy, in order to demonstrate that the workers interests were not aligned with the company. Once the workers council developed a strong foundation amongst the workers, they would advocate strategies that "builds capacities among them to interfere with the working conditions". The TIE points out that the success of the effort depends on self-conscious leaders, who can win the workers confidence and help them to actively engage in the labour-process. Their approach was to avoid larger campaigns until a significant majority had been consolidated on the work councils. The TIE can transform the way that we think about unions, which

> is not only about campaigns and much less about the institution but has to become a collective space where workers can discuss, learn from each other, strategize and develop the necessary capacities to change themselves, their workplace and in the end the society.[13]

The collective space created through the TIE campaign gave workers a space where they could break through corporate indoctrination. Once a strong union of retail employees had been created, the organisers sought to create an alliance with garment unions in countries where the clothing sold in H&M is produced. The TIE created a working relationship between their workers councils and the National Garment Workers Federation (NGWF) in Bangladesh. One of their most successful campaigns was a delegation of German retail workers from Zara, H&M, and Metro who travelled to Bangladesh to meet the workers that produce shirts sold in their shops. Their slogan was "solidarity along the supply chain: from production to retail, workers unite!".[14] The effort was endorsed by

12 Transnational Information Exchange 2017

13 *ibid.*

14 Transnational Information Exchange 2011

the German trade union federation and was organised jointly by the TIE and the NGWF. As they point out, the purpose of "the trip was designed to enable a direct encounter with the working and living conditions of the workers who make the clothes that we are buying and selling in Germany on a daily basis."[15]

The German retail employees had the opportunity not just to read about the working conditions, but to directly encounter the effects of extremely low wages and the unsafe environments of the garment workers. They got to meet with workers and union activists of the NGWF, and visit the H&M, Next, and Metro supplier factories. They participated in a seminar on Occupational Safety and discovered that the Bangladeshi and German workers experienced many similar problems at work, such as low wages, health issues, and precarious contracts. As the TIE states,

> Although their working and living conditions are different, colleagues from both countries exchanged experiences which are indeed comparable: experiences of humiliation, annoyance at indecent conditions, and last but not least difficulties concerning union and workplace organising.[16]

This shared work-experience was incredibly important in strengthening the bonds of solidarity between the Northern and Southern workers and uniting around a common plan of action to fight the multinational corporations that exploit them all. The meeting enabled them to unite around three primary goals and formulate a long-term campaign. First, they sought to pressure the multinational companies to be transparent about their suppliers, as this would strengthen the union's ability to create transnational networks. Second, the campaign demanded higher wages through a higher price of the shirts produced by the Bangladeshi garment workers. The multinational companies make huge profits through gaining access to the extremely cheap labour of Southern workers. The German retail workers would organise directly with the NGWF to unite with their Bangladeshi comrades to fight for a living wage, which would enable them to purchase basic goods, pay rent, and additional goods such as entertainment and holidays.

A major aspect of the campaign was the fight for a code of conduct, which H&M would be required to sign on to if they continue working with the supplier. Furthermore, in order to ensure higher wages, the union demanded that

15 *ibid.*
16 *ibid.*

the multinational companies pay higher unit costs for the garments. The third goal of the seminar was to defend Bangladeshi workers' right to organise a union, which is constantly combated by the owners of the supplier factories. The German workers therefore demanded that "major buyers and retail companies include union access rights to the factories in their codes of conduct, and to implement them with their suppliers."[17] After the Rana Plaza Factory disaster in 2013, in which 1200 Bangladeshi garment workers died when the factory collapsed as a result of negligence, the H&M works councils organised protests across Germany. In coordination with the National Garment Workers Federation (NGWF), the works council argued that the primary reason that the disaster happened was because H&M and other multinational buyers have sought the lowest costs, which has not created enough profit to invest in factory maintenance.

There are two major lessons from the experience of organising workers in German clothing retailers. First, socialist organisers should create a collective space that enables workers to transform their precarity into a struggle campaign. Unless the precarity of zero-hour contracts becomes a campaign combatted directly by the workers, it will be difficult to organise them into a self-conscious, active union. Second, uniting stage one and stage two workers is vital to organising retail workers. This requires contact between workers in peripheral nations such as Bangladesh with retail employees in the imperialist centres. Building effective anti-imperialist campaigns is only possible through the organisation of solidarity networks, which break through the corporate propaganda of the retailers. It is by organising contact between workers in the North and South that corporate propaganda can lose its hold over the minds of the workers and facilitate an international united front against monopoly capital.

The anti-imperialist approach of the TIE is important in that it overcomes some limitations in recent campaigns at McDonalds, UberEats, Weatherspoons, and WalMart. In the 2020 winter issue of *Capital and Class*, there were a number of articles by young scholars that used Marxist theory to analyse these actions.[18] A recurring theme in their work is that the belief that service and workers are positioned to engage in short-term actions (i.e., strikes, demonstrations, etc.), but lack the ability to form trade unions. Cant and Woodcock, for example, point out that service workers should organise "for action instead of for representation."[19] While they are very sensitive to how the nature of

17 *ibid.*

18 *Capital and Class, Vol 44 No 4, 2020.*

19 Cant and Woodcock 2020, p. 514.

service work requires innovative organising strategies, their autonomist approach makes the organisation of trade unions very difficult. This approach, which comes from Italian anarcho-syndicalism, is highly localist in its orientation and neglects the work of building international relationships between workers. The TIE's approach, which combines autonomist theory with anti-imperialism, overcomes this, for it equips retail workers with the tools needed to break through the ideological barriers to organisation. Instead of using local strike actions to organise trade unions, the TIE creates an international organisation across the value chain. By strengthening international solidarity, a long-term organisation is more likely to emerge, actions are coordinated by workers internationally, and strikes are more likely to be successful. Instead of a localist and short-termist focus, the TIE has developed an organising model that will result in a long-term, international organisation. This in no way entails that organisers should not also focus on the local conditions of workers they are organising but seek to foster a spirit of proletarian internationalism by building a strong solidarity network. Such a solidarity network is not new but has always been an important part of socialist politics. What is new, however, is the TIE's innovative approach to viewing the solidarity network through the transnational supply chain of multinational corporations such as H&M. While it might be difficult to organise such a network of solidarity, it is vital to empowering retail employees to break through corporate propaganda and unite with working people in peripheral nations.

2 Cleaners in Struggle

In the United States and Canada, the union most closely associated with cleaning workers (usually referred to as 'janitors') is the Service Employees International United (SEIU). Some may be aware of the SEIU through its campaigns, such as Justice for Janitors and the Fight For 15. Since its founding in the 1920s, the SEIU has been at the foreground of organising cleaning workers and has significant experience with strike action. Although it has some very militant members, the SEIU today often prefers a collaborationist approach to organising that does not involve member-led action. The union has a very close relationship to the Democratic Party in a way that is similar to Unison's relationship to the Labour Party in the UK. Despite this fact, the SEIU's campaigns to organise cleaners should be the starting point for an examination of cleaning workers in struggle.

In 2012, the SEIU launched one of the largest janitors strikes ever in Houston, Texas. Over 3500 unionised cleaners who clean the corporate offices of Exxon

Mobile, Chevron, and Shell decided to go on strike when their employers refused to renew their union contract.[20] The janitors demanded not just a renewal of their contract, but a $10/hour wage and expanded jurisdiction for the union. What made this strike interesting was the variety of tactics it used to advance its demands. First, the union focused on winning the community over the janitor's strike and making their invisible labour visible. In addition to large pickets and marches around the downtown area of Houston, the janitors engaged in planned civil disobedience. One of these involved a large circle of people who occupied the middle of the busiest intersection and shut down traffic during rush hour. During late July, the union organised marches with thousands of people and multiple street sit-down strikes, causing major disruptions to traffic. This got significant media attention and gave the union the power to speak about the campaign to thousands of people on TV. Their goal was to win the community to the demands of the strike, as well as the local council and the mayor. Furthermore, in seventeen cities, trade unions and activist groups organised solidarity events to cast a nationwide spotlight on the janitor's strike. The campaign was tremendously successful, as the mayor of Houston intervened and called upon their employers to give into their demands. Not only did the union win a significant pay increase, but it won the ability to expand its jurisdiction, resulting in thousands being eligible for union membership. Since the 2012 janitors strike in Houston, Texas, there have not been any janitors strikes on this scale anywhere in the US or Canada.

For most employees who work in offices and schools, little thought is given to the invisible labour of cleaners who ensure that the building is clean before the working day. The janitors strike was unique because it made this invisibility visible, and thereby exposed the horribly low-wages, insecure employment, and exploitation faced by the cleaners. No longer were the cleaners working late in the night, hidden away in office buildings. Now they could be seen marching through the streets and giving interviews on TV. What distinguished this strike from other smaller ones and made it so effective was thus that it mobilised significant sections of the community and local politicians. Instead of just winning over other trade unions, the campaign sought to create

20 This strike is very personal to me, as I was a participant and is what got me thinking about the issues raised in this book. I was one of the only non-union members invited to the SEIU meeting, in which they voted whether to accept a $9.25 wage increase and celebrate their victory. At the time, I was a journalist for Peoples World, and wrote two articles under my penname, Fabian Sneevliet: "Texas Janitors on Strike" (Peoples World: 25 June, 2012) and "Janitors Strike Rocks Houston, Forces Employers to Talk" (Peoples World: 6 August, 2012).

a worker-consumer alliance. In this case, the consumers are the entire community who benefit from the cleaning labour of the janitors—the office workers, teachers, and local residents. When they are won to the side of the workers, it creates a united alliance against the employers and puts significant pressure on them. This alliance is tremendously effective because it puts significantly more pressure on the employers, who risk harming their image if they do not concede. It makes it much more difficult for the employer to fire a worker who participates or a manager to engage in bullying. A worker-consumer alliance empowers precarious workers to take action against their employers to improve their material conditions. On their own, outsourced workers take a significant risk when they take any industrial action, for they can have their hours cut or fired without question. It is the pressure created by potentially lost consumers and negative publicity that gives outsourced cleaners the security to take industrial action.

Although the SEIU has not done any large actions like this since the janitor's strike, they have been at the forefront of developing strategies for organising service workers. One of their most popular campaigns has been the Fight for 15 (FF15), which demands a federal minimum wage of 15 dollars per hour.[21] The target of their campaigns has been retail employees at WalMart, and fast-food workers at McDonalds, Burger King, and other chain restaurants. These companies are notorious for paying the lowest wages and firing workers who attempt to organise a union. The SEIU has used the worker-consumer alliance strategy for this campaign, and it has proven effective. In order to win both the workers and the consumer over to the union demands, the SEIU has organised large pickets at popular fast-food chains. When more militant leaders are in charge of these pickets, the activists will enter the fast-food restaurant early in the morning, and march around for a few minutes, escaping right before the police arrive. Local residents are organised to join the picket and publicly boycott the fast-food restaurant. The union is very effective in combining these actions with mass marches that often contain thousands of people. Sometimes, the union will utilise civil disobedience, such as chaining themselves to a door or occupying a street in order to gain media attention. This exposure campaign tactic has two primary goals. First, it is designed to win the consumer over and get them involved in the direct actions. By exposing the exploitation of retail workers through a kind of political theatre, the public image of the company is harmed. The second goal is to empower the workers to utilise this solidarity network to take action by calling a strike and forming a union. By giving the

21 For details about the FF15 campaign, see their website: https://fightfor15.org/.

workers clear demands and a strong basis of support, the SEIU gives the workers the confidence that they need to take industrial action. In many cities, the SEIU's innovative tactics have been very effective, resulting in fast food workers forming unions, as well as Amazon employees and adjunct professors.

Although the FF15 campaign has had some successes, it has been the subject of some criticism, which is summarised by Alex J Wood. Wood makes two criticisms of the Fight For 15 campaign (FF15). First, he points out that the campaign focused too heavily on mobilising while neglecting the work of organising. Instead of seeking out organic leaders at McDonalds, Burger King, and other fast-food restaurants, Wood claims that the FF15 campaign sought exclusively to organise large actions that engaged the community in defence of the workers. Second, he criticises the large amount of money—23 million US dollars—that went into funding the FF15 campaign. Wood thinks that the FF15 exploited the struggles of low wage workers to promote the SEIU and get profits for the PR companies it used.[22] Wood's criticism misses two crucial elements of the FF15 campaigns organizing strategy. First, its attempt to mobilize people was designed to empower precarious, low-wage workers to organise themselves and take industrial action. The function of their large demonstrations and marches was to create a solidarity network, which the workers could rely on in the absence of numerically large forces. While it is true that the traditional trade unions have a tendency towards careerism, the FF15's goal of using PR companies was to create media that would empower workers to form unions. By making millions of people aware of the plight of low-wage workers, and winning the support of progressive Democrats like Bernie Sanders, the FF15 campaign played a role in initiating worker organisation. Although it has not been successful, Sanders introduced a bill in congress to raise the minimum wage to 15 dollars per hour with the support of a number of Democratic politicians.

Wood contrasts the organizing model of the FF15 campaign with #McStrike, which followed a few years after the FF15 actions. In 2017, small actions centred around management bullying erupted at two McDonalds locations, which quickly turned into a Britain-wide McStrike. They built on some of the successes of the FF15 campaign, while relying less heavily on the traditional trade unions for support. Although the McStrike took place mostly in Britain, it was the earlier efforts by FF15 campaigners in the United States that created the social horizon in which their struggles took place. Wood fails to see how a large, worldwide solidarity network had been created by the FF15 campaign,

22 Wood 2020, p. 497.

which enabled McDonald's workers to take action in 2017.[23] It is this creation of a solidarity network that we should take as a valuable contribution of the FF15, irrespective of whether it resulted in the creation of new unions or even significant victories. Such a solidarity network turns public opinion towards workers in precarious, low-wage service jobs, and enables them to take action to form unions.

3 Exposure Campaigns and Workers Power

Before ending this chapter, I would like to discuss a bit more how an exposure campaign can empower workers, especially in the service sector. Alex Wood points out that "reputational damage offers workers an alternative opportunity to traditional collective bargaining."[24] An incredibly powerful weapon to organizing in the service and retail sector is the use of systematic exposure campaigns. Actively engaging workers to destroy a corporation's reputation is the most effective way to break through corporate propaganda. To briefly highlight the power of exposure campaigns, I would like to use the example of Starbucks. Like many corporations, Starbucks invests significant capital into its image, which functions as an advertisement for its coffee. What it fears most is bad press, which would hurt its sales targets, but empower its workers to action against it. In their 2018 financial report published by the UK's Companies House, Starbucks reports that one of its primary risks and uncertainties is "adverse impacts resulting from negative publicity regarding the Company's business practices."[25] To prevent such 'adverse impacts', Starbucks places propaganda in its shops about its humanitarian work, and allows the customer to participate in philanthropy by purchasing special water bottles for which a very small amount of the profit is donated to charity. Starbucks claims that its Ethos water

> is a brand with a social mission—helping children around the world get clean water and raising awareness of the World Water Crisis. Every time you purchase a bottle of Ethos Water, Ethos Water will contribute US $0.05 (C$0.10 in Canada) toward our goal of raising at least US $10 million by 2010. Through the Starbucks Foundation, Ethos Water supports humanitarian water programs in Africa, Asia and Latin America. To date,

23 Wood 2020, p. 498.
24 Wood 2020, p. 500.
25 Starbucks Financial Report 2018, page 3.

> Ethos Water grant commitments exceed $6.2 million. These programs will help an estimated 420,000 people gain access to safe water, sanitation and hygiene education.[26]

In an article on consumerism, Slavoj Zizek points out that Starbucks seeks to conceal the contradictions of commodity production by encouraging us to purchase commodities (Ethos water). By consuming Ethos water, our own suspicions against Starbucks well-known imperialist exploitation of developing nations are demobilised.[27] Campaigns like Ethos water are designed not just to win over the consumer, but the coffee baristas, who are won over to Starbucks humanitarian ideology through selling the water bottles.

An organised campaign to expose how Starbucks engages in neo-colonialism in countries like Indonesia, the Philippines, and China could potentially bring the 'adverse impacts' that it fears on its operation. It is for this reason that the workers employed in a company like Starbucks must be organised to form links with the victims of imperialism in developing nations that produce the coffee. Although they should form concrete bonds of solidarity with the coffee-farmers, they should also be politically educated about imperialism and neo-colonial domination. Doing this is extremely difficult, as Starbucks has a carefully crafted ideology that is designed to neutralise such efforts. Advanced workers who even try to organise a meeting to discuss issues affecting Starbucks employees will come under the watchful gaze of management. Breaking through their corporate propaganda is very important, as the success of organising Starbucks baristas depends on it. Socialists who want to empower Starbucks workers to take industrial action should organise a carefully constructed exposure campaign as a central task to winning over both workers and consumers. Before proceeding, they must research Starbucks crimes and produce propaganda that creates negative publicity for the company. It should highlight everything from exploitative labour practices, such as using child labour on its farms, to the low wages received by its baristas. The best way to ensure that the campaign is effective is for it to provide truthful, well research material in a popular form that is easily accessible by the masses. If the campaign is effective, it will prevent the realisation of surplus-value by Starbucks. When it begins to lose customers as a result of the exposure campaign, socialists should then distribute leaflets to the baristas. These should call meetings where the baristas can vent their frustrations and organise actions against

26 Qtd. By Zizek 2007

27 *Ibid.*

Starbucks. Raising class consciousness also involves explaining to the baristas their place within the value chain by putting the concepts of surplus-value and exploitation at the centre of the conversation. Most importantly, socialists should organise contacts between the baristas and the coffee farmers, as well as the workers in the coffee processing refineries. Doing this assists the creation of a solidarity network, consisting of workers across the value chain and consumers, which empowers the baristas to organise themselves into a union. Without such a solidarity network, the baristas will be left powerless to take action and continue working in a very exploitative environment.

4 Conclusion

In this chapter, I have discussed two effective strategic considerations for organising service workers. Both examples highlight the importance of devising innovative tactics when organising service workers. These tactics must correspond to the specific form of the labour process rather than an abstract model devised by paid union organisers. The first example of H&M retail workers shows that we must be attentive to the particular place that a worker occupies in a value chain. Workers who are in stage two of the value chain are responsible for realising the surplus-value contained in the commodity. Significant marketing, consumerist propaganda, and sales tactics are utilised to ensure that the commodity is sold. The strategy of transnational organising helps to create a solidarity network across the value chain, which is the direct result of imperialism and the globalisation of the labour-process. Doing this allows workers employed by multinational corporations to coordinate successful campaigns against their employers in order to improve their material conditions. In the case of outsourced workers such as cleaners, the strategy of a worker-consumer alliance is necessary to give workers the support needed to take industrial action. By creating an exposure campaign, the image of the corporation is harmed through the proliferation of negative publicity. Through constant threats of more bad publicity, they are under pressure to give into the demands of the workers. These two tactics directly follow from the labour process of retail and service workers, which differs significantly from those who work in factories or on farms. In the next chapter, I will discuss how a socialist revolution and the creation of a socialist state will radically transform the lives of service workers. This will require us briefly to reflect on what constitutes socialism and what role service workers have played in former socialist countries such as the Soviet Union.

CHAPTER 11

Service, Retail and Transport under Socialism

So far, I have examined the role played by service and retail workers in the production and realisation of surplus-value. I have argued that they represent an important segment of the working class and have the potential to become a militant political force if organised properly. All this, however, has been articulated within the horizon of capitalist social formations and the exploitation of labour-power. In this chapter, I want to discuss the role played by service and retail workers in socialist social formations that have gone beyond capitalism.

Historically, the theorists of socialist planning—both in the socialist countries and outside of them—have not given enough attention to service labour. Fiona Tregenna points out that

> the measures of National Material Product (used instead of GDP) reported under the Material Product System in the former Soviet Union and eastern bloc countries included the production and distribution of physical goods but not services.[1]

Socialist planners did not include services in national accounts because they were not an object of economic planning. Although the socialist countries did account for services in other ways, they did not figure into national economic plans. What has been known in scholarly literature as the 'second economy'—an informal, unplanned part of socialism—often were related to services. Because these services were not an object of planning, they had the effect of undermining socialism. In this chapter, I will argue that we must take service labour seriously, not just for grasping the capitalist present, but for theorising the socialist future.

My analysis will rely on traditional Marxist theory combined with examples from former socialist countries—the USSR, the German Democratic Republic, the Polish People's Republic, and the People's Republic of China. While they had many problems, the history of socialist construction contains many lessons that can inform theory for future socialist construction. In the Marxist critique of writers such as Trotsky, Schachtman, and Bettelheim, there is sometimes a tendency to dismiss the Soviet experience with terms such as

1 Tregenna 2010

 | DOI:10.1163/9789004469624_012

'Stalinism', 'revisionism', and 'state bourgeoisie'. Although these writers made important observations about the contradictions of socialism, and foresaw the downfall of many socialist states, their approach sometimes neglects a serious enquiry into some of the progress made under socialism. Despite the tremendous problems with the Stalinist model—which should be criticised relentlessly—socialist social formations were able to experiment with new ways of living and innovative forms of social property. Although their criticisms are often justified—especially Trotsky, whose brutal treatment by Stalin made him very critical of socialism in the USSR—it is necessary to explore how socialist societies have attempted to transform social relations. My analysis is informed by the work of Albert Szymanski, Roger Keeran, Thomas Kenny, Paul Baran, Clive Thomas, Kirsten Ghodsee, and Victor Grossman. For these writers, the history of socialist societies contains general theoretical principles, which can be used to think about *what* socialism *is*. If their work is combined with the critical work of Leon Trotsky, Paul Sweezy and Charles Bettelheim, significant progress can be made towards the understanding of socialist social formations. As an entire book could be written on these theoretical principles, I will only focus on what principles can be deduced with respect to service workers under socialism.

I will begin this chapter by developing a definition of socialism so that it is clear to the reader how I use the term. I will argue that in a socialist society, the division between industrial and service workers gradually disappears. The majority of working people under socialism will both produce goods and perform service labour as a result of a transformation of the division of labour. This is because *all* workers will be trained in the science of economic planning and industrial management, which transforms the relations of production and creates worker's power. Furthermore, in a socialist society, the private service industry will gradually disappear and become part of the public sector. Service labour such as domestic cleaning, food and drink preparation (in a cafe or restaurant), and transportation will be conducted by state employees. Also, I will argue that because socialism strives for the integration of the socialist bloc, it eliminates the inequality between the stages of production and abolishes unequal exchange. Instead, it encourages cooperation between socialist countries and creates the foundation for real equality between nations.

1 What Is Socialism?

Socialism is a word that is used frequently in mainstream politics by many different types of people. Young people often find the idea of socialism appealing, and many have become members of the British Labour Party, the Democratic Socialists of America, and the Workers Party of Brazil. Although neither Bernie Sanders, Jeremy Corbyn, nor Lula managed to win state-power in recent elections, all received significant support for their 'socialist' policies. For them, socialism means a society with free healthcare, cheap housing, and public ownership of parts of the economy. They view socialism as a society with strong trade unions, high wages, and state subsidies for small businesses. While Sanders and Corbyn are preferable to the (American) Republicans or the (British) Tories, they are neither socialists nor do they aspire for a socialist society in the Marxist sense. Their social democratic policies, even if informed by Keynesian Modern Monetary Theory (MMT), does not end the exploitation of labour, nor does it weaken the power of the monopolies and eliminate outsourcing.[2] At most, they can slightly improve the lives of the working class without abolishing capitalism. Corbyn and Sanders, if elected, would certainly represent a victory for the working class, but this would not mean that a socialist USA or a socialist Britain would emerge. What then, is socialism? I will answer this question with four propositions.

1.1 *Workers Power*

The first feature of socialism that I will discuss is the necessity of workers power and the construction of a socialist state, in which the working class holds an exclusive monopoly on state-power. Socialism requires that the working class, in alliance with the popular masses, make a socialist revolution. Lenin points out that "the passing of state power from one *class* to another is the first, the principal, the basic sign of a *revolution*".[3] A socialist revolution led by revolutionary workers does not miraculously arise, but requires what Lenin calls a 'revolutionary situation'. Sweezy notes that a revolutionary proletariat

> is one which has the potential to make a revolution, but which can actually make it only once under favourable conditions (the so-called revolutionary situation).[4]

Such a situation is one where the capitalist class has gone into such a crisis that it can no longer rule and where the popular masses do want to continue living in the same way. If the working class has developed its own *revolutionary* political party and has won significant support from the popular masses, then

2 See Mitchell and Fazi 2017 for a thorough discussion on MMT.
3 Lenin 1917
4 Sweezy 1972, p. 157.

there is a chance a socialist revolution might occur. In a socialist revolution, the working class seizes state-power, creates a new socialist government with its own institutions, and begins the transition to a planned economy designed to meet the needs of the people. In Lenin's understanding, socialism is a transitional society with the final goal of communism, which is a social formation characterized by a withering away of the state and the disappearance of classes. Socialism is thus not an end in itself, but only a means to achieve a communist society.

During a revolution, the oppressed class seizes state-power and uses the state to create a new kind of society. The apparatuses of the previous state are abolished in order to create new institutions, political documents (i.e., constitutions, manifestos, statements, and policies), laws, and an internal security force to defend the revolution. These new institutions are an expression of the revolutionary power of the new dominant class and are important sites of political struggle during a revolutionary situation. After a revolution, a parliament or constituent assembly are sites where the masses take control of society and organise the conditions for their emancipation. The result is usually a new constitution, documents stating the rights of the people, and an entirely new legal apparatus. The constitution from the former capitalist society is replaced with a new socialist constitution, and the masses are mobilised to help produce this new constitution. This legalises the illegality of the revolution and encourages the growth of proletarian power across society. The new constitution inscribes the class struggle into a textual form, specifying the allies of the new dominant class as well as its enemies. A new security force, whether consisting of armed citizens or a police force, protects the revolution and allows for the repression of its enemies.[5] A transition to socialism can thus only begin once state-power has passed from the bourgeoisie to the working class. As both Lenin and Trotsky understood, a socialist revolution and the creation of a socialist state is only the first stage and will require revolutions in the advanced capitalist countries in order to make further progress. For a revolution to be successful, a federation of socialist states that support each other and share resources must emerge. The experience of the USSR in the thirties has shown that it is very difficult to build socialism in a single country, especially if the productive forces are underdeveloped as a result of economic backwardness. As Trotsky says in his *Permanent Revolution*,

5 See Lenin's *State and Revolution*, chapter 1, for an exposition of the Marxist theory of revolution.

> The socialist revolution begins on the national arena, it unfolds on the international arena, and is completed on the world arena. Thus, the socialist revolution becomes a permanent revolution in a newer and broader sense of the word; it attains completion, only in the final victory of the new society on our entire planet.[6]

To illustrate the process of socialist revolution, let us take the example of Poland's road to socialism after the Second World War. Once the Nazi's had been driven out of Poland after the war, a long period of reconstruction unfolded, which lasted from 1945 to 1952. During the war, the Polish bourgeoisie and its pre-war government were in exile in London, with only a small minority of Polish capitalists remaining in the country. Polish communists—especially Bundists— and progressive nationalists led the resistance against the Nazi's, and therefore were perceived positively after the liberation of Poland in 1945, allowing them to democratically seize power. In post-war Poland, communists and socialists formed an alliance through the Committee for National Liberation, which involved workers, peasants, and small businesspeople to draft a new socialist constitution.[7] The new constitution of the Polish People's Republic established that the socialist public sector would be primary and significantly limited private enterprise, allowing only those with 50 or less workers to operate privately. This constitution enabled the socialist state to nationalise key industries needed for reconstruction—transportation, mining, heavy industry, communications, and public utilities. Also included in the constitution were land reforms, which created co-operatives across the countryside. Land was expropriated by the state from big landowners and redistributed to small farmers and agrarian labourers. Because the country had undergone a horrible war, with millions of people murdered by the Nazi's, the socialist state was cautious with nationalisations and land expropriations. Industries and farmland that was owned by Germans or by Polish Nazi collaborators was expropriated without compensation. However, Poles who owned large amounts of land or were members of the bourgeoisie received compensation, and some were allowed to continue owning a smaller portion of land. Douglas points out that this approach made the Committee for National Liberation popular in the eyes of the Polish people and ensured a strong foundation for democracy in socialist Poland.[8]

6 Trotsky 2020, p. 166.

7 Douglas 1972, pp. 44–57.

8 *ibid.* pp. 47–48.

The above example demonstrates why socialism requires a revolution that puts the working class in power. In the case of Poland, the revolution was fought by communists—with assistance of the Soviet Red Army— in the process of liberating their country from the Nazi's. Although Polish communists used parliamentary methods to take power after the war, the process itself was a revolutionary one that was met with significant opposition by the former bourgeoisie. Only a new constitution, which legalised the revolution and created new socialist institutions, enabled the workers and peasants of Poland to take the socialist road. Had the pre-war Polish government returned to Poland and re-established itself on the basis of the old constitution and institutions, it would have been impossible to build socialism. Hence, a socialist revolution and the establishment of a socialist state is necessary in order to embark on a process of socialist construction. As Goran Therborn puts it, "the working class becomes the ruling class by destruction of the power of the bourgeoisie and the construction and defence of a socialist mode of production."[9] A socialist revolution can take many forms—some violent, others more peaceful—but they all involve the passage of state-power from the bourgeoisie to the working class.

The process of decision making and socialist planning—if done correctly—is a democratic process that involves planning agencies, workers, peasants, and sections of the petty-bourgeoisie. The creation of a socialist state is not designed to alienate the masses from the government. One of its primary functions is to develop a state apparatus that can provide basic services to the people, address problems, and plays an important role in the planning of the economy. A socialist society must develop a system of accounting, planning, and distribution to ensure the material needs of the people. This is done at the level of the state and can take extremely varied forms. Only a socialist state can carry out large-scale nationalisations and land expropriations, which are a necessary condition for socialist planning. Unless the socialist state holds a monopoly on land, it is not possible to plan the production of food and other agrarian products. Without public ownership of the means of production in key industries, socialist planning cannot effectively function. If capitalist production remains dominant and the primary purpose of production is the appropriation of surplus-value, socialism will not be able to develop.[10]

Although a socialist society is more democratic than a capitalist one, it is not free of contradictions. One of the writers to clearly perceive the problems

9 Therborn 1978, p. 44.

10 See Bukharin and Preobrazhensky [1923] 1966, ch. 12.

facing the USSR in the thirties was Leon Trotsky, whose *The Revolution Betrayed* is a very honest and sober confrontation of the contradictions that existed in the Soviet Union. Trotsky argues that because the USSR was isolated in the thirties and surrounded by hostile capitalist states, an undemocratic Stalinist faction took command of the Communist Party. It made decisions in a highly administrative way, and while the material conditions did improve compared to pre-revolutionary Russia, there was a high level of social inequality. Trotsky shows how the Soviet bureaucracy exploited the planning system not to meet the needs of socialist society, but in order to advance its own material privileges.[11] In his *Post-Revolutionary* Society, Paul Sweezy identifies some of the privileges of the Soviet bureaucracy, which included a stronger educational background, a more cultured family, higher self-confidence derived from one's parents, and connections to those in power. He points out that such a ruling stratum "finds ways to preserve and protect its vested against mass invasion from below".[12] Instead of using democratic methods to resolve contradictions among the people, the Stalinists preferred to repress them using the police. This demoralised many honest communists and alienated the Soviet government from the masses of the people. Sweezy argues that these problems can be overcome if a socialist state invests its resources into raising the political education of the entire population so that any member of society can take up a job in the state. If all working people are taught how to think and act in a communist way, then levels of political education are no longer a privilege that one can use to join the bureaucracy. A good socialist policy is also to keep the wage of a state official at that of a wage worker, and to create a high level of transparency. Through transparency and the method of criticism and self-criticism, it becomes more difficult for corruption and nepotism to emerge in the socialist state. Sweezy thinks that such a struggle against the bureaucracy and its bourgeois ideas is indispensable to the existence of a socialist state. Following Charles Bettelheim, Sweezy thought that a socialist society is strongest when it 'puts politics in command', which means "giving priority to transforming human beings and their relations with eachother".[13] When politics govern decision making, it enables workers to take over the production process and play a more active role in socialist construction.

Throughout his writings, Trotsky predicted that the USSR would be pushed to become more democratic and change its policies only with the emergence of new socialist states in Europe. This would bring the USSR out of its isolation,

11 Trotsky 2004, ch. 6.
12 Sweezy 1980, p. 26.
13 Sweezy 1980, p. 61.

improve its material conditions, and create a federation of fraternal socialist states. In many ways, Trotsky's predictions were confirmed in post-war Europe, in which many new socialist states emerged. By the 1960s and 1970s, the USSR had become far democratic as a result of the growth of the socialist bloc. While it still suffered from a sometimes-bureaucratic approach to decision making, the 1970's Soviet state had improved its ability to involve the popular masses in socialist planning. As Szymanski shows in *Is the Red Flag Flying*, the Soviet government involved its citizens in many aspects of decision making, and the Communist Party often found unique ways to consult the public about its policies. During the sixties and seventies, the Soviet state tried to consult working people when constructing its economic plans in a democratic way. Gosplan, which was responsible for national economic planning in the USSR, generally sent its plans to factories to be discussed and commented on by workers through their trade unions. Their criticisms were then used to modify economic plans so that they reflected the input of the workers and trade union leaders. Furthermore, a new five-year plan was published in *Pravda*, and citizens were encouraged to give their opinion on the plan; *Pravda* often received thousands of letters, which it carefully studied and conveyed to government bodies.[14] Because the dictatorship of the proletariat puts the majority of society—the working class—in command of the state, it thus is far more democratic than even the most democratic capitalist states. It creates opportunities for society to experiment with new forms of democracy, which far exceed casting a vote at a ballot box.

Another reason why a socialist state is necessary is to defend the revolution from its enemies. Every revolution—in Russia, Cuba, China, Poland, the GDR, etc.—faced opposition by the former bourgeoisie, which resorted to sabotage, organised violence, and other forms of conspiratorial activity against socialism. Without a socialist state, it is impossible to repress counterrevolutionaries who are conspiring to overthrow the communist government. A socialist society must have an internal and external security force to establish the rule of law and respond to external threats. This can involve arming citizens and training them to address problems in their community, or it can involve the creation of a police-force (although this is highly limited and can cause serious problems if not done correctly). The role of law-enforcement under socialism is to protect the working class and secure the gains of the socialist revolution. It is vital that the governing socialist party encourages criticism and self-criticism to ensure the accountability of law enforcement and the army. As Trotsky and

14 Szymanski 1979, pp. 37–41.

other critics of Stalinism correctly perceived, this was often not done in the Soviet Union. Kostas Mavrakis points out that

> Stalin did not see enemies who had to be defeated ideologically and politically by the revolutionary mobilisation of the masses but only spies, murderers and wreckers to be dealt with by the police and the courts.[15]

Instead of encouraging an environment of discussion and debate, the Stalinist bureaucracy in the 1930's preferred to use the police to repress differences in the Communist Party. In a socialist social formation, using the police to address political differences is a violation of socialist legality and harms the process of socialist construction by demoralising working people. Without a state-apparatus, it is impossible to create a legal system with courts and produce socialist legality. However, without democratic accountability of state officials and the police, socialist legality cannot exist and be used to advance the needs of the revolution. Therefore, a future socialist society must aspire to create democracy at all levels by encouraging discussion, debate, and criticism rather than using repression to deal with problems.[16]

In this sub-section, I have argued that a socialist society is only possible through a working-class revolution, which seizes state-power and creates a socialist state. This differs from 'democratic socialism', which neither seeks to end capitalism nor create a socialist planned economy. Opposing a revolutionary road, democratic socialists imagine that they can radically transform society by introducing a series of reforms—free healthcare, strong trade unions, and social welfare. While all these things are certainly desirable under capitalism, they are not socialist demands because they do not involve seizure of state-power by the working class. I will now examine the second element, which addresses the mode of production and social formation under socialism.

1.2 *Socialist Mode of Production*

One major way that a socialist society differs from capitalism is that the socialist mode of production is dominant, while pre-socialist modes of production, such as capitalism and feudalism, gradually dissolve. Capitalism and other pre-socialist modes of production are not immediately abolished, but gradually overcome and replaced with socialist production forms. In order for this to happen, the working class must control the state and use the state to create

15 Mavrakis 1976, p. 92.

16 For a discussion on possible ways to improve socialist democracy, see Poulantzas (1978) and Therborn (1978).

policies that favour socialist production. Progress in the expansion of socialist production depends on the policies of the government and its ability to stimulate enthusiasm for socialism in the masses. Also, it requires that the state exercises effective law-enforcement to prosecute illegal economic activity, such as private appropriation and abuse of state-funds. Socialist production entails that workers control the means of production and play an active role in socialist planning, distribution, and socialist expansion. Socialist relations of production are expressed through socialist planning, workers control of production, agrarian co-operatives and collective state farms. It is important to emphasise that workers ownership of the means of production does not generally happen immediately and can take a long time to develop. Historically, after a socialist revolution, a transition period will unfold that strengthens socialist production and causes non-socialist forms of production to dissolve. Mistakes are made when this is done too quickly or without support from the masses of people.

It generally takes a long time after a socialist revolution for socialist relations of production to fully develop. To make this point clear, I would like to turn to a helpful distinction from the Greek Marxist, Nikos Poulantzas. Poulantzas makes a distinction between formal ownership and real ownership in a socialist society.[17] During the period of transition from socialism to capitalism, the working class uses the socialist state to transfer ownership of the means of production from the bourgeoisie to the working class. In the first stage, there is generally only formal ownership of the means of production, which means that the socialist state owns or controls the means of production. For example, a factory, office, workshop, warehouse, or farm is owned by the socialist state. In the period of formal ownership, the state actively works towards putting the means of production under the control of the working class. In order to do this, they must educate them on how to collectively manage production, participate in drafting and carrying out state plans, and participate in distribution. It is only when the workers have been trained in the science of self-management that ownership can pass from formal to real ownership. Real ownership is when the workers actively manage production and where production is entirely carried out on a socialist basis. A major role of the socialist state is to develop socialist relations of production and put an end to capitalist production by creating real ownership of the means of production.

Trotsky wrote a lot about the struggle to strengthen self-management in order to improve the quality of life under socialism. Throughout his writings of

---

17 Poulantzas [1977] 2008

the thirties, Trotsky argued that instead of aspiring to build a fully developed socialist society within the confines of the USSR, the Soviet government should instead have sought to make the workers and peasants more active in socialist construction. This would have involved a more concerted attempt to raise the level of political education across the USSR, which does not mean training people to regurgitate passages from Marx and Lenin but to learn to apply them in socialist practice. Trotsky was convinced that this would only be possible in a democratic environment where people are free to say what they think so that their political consciousness develops in a natural way. The often-hostile environment in the USSR of the thirties (as well as later periods, which improved but were scarred with their Stalinist past), where debates were conducted using quotes from the holy canon of Marxism-Leninism, made real political education impossible. In the Party schools in the Soviet Union, students were trained to be good ideologues, well-versed in the 'science' of Marxism-Leninism, but unable to engage in real debate. The result was that while many people may have joined the Communist Party, few people possessed a real political education. Their 'Marxism-Leninism' was a very vulgar simulacrum of Marxist theory, which transformed the teachings of Marx, Engels, Lenin, and Stalin into a doctrine rather than a guide to action. Without socialist democracy, it is very difficult to raise the political level of working people and train them to manage industry.

A frequent symptom of failing to devote time to political education is a tendency known as 'economism', which imagines that improving the material conditions through developing a society's productive forces will automatically create socialist consciousness. This 'economistic' view, held primarily by Stalin and his supporters, argues that a society with full employment, a decent living standard, and good education is sufficient to make working people embrace socialism.[18] While Party schools may train workers to become ideologues who are well versed in Marxism-Leninism, economism places its primary faith in the development of the productive forces. An example of economism can be seen in the ideology behind socialist urban planning, in which architecture was designed to encourage collective activity and spaces for public meetings were created. One example of this is Halle-Neustadt, which was built in 1967 entirely by the state in order to give chemical workers in Halle their own city. Workers and youth were involved in its construction, and a vibrant socialist community was built, with shops, leisure centres, and entertainment venues. The idea behind this was to prove to the people of the GDR that socialist

18 For an excellent discussion of economism, see Bettelheim 1976, pp. 32–45.

housing is superior to privately owned accommodations and to discourage renting from private landlords (which were a minority in the GDR). This could then result in a popular demand for the expansion of socialist housing, and new confrontations with landlords through expropriation.[19] There is certainly nothing wrong with socialist urban planning, for it can play an important role in changing how people think about themselves and their relationship with other people. A socialist city such as Halle-Neustadt that encourages more collective forms of life can create behaviour patterns that are compatible with socialism. The primary issue with economism is that it imagines the improved material conditions of socialism are sufficient to convince working people of the truth of Marxism.

One of the critics of economism was Paul Sweezy, who wrote numerous articles (influenced by Charles Bettelheim) that criticised economism for being detrimental to socialist construction. While it is true that a socialist mode of production will change people's beliefs and make them favourably inclined towards a socialist government, Sweezy thought economism was mistaken, for it can easily produce consumerist ideas in the minds of communist leaders and neglect the work of ideological consolidation. Although improving material conditions should be an important goal of a transitional social formation, a socialist government should not subordinate all its activities to economic development. Sweezy reminds us that proletarian revolution is "not a process by which the proletariat seeks to improve its own lot as a class, but one by which it seeks to do away with itself as a class."[20] By organising campaigns against capitalist ideas, training workers to manage production, and actively supporting revolutionary movements abroad, a communist government puts the proletariat in a better position to continue its revolution.

Sweezy elaborates this critique by examining how Soviet economism created the foundation for capitalism to be restored in the Soviet Union. In 'Lessons of the Soviet Experience' written in 1967, Sweezy observes that the USSR had become a depoliticised society dominated by private incentives to stimulate production. He argues that although income inequalities were significantly lower in the Soviet Union than in the capitalist countries, inequality existed because of the Soviet policy of *private* distribution of consumer goods. This began in the early sixties because higher income strata of society were demanding more consumer durables such as automobiles, refrigerators, washing machines, and other such goods. In order to respond to this demand,

19 https://en.wikipedia.org/wiki/Halle-Neustadt.
20 Sweezy 1980, p. 65.

the Soviet leadership began using material incentives—wage inequalities, bonuses, etc.—to simulate production. Those who produced more and worked harder were rewarded so that they could attain these goods, while those who did not, had a lower material standard of life. A major effect of Soviet consumerism was a significant increase in private car ownership and a corresponding individualistic lifestyle. As Sweezy observes, this new car-centric lifestyle created a demand for a variety of new goods and services, such as tourist resorts, camping equipment, and sporting goods.[21]

The unfortunate result of Soviet consumerism was the "hardening of material inequalities in Soviet society".[22] The automobile became a major signifier of material privilege, increasing selfishness and envy in Soviet society. Sweezy observes that Soviet consumerism depoliticized socialist society and created a new ruling stratum that used the Soviet state to protect its material privileges. He is careful not to call them a 'state bourgeoisie' or a new 'ruling class' because he thought there was still a possibility of repoliticising Soviet society and changing its trajectory. There was still the chance that an intervention by leftists in the Communist Party could result in a kind of 'cultural revolution', and the reinvigoration of Soviet socialism. Sweezy points out, however, that if this does not happen and Soviet society continues along a consumerist path, the ruling stratum will turn into a new class that sets up barriers to entry. This is unfortunately what happened in the Soviet Union and Eastern Bloc countries (i.e., the GDR, Peoples Republic of Poland, etc.) in the late eighties, and was an important factor in the end of socialism.

It is very important for a socialist state to actively work towards ending private property and not neglect the work of creating popular support for socialism. Historically, the failure to do this has resulted in serious crises and the emergence of latent bourgeoisies. One way that this can happen is through the growth of the black market and the growth of a second economy. In *Socialism Betrayed*, Keeran and Kenny argue that one reason that the USSR collapsed was due to negligence of the second economy during the Khrushchev and Brezhnev years. Soviet economic reforms tended to privatize agriculture and encourage profiteering from the sale of products. Keeran and Kenny show that the growth of the unplanned, second economy made socialist construction much more difficult, as it undermined socialist planning. Had Soviet leaders involved the masses in tackling the second economy, exposing corrupt Party officials and prosecuting illegal economic activity, it is possible the socialist

21 Sweezy 1980, pp. 24–25.
22 Sweezy 1980, pp. 24.

mode of production could have expanded. Instead, a petty-bourgeois stratum developed in the Soviet Union, which demanded the restoration of capitalism and the destruction of the socialist state. While they called for more 'freedom', they were hostile to workers power and actively opposed socialist relations of production. Hence, as a result of Khrushchev and Brezhnev's policies, the means of production never passed from formal to real ownership. Keeran and Kenny argue that this created an audience for Gorbachev's Perestroika reforms, and the gradual destruction of the Soviet state between 1987 and 1991.[23]

In *Post-Revolutionary Society*, Sweezy makes some suggestions on how to ensure that future socialist societies do not make the same mistakes. First, he argues that socialist economic policy should prohibit or significantly reduce private distribution of consumer products in order to combat consumerism. Instead of using material incentives to stimulate private consumption, socialist policy should use moral incentives and collectively distribute consumer goods. For example, it should significantly reduce private food distribution and instead distribute food through public canteens. This gives a socialist society the ability to more effectively plan people's diets, reducing unhealthy consumption and improving public health. Sweezy thinks that a transitional workers state should invest its resources into developing a highly advanced system of public transportation and significantly limit or even abolish private car ownership. The result is that people will travel on the same trains, buses, and trams and eliminate the bourgeois ideas that result from having one's own private mobility. This would be significantly better for the environment, as it would give the leaders of society the ability to more effectively plan its ecological policy. If it wanted to reduce greenhouse gases, it could invest state funds into research about clean energy and fully utilise its existing resources to ensure a green society. Sweezy thus holds that a principle of socialist policy should be that "private needs and wants should be satisfied only at a level at which they can be satisfied for all."[24] When goods are distributed collectively, Sweezy argues that a different pattern of production relations will be made possible. If one cannot use one's income to privately acquire material goods, it will no longer be possible to use material incentives to stimulate production. Instead, it will be necessary to educate the popular masses and generate an enthusiasm for building socialism. Furthermore, such moral incentives would enable the working class to manage production and take a more active role in socialist construction. The result is a politicisation of society, a conscious

23 Keeran and Kenny 2010

24 Sweezy 1980, p. 22.

reduction of consumerism, and a significant improvement in the material standards of living for all.[25]

In this sub-section, I have argued that after a socialist revolution, a transition period generally exists before socialist relations of production begin to emerge. A socialist state must actively create popular support for socialism and consciously involve the masses in socialist construction. Failure to do this can strengthen bourgeois elements in society and result in the restoration of capitalism, as happened in the Soviet Union in 1991. In the next sub-section, I will discuss some of the aspects of socialist planning, which can take many forms and are diverse in their application.

1.3 *Socialist Planning*

One way that socialism differs from capitalism is that a socialist state plans production, the distribution of goods, and the allocation of housing. In a socialist society planning agencies exist in order to create a planned economy that meets the material needs of the people and to puts an end to the production of surplus value. There is still an economic surplus, but this economic surplus is invested into the expansion of socialist infrastructure. In a socialist society, workers do not produce surplus-value but rather an economic surplus that returns to them in the form of goods and service. A socialist state actively pursues policies that dissolve the capital relation and put an end to exploitation of labour through the appropriation of surplus-value. Although some remnants of capitalist production may still exist in an early stage of socialism, capitalist exploitation is no longer generalised because socialist planning is in command of production decisions. As socialism develops, socialist production grows, and socialist relations of production become dominant. Surplus value thus becomes a thing of the past, but there continues to be an economic surplus that has to be dealt with by the socialist planning agencies.

In his *Political Economy of Growth*, Paul Baran introduced the notion of a potential economic surplus to envision how a socialist society would conceptualise surplus value. He defines the potential economic surplus as

> the difference between the output that could be produced in a given natural and technological environment with the help of employable resources, and what might be regarded as essential consumption.[26]

---

25 For a discussion about the use of moral incentives under socialism, see Wheelwright and McFarlane (1970), ch. 8.

26 Baran 1957, p. 23.

The potential economic surplus are all the things that are wastefully used under capitalism, such as marketing, advertising, and packaging.[27] Since a socialist society produces goods and services to meet the needs of the people rather than for profit, it no longer needs to stimulate a demand for goods like cars, washing machines, smart phones, computers, etc. Rather, the state produces these things and makes them available to the working class at an affordable price. As a result, it is unnecessary to invest significant funds in advertising and marketing in a socialist society. Socialism therefore puts an end to wasteful usage of society's resources and discourages toxic consumerist behaviour. Growth does not result from the anarchy of the market, but from the liberation of the production forces through socialist planning.

Socialist planning agencies do not have to plan every aspect of production and can allow some levels of decentralisation. Syzmanski points out that although planning was heavily centralised in the USSR, there was always decentralisation with respect to local decision making. Furthermore, although the planning agencies create economic plans, it was the masses that carry out the plan. Historically, this involved divergences from the plan through criticism directly from the workers. Ideally, a socialist government should try to involve workers in the process of planning, carrying out the plan, and celebrating advances in socialist production. Socialist planning utilises elements from capitalist accounting, but also creates new theoretical models designed to encourage socialist relations of production. The Soviet Union used the theories of Leontiev, which were based on Marx's schemas of social reproduction. These models of socialist planning viewed production, circulation, and distribution as interrelated spheres that each had an effect on each other.[28]

Managerial practices might still exist in an early stage of socialism, but they take a form different from capitalism. Under capitalism, management exists to extract as much surplus value from the workers as possible. Capitalist management has a repressive and disciplinary function and involves a high level of labour surveillance. Szymanski argues that in the USSR, management existed to encourage workers to participate in the construction of socialism. Although sometimes they abused their power, socialist managers tried to motivate them to carry out the plan and help transfer ownership to the workers. Often, these managers work in the very factory that they help manage and are elected by their trade union to receive training in socialist management.[29] It is tremendously important for a socialist government to create policies that ensure

27 *Ibid.* pp. 22–24.

28 Syzmanski 1979, pp. 34–58; Nove 1972, pp. 309-318

29 Syzmanski 1979, pp. 40–41; Nove 1972, pp. 319-334

these managers are accountable. This can be done by creating party committees in workplaces, in which workers are given the opportunity to raise issues and criticise them. A socialist manager should also not receive a higher wage than a worker in order to prevent them from deriving material privileges from their managerial position. A long-term goal of a socialist society should be to fully transfer management to the workers so that they no longer need to rely on individual managers. This requires political education, which can only be achieved in a democratic social formation that encourages collective values and builds strong solidarity between working people of all occupations.

Socialism makes it possible to create more advanced technology because the competition that regulates production under capitalism has been abolished. The socialist state will take goods like iPhones that are expensive under capitalism, and mass produce them under socialism so that all working people can have them. Companies like Apple will be expropriated and nationalised so that the competition between monopolies will no longer affect the way goods are produced. The best knowledge of computer production will be combined to create high-quality computers available to all working people. We will no longer have dozens of different apps for the same thing, but one app that combines the knowledge of all previous apps to create a socialist super app. Socialism thereby transforms consumption and allows all working people to enjoy advanced technology, science, and consumer products at an affordable price. It does not thereby generate consumerist individualism, but drastically improves the quality of consumption by raising the material standard of living of all.

The same thing will be true for medicine, as the massive pharmaceutical industrial complex will be abolished. Socialism in the twenty-first century will encourage a healthy lifestyle and find a cure to many illnesses. Some illnesses, such as obesity, severe anxiety, and manic depression that are connected to high levels of stress and an unhealthy lifestyle will gradually disappear under socialism. This is because a socialist society will make gyms available to the public and encourage everyone to exercise, take walks, and eat healthful food. A good example of this is Cuba, which has one of the world's most advanced medical systems and encourages a very healthy way of living. Past socialist countries—the USSR and the GDR—put tremendously high value on sports and won many international competitions.

In a socialist society, workers thus still produce an economic surplus, but they are no longer exploited. Rather, the economic surplus they produce is realised in the goods and services distributed by the socialist state.[30] A steel worker who produces a thousand pounds of steel will realise his surplus in free

30 Foster 2014, pp. 194.

healthcare, an abundance of healthy food, free gyms, high quality electronics that he can afford, and a high level of cultural wealth. Socialist planning agencies encourage the steel worker to be active at work, not in order to valorise the profits of the few but to contribute to the material prosperity of socialist society. The government also encourages the steel worker to participate in the creation of the plan as it relates to steel production, the implementation of the plan, and criticism of mistakes made. Under socialism, the worker thus realises the products of his labour in material goods and services, and exercises his socialist freedom in the participation of building socialism.

This brings us to a complete, final definition of socialism: *a socialist social formation is one in which the working class holds a monopoly on state-power, exercises internationalism by promoting revolutions abroad, creates a state that plans the economy to meet the needs of the people, organises socialist relations of production, and puts an end to the exploitation of labour-power.* Socialism drastically improves people's lives, eliminates the material basis of racism and sexism, and allows every citizen to contribute to socialist construction. Through organising an integrated socialist bloc, it puts an end to unequal exchange and encourages the levelling out of nations so that they can exchange products on an equal basis. What socialist planning makes possible is the orientation of all production towards creating use-value and social ownership of the means of production. One of the goals of socialism is to produce high-quality goods that are available to everyone in society and improve the material conditions of the population. Socialist planning eliminates surplus-value because it removes the capital-relation from the production process. Instead, it plans an economic surplus, which is reinvested to expand socialist infrastructure and constantly improve the quality of people's lives. By means of a long process, it gradually transfers management of the production process directly to the workers, who become the masters of society. Socialism therefore ends the exploitation of man by man and improves the material conditions of all of society's members.

Socialism—as understood by Marx, Lenin, and Trotsky—was not intended to be utopian. In their time, they were very hostile to utopian speculation about what socialism would be like. Instead, they argued that socialism would have to be built on the foundation created by capitalism. As Goran Therborn puts it, "the future has to be built on the foundation of the past and the present, not merely constructed in thought out of ideals".[31] Although a socialist revolution could occur in an underdeveloped nation—and did in the case of Russia—its success will be guaranteed by revolutions in the advanced capitalist centres.

31 Therborn 1978, p. 18.

Since technology, management, logistics, and science is most advanced in the capitalist centres, they provide a strong foundation on which to build a new socialist society. In the next section, I will discuss how a genuine socialist society will gradually transform the labour process for the service workers discussed in this book. As it turns out, the advanced technology created by capitalism contains a revolutionary potential to transform the lives of service workers in a socialist social formation.

2 Food Consumption under Socialism

In a socialist society, food consumption will significantly change by making it collectively distributed through public restaurants. If a revolution occurs in an advanced capitalist country like the United States or Britain, it will be possibly to immediately move towards collective distribution of food. In an early stage of socialism, the distribution of products may still involve money, although the prices will be set by the state and kept as low as possible. Although grocery stores will still make it possible to acquire food, a socialist government will encourage people to have their meals in public canteens. As Kollontai and Trotsky point out in their writings, public canteens will take the burden off of women to prepare food and free up time for more enriching activities. Trotsky notes in *The Revolution Betrayed* that

> the complete absorption of the housekeeping functions of the family by institutions of the socialist society, uniting all generations in solidarity and mutual aid, was to bring to woman, and thereby to the loving couple, a real liberation from the thousand-year-old fetters.[32]

Instead of being under pressure to perform a second housework shift, a socialist woman will be able to enjoy her meal in a public canteen and participate in political life. While she eats dinner with her comrades, the canteen will organise activities for her children. The collective distribution of food enables women to live a more fulfilled, meaningful life under socialism. Her children will have opportunities to participate in enriching activities, which will be entirely provided by society and not cost her a penny.[33]

---

32 Trotsky [1936] 2004, p. 119.

33 For an excellent history of women's liberation under socialism, see Ghodsee (2018).

After a socialist revolution, restaurants will become publicly owned and unhealthy food will gradually disappear from people's diets. Under capitalism, working people who do not have time to cook can often only afford cheap fast food from places like McDonalds. This results in super profits for fast food chains and health issues for workers, such as diabetes and obesity. In a socialist society, the government can employ culinary specialists to train hospitality workers how to produce healthy food from a variety of culinary traditions. Public canteens can become not just places where food is consumed, but where workers organise cultural activities in order to create friendship between nationalities. For example, in order to combat antisemitism, workers can learn about the history of the Jewish people at a public canteen while they enjoy a kosher meal with Hasidic music. This transforms anti-racist politics into an engaged practice through the politicisation of food consumption. Historically, this was done by the Black Panther Party, who used their breakfast programme as an opportunity to improve the health of African American children while teaching them about the history of African Americans. While eating a healthy meal, children in the Black Panther Party could learn about a slave revolt or about the history of a new post-colonial African nation like Ghana. What made the Black Panthers extremely popular was not their use of arms, but their creative attempts to politicise consumption while fulfilling the material needs of the working class.[34] Socialism has the potential to drastically transform consumption so that it becomes a way to spiritually uplift people, providing them with cultural and political education in the process of eating food.

After the proletariat seizes state-power, the socialist government can begin transferring management to the workers and create socialist relations of production. In some industries, especially those with complex logistical systems, this process will take time as workers will need to be trained to take up management of industry. However, with many service industries, it will be possible to rapidly transform management to the workers and create collectively run workplaces. As I discussed earlier, in service industries such as hospitality and cleaning, workers already partially manage their workplace even under capitalism. They do not have a voice in major economic decisions, nor do they get to choose their wage or working conditions. However, a camaraderie exists between the workers of a large restaurant, and they have a system of managing a large operation. In a new socialist society, the management structure will certainly change, but the existing system of camaraderie that exists in

34 For an excellent article on the BPP's breakfast program, see Potorti (2014)

the hospitality sector will be relied on in the transfer of power to the workers. What will change is the division of labour in the restaurant and also the very way that food is distributed.

A socialist government has the potential to give every restaurant worker—whether a waiter, cleaner, engineer—an education in the culinary arts. Their education will train them so that every worker can become not just a chef, but also skilled in the logistics of food distribution and dietary science. Instead of sending them to a university separated from their workplace, specialists in the culinary arts, logistics, health, etc. will visit their restaurant and teach them on the job. A major part of their education will include socialist theory, which will demonstrate how Marxism is behind the socialist revolution in education. Also, their education will make them sensitive to culturally specific diets (i.e., kosher, halal, etc.) and the importance of providing this to the community. They will learn the principles of collective self-management, which will develop as they learn to apply it in their labour-process. In this way, the oppressive division of labour from capitalism will gradually be replaced with collective management of the production process. Each worker in the new socialist restaurant will be greatly uplifted and take great pride in the drastic improvement to their material conditions. What under capitalism was just a job to pay the bills will become a collective service to society and an integral function of socialist construction. Most importantly, socialism liberates them from the capitalist division of labour and opens up opportunities for personal, spiritual, and cultural enrichment.

Socialism has the potential to drastically transform food consumption. Instead of just being the satisfaction of a biological need, every meal can become an opportunity for improving people's lives. By providing healthy, quality food, society can gradually put diabetes and obesity in the dustbin of history and proceed to create healthy, thoughtful people. This will take time, and its success will depend on whether the revolution has succeeded in collectively distributing food. If it proceeds too gradually, it will prevent the transformative elements contained within public canteens from emerging. On other hand, if it proceeds too rapidly without educating people properly, it may harm future attempts to proceed to the socialist transformation of consumption. The surest way to ensure progress in the transition to socialism is by first transferring management of production to the workers and then gradually introducing public canteens. While this is occurring, the socialist leadership can begin to educate people on food health and encourage people to eat in government owned restaurants.

Historic revolutions have shown that agrarian policy is tremendously important for the success of socialist food distribution. In the advanced capitalist centres, farming is mostly conducted by large-scale capitalist agribusinesses. It is often the case that the imperialists exploit the agrarian resources of developing nations to get cheap food while the people of that country starve. A major task of socialist construction is creating full food sovereignty so that it becomes unnecessary to gain crops from abroad. With the growth of socialist revolutions, trade between socialist nations can significantly increase the quality of food and the possibilities for collective food distribution. A socialist revolution would have to include major land reforms as a central task of developing socialist relations of production. In countries where farming is conducted by large agribusinesses, the socialist state would have to expropriate their land while gradually setting up a collective farming sector. This might mean that the former owner of the agribusiness will have to continue working on their farm until farming can be fully collectivised. One way to transform agriculture is to encourage hospitality workers to work on farms in order to learn farming and directly produce the food that they prepare in their restaurants. A socialist social formation that collectively distributes food could create a new type of chain restaurant that is directly connected to a particular collective farm. Every restaurant could have its own collective farm where it grows the vegetables, raises cattle, and gains the primary ingredients used in its food. It would probably take significant time to develop and require the existence of generalised enthusiasm for socialist construction. In this way, the distance separating a chef from a farmer is drastically reduced, and the distinction between 'town and country' is gradually abolished, which was one of the major programmatic points in Marx's *Communist Manifesto.*

3 Socialist Integration and Retail Labour under Socialism

In an earlier chapter, I made a distinction between the stage in which surplus-value is produced, and a stage in which the surplus-value is realised. In the first stage, raw materials are extracted and the commodity is manufactured, resulting in a physical product. As I showed, in the era of monopoly capitalism, this generally takes place in peripheral nations such as Bangladesh, India, and Cambodia. In the second stage, the product is shipped to warehouses, and distributed to shops where the commodity is sold. Significant labour is required to sell the commodity, which can include advertising, stocking shelves, and sales tactics. During this stage, new surplus-value can be produced, but its main purpose is the realisation of surplus-value. I showed that most of the sales-effort is conducted in the imperialist nations, where the multinational corporations have their headquarters and direct the entire process.

The two-stage process assumes the primary features of a capitalist social formation, in which the capitalist class holds state power, and uses the state to reproduce these capitalist social relations. It is only possible in a society where the primary aim of production is the creation of surplus-value and its transformation into profit. This requires that the capitalist class owns the means of production, which allows the capital-relation between a worker and a capitalist to exist. It is irrelevant whether the means of production are owned by the capitalist state or by private firms. So long as workers sell their labour-power to capitalists in exchange for a wage, their labour will create surplus-value, which will need to be realised through the sales-effort. Therefore, a primary goal of a socialist society will be the abolition of the capital-relation through the organisation of production according to a plan.

A major effect of a planned economy is the integration of all sectors of economic life. Unlike capitalism, in which the capitalist centre is deindustrialised and exploits low-wage labour in the periphery, socialism integrates the production, circulation, and distribution of goods. Although socialist countries can still trade with non-socialist nations, they prioritise the development of their own industrial capacity through trade with other socialist countries. This was the case in the former Soviet Union, which placed a high level of importance on its own industrial capabilities so that it could produce its own raw materials and manufacture goods. The USSR led the creation of an integrated socialist bloc after the war, which included Eastern European 'people's democracies' (i.e., Poland, Hungary, Czechoslovakia, GDR, etc.), Cuba, Vietnam, the DPRK, and socialist states in Africa (i.e., Angola, Congo, Mozambique). These countries would trade with each-other on an equal basis, exchanging products in equal quantities determined by scarcities in their own economies. At the same time, the more economically developed USSR would share its resources to help develop the newer socialist countries.[35] One example of socialist integration is how the socialist bloc related to the DPRK after the imperialist war in Korea. Armstrong shows that after the Korean War, the Soviet Union and the German Democratic Republic devoted significant resources to help North Korea with post-war reconstruction. The GDR sent engineers to help with housing and infrastructure construction, while the Soviets sent thousands of workers, teachers, economists, and scientists. Their approach was to train Koreans so that they could take up the management of all elements of society, from economic planning to scientific research. Within ten years, Pyongyang

35 Senin 1973; Szymanski pp. 120–131.

was transformed into a thriving socialist city, and North Korea was to become one of the most successful socialist countries in Asia.[36]

Socialist integration and economic planning transform the relationship between stage one and two of production and circulation. The production of goods and their distribution are conducted within the same socialist country, or between socialist nations (i.e. CMEA, Comecon).[37] Multinational corporations such as H&M and Starbucks are nationalised, and are unable to outsource their production to a low-wage capitalist country. Instead, the socialist state builds its own garment factories, planning both the number of shirts that need to be produced and the desired economic surplus. These garment factories gradually become managed by the workers, who learn not just how to produce shirts, but the logistics of distributing them and the art of fashion. Socialist garment workers will gradually become logistic specialists and fashion designers. The workers produce both what is needed to meet society's clothing needs, and an economic surplus to allow for the expansion of socialist production. The workers are compensated for the labour that they perform, and wage increases are directly tied to increased productivity. However, they are not exploited in producing this surplus, as it returns to them in the form of more services, entertainment, better housing, and improved infrastructure. Although socialist enterprises have some autonomy in business decisions, the socialist state sets wages, the prices of goods, and allocates capital to them.[38] Enterprises can have managers, but a socialist state actively promotes workers to managerial positions in order to train workers how to manage production.[39] The long-term goal is the complete management of all enterprises by the workers themselves so that they no longer need individual managers. Therefore, the first stage of production under socialism does not involve exploitation and eliminates the oppressive conditions of labour that exist under capitalism.

The distribution of the means of production (i.e., raw materials and machinery) under socialism differs from the distribution of consumer goods. Industrial equipment, agrarian machinery (i.e., tractors), and other means of production are directly transported to factories and farms. The socialist state owns the factory where a tractor is manufactured and the collective farm in which it is used. Therefore, once the tractors are built, they can be immediately used on collective farms without any market exchange taking place between the two departments. Their exchange is mediated by a central plan, which

36 Armstrong 2015.

37 Senin 1973, chapters 1–2.

38 Syzmanski 1979 pp. 43–36; Liberman 1962, (in Nove 1972, pp. 312–315).

39 Szymanski 1979, pp 38–41 and pp. 66–67.

determines their production, circulation, and consumption from beginning to end. Historically, the USSR engaged in multilateral planning with other socialist countries, especially Hungary, Bulgaria, and the German Democratic Republic.[40] In this way, multiple socialist countries could plan together and become integrated in order to exchange products without disrupting socialist equilibrium. As the socialist countries usually provided lower prices to their allies, there was an incentive for socialist countries to trade raw materials and machinery in order to help each-other to develop their productive forces.

Retail under socialism differs significantly than under capitalism. First, socialist countries use economic plans to determine the allocation of goods but can use markets to distribute them.[41] In an early stage of socialism, goods are *sold* in socialist markets, but their prices are set by the state through planning agencies. Enterprises do not compete, which means that there will not be multiple brands of the same product. People use money to purchase these goods, which is printed by the state and returns to it through the exchange of products. Money is a means to circulate goods and distribute the social product but cannot function as capital under socialism. A retail employee in a socialist shop does very little sales work, as it is less necessary to stimulate demand for products. Retail workers act more like accountants, recording the products that are sold, and working with planners to account for goods sold. As I will show in a moment, a more advanced stage of socialism gradually eliminates retail by collectively distributing all products and transforming the quality of consumption.

Socialist retail workers may also play a role that is similar to product development under capitalism and carry out the socialist equivalent of market research. As a way to carry out the mass line, retail employees can hold meetings with consumers to find out what kinds of products they want. Using advanced research methodologies, they can evaluate how consumers rate a particular product in order to find out how it can be improved in order to better serve the people. Consumers have a far greater say in what is produced in a socialist society, for the purpose of producing consumer goods is not profit but consumption. A shop under socialism can become a space where new products are developed with the help of consumers. Consumers can be organised under socialism, giving them a greater voice in what is produced. It is no longer necessary to use manipulative marketing techniques to stimulate demand, but rather the input of the masses. This approach was used in socialist China

40 Szymanski 1979 pp. 128–130.

41 Syzmanski 1979 pp. 42–43; Lieberman 1962.

during the 1960's when the Chinese Revolution was at its height. Researchers E.L. Wheelwright and Bruce McFarlane visited a large department store in Shanghai during China's Cultural Revolution. They noted that:

> It employs 2,000 shop assistants and staff members. The retail stores are invited to exhibitions of different goods, which shop assistants attend to put forward ideas on what they think customers will want. Where a factory produces something new, the store will set up a special experimental counter to receive suggestions from customers. Such suggestions are meticulously recorded, and go to the wholesale purchasing agencies and, in the case of big retail store, directly to the factories.[42]

Interestingly, they note that in more rural, underdeveloped parts of China, shop assistants will sometimes live with peasant communities for extended periods of time to research consumption patterns. Wheelwright and McFarlane point out that because China contains hundreds of nationalities, this approach is very important because it enables the satisfaction of everyone's needs. Although some factories produced basic, generic products, some of them produced goods for specific national groups. Although the leadership of the Communist Party of China was often sectarian during the Cultural Revolution, it is clear that they were trying to maximise use-value by satisfying the material desires of the masses. When this research was carried out, China was still at a very early stage of socialism, for the productive forces were at a low-level and were still in the process of development. Unfortunately, China's socialist revolution was betrayed in the eighties by a pro-capitalist faction in the Communist Party of China headed by Deng Xiaoping, which makes it impossible for us to know how socialist retail would have further developed in China.[43]

In the more advanced stages of socialism, the retail sector can be drastically transformed, and it is likely that retail employees will be shifted to more enriching forms of labour. It is conceivable that the work of stacking shelves, managing cash registers, and managing a shop can be fully automated in a socialist society. Already under capitalism, Amazon is experimenting with entirely automated shops that use an electronic system to ensure the proper exchange of goods. Amazon shops do not contain cash registers or even a self-checkout system, but rather use the Amazon system to centrally exchange goods. A socialist society could utilize this technology to liberate retail workers

42 Wheelwright and McFarlane 1970, p.13.

43 See Hart-Landsberg and Burkett (2005) for a discussion of the process by which capitalism was restored in China.

from the dull labour of spending the entire day in a shop. The 2020 coronavirus outbreak has shown that it is entirely possible to acquire goods without spending time inside a shop. Today's technology has made it possible to transfer all shopping to the internet so that one can acquire everything one needs without going inside a store. However, shops only closed in 2020–2021 because of the public health crisis and are already in the process of reopening. Although some retailers like Amazon profited from this, most capitalists prefer to run shops because it allows them to stimulate consumerist desires and encourage consumerism.

A socialist society would gradually generalise online shopping, so that acquiring necessities such as water, clothing, food, etc. would be selected on the internet and collected at an office. Since public canteens would gradually replace private food preparation, people would need to spend less time shopping for food. In an early stage of socialism, people will still probably want to acquire things like video game consoles, TVs, books, and other goods required for entertainment. With the development of the productive forces, each of these things can gradually be collectively distributed in order to eradicate shopping all together. Young people will have access to advanced community centres that will be equipped with everything needed for an enriching entertainment experience. Instead of playing video games at home, young people will have access to free entertainment venues where they can play every video game ever created. The state will discourage unhealthy, violent video games while encouraging those that stimulate people's mind. New video games will be created, which are playable in groups and require cooperation rather than competition. Such video games occasionally appear under capitalism, such as Mario Party, which contains a variety of games that require cooperative activity. However, a large majority of video games are highly competitive, violent, combative, and not conducive to social development. The only way a socialist society can remove these negative video games from the planet is by providing young people with enriching alternatives that stimulate their creative potential.

It is unlikely that a single socialist country alone will be able to collectively distribute the entirety of the social product. With each new revolution, however, the potential for more collective forms of living will grow and shopping will gradually become a thing of the past. In a federation of socialist countries—which include the former advanced capitalist centres—young people will not find shopping particularly stimulating and they will not want to spend a lot of time alone. Instead, their lives will be bound up with others, with whom they will coexist and develop strong bonds. As a result, the revolution will permanently dissolve the retail sector and gradually replace it with collectively distributed products. These products will be superior in quality to those produced under capitalism, for they will contain potentials for personal growth and self-expression. None of this is utopian speculation, but rather a deduction of what is possible from the foundation created by advanced modern technology. For these possibilities to be fully realized, a long transitional period will exist, which include a struggle to win people over to collective forms of living and to defeat consumerist ideology.

4 Residential Cleaning under Socialism

Under socialism, there will not be cleaning industry and the relationship to housework will be significantly transformed. As I have argued, a socialist state will organise opportunities for people to form relationships based on collectivity. What under capitalism is solely a private, individual task will under socialism become a collective activity that builds strong relationships between people. One of these tasks is housework and cleaning, which under capitalism is often performed by women who are under pressure to perform a 'second shift' when they get off work. Only women with a higher income can afford to purchase cleaning services from companies like Molly Maid. Socialism has the potential to transform housework and cleaning into a collective activity designed to stimulate a socialist consciousness and respect for one's everyday environment. As Angela Davis observed in *Women, Race, and Class*,

> A substantial portion of the housewife's domestic tasks can actually be incorporated into the industrial economy. In other words, housework need no longer be considered necessarily and unalterably private in character. Teams of trained and well-paid workers, moving from dwelling to dwelling, engineering technologically advanced cleaning machinery, could swiftly and efficiently accomplish what the present-day housewife does so arduously and primitively.[44]

In an early stage of socialism, cleaning can be made part of the public sector through the nationalisation of cleaning companies like Molly Maid and Bidvest-Noonan. Just like healthcare, a socialist state can make housecleaning a public service that it distributes to every household for free. Instead of just cleaning, however, the workers of a state-owned cleaning company can offer

44 Davis 1982

courses in public hygiene in order to educate people on the importance of keeping their living space cleaner. Just like workers in a public canteen, cleaners under socialism will become specialists in issues related to recycling, the environment, and health. They will not simply clean but play an active role in improving the quality of people's everyday lives. A public cleaning service, in addition to a public canteen and public day-care, will liberate women and give them the time necessary to fully participate in society.

At a more advanced stage of socialism, cleaning can be fully collectivised, which will be made possible through the reorganisation of neighbourhoods and housing. Instead of relying on a property factor, a landlord, or housing officer, a socialist state will gradually transfer housing management to the residents through residential committees. Although families can continue living in their own flat, apartment buildings will have spaces where people can meet to organise flat maintenance and address issues affecting the residents. In these socialist communities, group-cleaning of the entire building becomes a weekly activity that involves all the residents—men and women, children and adults.[45] Regular meetings create a sense of belonging to a collective and makes each resident accountable. If someone is frequently littering or neglecting the care of their home, the residents can criticise this person and help them to change their behaviour. Instead of harshly punishing them, the community can identify why they are being negligent and help them to become better people. By making housework a collective activity taken up by *all* the residents, traditionally gendered activities begin to break down. Men and boys will be required to clean, vacuum, scrub the floors, and dispose of trash just as much as women and girls. By making the cleaning of the entire building a collective task, it prevents the residents from hiding things that could be harmful to socialist construction. For example, if one of the residents has misogynistic posters, anti-communist literature, or racist leaflets, it will be less hard for them to hide these things if other residents enter their home regularly.

By making life more transparent and subordinating residential life to a housing committee, it empowers women to confront domestic abuse and reduces the chance that it will happen. Because the residents meet regularly to discuss not just cleaning, but *all* issues affecting the community, women under socialism have a stronger support network and can more easily expose abusers. First, an abuser will find it much harder to hide material evidence of his abuse if he knows that other residents will regularly come into his flat for cleaning. Second,

45 See Grossman (2019) for an excellent discussion of how the German Democratic Republic addressed daily living and tasks related to social reproduction.

the knowledge that his partner could report him to the residential committee and denounce him at a public meeting itself will weaken his power over his partner's body. Women in abusive relationships will no longer have to live in fear, as their fellow comrades will be next door if they need them. The same is true of children, who will receive far more support from both the state and the community under socialism. Children will be empowered to criticise abusive parents and teachers in much the same way that women will be empowered to criticise abusive men. Through a process of gradually collectivising private life, some of the worst forms of abuse can be gradually abolished. In *The Revolution Betrayed*, Trotsky beautifully formulates this, saying that "socialism, if it is worthy of the name, means human relations without greed, friendship without envy and intrigue, love without base calculation."[46]

Although some of the above social relations might be possible even under capitalism, they can never be generalised because of private housing and landlords. A socialist state is able to generalise housing committees to create strong socialist communities. Cleaning and other forms of care are no longer private activities, but become a collective activity that can have positive ideological effects and contribute to women's liberation. The community in which one lives will be empowered to look after children and create a greater level of accountability on each resident. It will take time to organise housing committees, as people under capitalism have learned how to relate to their neighbours in an alienated way. In an early stage of socialism, most people would probably not be comfortable leaving their doors unlocked and allowing other residents into their homes. Residential committees can begin by organising weekly meetings and cleaning common areas, while making the cleaning of private flats an optional service provided by the community. Over time, they can become fully functioning organisations that address problems faced by the community, an outlet for residents to confront abuse, and a way for residents to organise fun activities.

One might think that I have constructed an ideal that will not be likely to be fulfilled in any actual society. This is not true because the experience of socialist construction shows that nearly every socialist country—even the least economically developed—developed such communal practices, which were often the most developed in neighbourhoods and housing. Bruni de La Motte and John Green both spent significant living in the German Democratic Republic and produced a very balanced account of East German socialism. They point out that in socialist housing establishments

46 Trotsky [1936] 2004, p. 117.

> tenants were themselves responsible for the cleaning of the communal areas: the corridors, staircases, airing, washing rooms in the cellar, and other communal areas. Where applicable, tenants also took responsibility for caring for the surrounding area which could include lawns, shrubbery and flowerbeds.[47]

They note that the community often also took a role in looking after children. If a family needed extra care for their child, it was very common for neighbours to help with this effort. Because strong bonds of trust existed between people in the GDR, mutual aid and care was made possible. Victor Grossman, an American communist who lived in the GDR for almost its entire existence and had a very average life, says that a strong environment of solidarity and trust characterised relationships between people in the GDR. Throughout *Socialist Defector*, Grossman highlights that life was at times challenging and that there were sometimes negative censorship trends.[48] However, he points out that this was not always the case, for he had more freedom of speech in the GDR than in the United States, whose FBI wanted to prosecute him for his involvement in the American Communist Party. He claims that despite difficulties at times, he was never without work, had access to a great deal of culture, and was able to get a degree in journalism at Karl Marx University in Leipzig. Even the prime minister of Germany, Angela Merkel, claims that her "life in the GDR was sometimes almost comfortable in a certain way."[49] After socialism ended in 1991, life became very difficult and some of the best elements of socialism were systematically eradicated from society. While socialists have a duty to criticise the negative elements of life under socialism, it is important to also highlight the positive social relationships that were formed in socialist societies.

4.1 *Cleaning Outside the Home*

As I have shown, a socialist state will abolish the exploitation of cleaning workers and make caring for the environment the responsibility of the citizens. From a young age, socialist school children will not just be taught intellectual knowledge, but practical skills to look after their society. Together with teachers, school children will clean their school and look after its maintenance. Everything from the toilets to the classrooms will be managed by the students, teachers, and staff without relying on outside workers. They will take out rubbish, vacuum floors, empty bins, clean the kitchen, and sweep the floors. This

47 De La Motte and Green 2015, p. 33.

48 *ibid.*

49 Reuters 2018.

will create a strong consciousness on the importance of recycling, cleaning, and disposal of waste. As everyone in the school will be responsible for its maintenance, it will remove the idea that cleaning is a women's task. Boys and girls, as well as male and female teachers, will clean together, abolishing any gendered ideas about cleaning. This is something that may be possible even under capitalism and is actively pursued in Japan where pupils are responsible for school cleaning. As Fino Menzes explains,

> Many Japanese schools don't hire janitors or custodians in the traditional American role, and much of the school cleaning is done by the children themselves … Every class is responsible for cleaning its own classroom and two other places in the school, for example the nurse's office and the library. The class is divided into *han* (small groups), each of which is responsible for one of the areas to be cleaned.[50]

Socialism can utilise these progressive traditions of the Japanese school system and generalise them to every aspect of society.

Furthermore, maintenance labour such as plumbing will be used as an opportunity to teach school children practical skills. Although schools will have plumbers to fix toilet issues, the plumber will visit the schools and teach students the science of plumbing. The children will learn of the plumbing system in their school, and how to look after it properly. Boys and girls will receive practical plumbing education so that they do not immediately need to call a plumber if their toilet does not work. The same is true of all other maintenance activities, which will become integral parts of the student's education from primary school to the end of secondary education. This will make them knowledgeable so that they can be productive members of socialist society and contribute to the needs of their community. In the German Democratic Republic, the educational system embraced this model and developed what was known as the 'polytechnical principle'. De La Motte and Green note that GDR school children were encouraged "to observe the work of cooks or the caretakers and to appreciate how much effort is involved in essential work."[51] Also, East German schools taught children how to garden, plant seeds, and handle complex farming equipment. They were introduced to metalwork, handicrafts, and other forms of manual labour, which they were encouraged to take up as a career.[52] As a result of a strong educational policy, Victor Grossman—who learned both

50 Menezes 2019
51 De La Motte and Green 2015, p. 58.
52 *ibid.* pp. 58–59.

how to work as a manual labourer and as a journalist in East Germany—notes that in the GDR "working-class youngsters got a free college education, no one was jobless, and everyone was medically insured".[53] Although capitalist secondary schools may include welding or gardening as part of their curriculum, they tend to privilege intellectual labour that benefits capitalism and often denigrate manual labour. This is expressed in the way that people often use the example of 'flipping burgers' at McDonalds as the ultimate punishment for not performing well in school. Socialism differs in that it seeks to make every person capable of both manual labour and complex technical-scientific work. It values the work of hospitality worker as much as the scientist and tries to raise the educational level of every cook so that they can also conduct scientific research relevant to food production.

Many of the maintenance tasks that are completed by service workers under capitalism will thus be taken up by the community under socialism. Although there will still be some management structures, especially in the early stages, workers will be trained in the practical skills needed to look after their workplace. Because they will be required to work less than under capitalism, a socialist factory or office will set aside time for cleaning and maintenance work. Management, however, will be required to do the same labour as everyone else, which will be a general principle of socialist construction. This will empower workers to view their workplace as their own and give them the courage needed to gradually take over its management. Some workers will still be employed to provide necessary services—cleaning, maintenance, plumbing, etc. Although residents, students, and workers will play a more active role in looking after their environment, there will be additional workers who aid them. A service worker under socialism will help communities, schools, and workers to improve their skills so that they have to rely less on them. As I showed with the example of a plumber that shares their skills, service workers such as cleaners and electricians will become teachers of the people. State-employed cleaning workers may visit apartment buildings to provide additional support. Instead of just cleaning, they will offer suggestions on how the residents could more effectively clean and reduce their labour. Cleaners under socialism will act more like advisers to the community than its servants and be invited to attend residential committee meetings if they detect problems. Cleaners will also visit schools and offer workshops on cleaning techniques, incorporating singing and games into cleaning. For example, they may organise a competition between teams to see who can clean the best, and then give

53 Grossman 2019, p. 27.

the winning team a prize. This would train students to view cleaning not as a dreary task, but as something that can be fun, especially when done in a group. It would be a way of strengthening relationships between people and creating positive forms of group accountability. A cleaner under socialism will therefore gain the same dignity as all other working people and value their job. The alienated labour that Marx speaks about in his early writings will disappear by being replaced with more meaningful and fulfilling activities.

The socialist state will provide residents, schools, and workplaces with advanced cleaning supplies. Apartment building will receive things like vacuum cleaners, mops, cloths, and regular shipments of cleaning chemicals. In this way, individuals will no longer have to spend their income on cleaning equipment but receive it from the state. They will have access to the finest technology, from robotic vacuums to high powered mops, which accelerate the cleaning process and free up time for leisure. The same will be true in schools and workplaces, where public cleaning equipment will be owned and managed by the students, teachers, and workers. By providing them with cleaning supplies, the state can actively encourage the community to look after their society. Socialist governments can wage massive propaganda campaigns to encourage recycling and cleaning, putting up posters in cities encouraging people to put their rubbish in bins and clean up after themselves. De La Motti and Green point out that in the German Democratic Republic the local authority would provide housing committees with a fund for flat maintenance, which would be used to acquire equipment needed to clean flats. Also, they note that the GDR government encouraged recycling and would pay bonuses to housing committees in exchange for recycled goods.[54]

5 Transportation under Socialism

A defining feature of socialist construction is the importance given to improving public transportation. For some, the first thing that comes to mind when they think of the socialist past are Czechoslovakia's finely engineered trams, which operated in nearly every socialist country and are still used in the Democratic People's Republic of Korea. Socialist urban planners created cities that made transport available to all, while being sensitive to the environment and the experience of the city. Although private cars were still driven in the socialist countries—the iconic Trabant from East Germany, the Czechoslovak

54 De La Motte and Green 2015, p. 33.

Skoda, and the Soviet Lada—a major goal of future socialist societies should be their abolition. As I indicated earlier, the continued existence of private automobiles in former socialist societies was more symptomatic of harmful policies than a genuine socialist approach to transportation. In an advanced socialist country, people will not need private cars because excellent transport links will make their use unnecessary. A system of electric buses and self-driving cars, taxis, high-speed rail, trams, subways, and boats will replace private transportation entirely. This is more environmentally friendly and would give socialist societies the ability to combat climate change, reduce pollution, and conserve resources.

An effect of this is that significant working people under socialism will work in the transport sector, so that being a bus or tram driver, subway operator, taxi chauffeur, or train conductor will be major sources of employment. One way that their labour will differ from capitalism is that they will be trained not just to operate a vehicle but receive training on how to repair them and do maintenance. A socialist bus driver will not spend their entire life driving the same route, but also work in the garage doing maintenance on the buses. They will become highly knowledgeable about every aspect of the bus they drive, the materials out of which they're made, and the energy source they depend on. Socialist bus drivers will also become leaders in creating environmentally friendly transportation, receiving a detailed education on the environmental impact of public transportation. This will make them much more than a bus driver, but socialist environmentalists who connect their own labour-process to the fight to save the planet from climate change. Through a gradual process, transport providers will receive skills that make them capable of operating multiple types of vehicles, doing maintenance work on them, and becoming leaders in the improvement of socialist transportation. One of the results of the collective distribution of transportation is that it enables society to effectively combat climate change. Instead of depending on people's private consumption decisions, a socialist society can centrally plan its environmental policy by investing only in green transportation.

A major effect of the improvement of public transportation in a socialist economy is the acceleration of socialist integration. By making it possible to rapidly transport people in a cheap and efficient way, socialist countries can more easily engage in shared projects. Although national borders will exist until communism is achieved, socialist integration creates a strong foundation for equality and friendship between different nationalities. It allows the people of a socialist country to work on equal terms with the people of another socialist country. Such a socialist integrated alliance resulting from improved transportation significantly weakens capitalism internationally and puts the working class in a stronger position. When the stage of communism is achieved, the entire planet will be connected, and new forms of transportation will exist as result of the absence of borders.

6 Conclusion

In this chapter, I have argued that a primary feature of socialist society is economic planning, and the integration of multiple socialist countries into a socialist bloc. The success of socialism is bound up the victory of socialist revolution in multiple countries and every new revolution enables socialism to expand collective distribution. I have shown that service workers under socialism—cleaners, plumbers, electricians—will become important teachers in their community. Retail workers will no longer be sales employees, but highly trained people who play an integral part in socialist accounting, as well as the development of new products. When socialism has achieved a more advanced stage, collective distribution will fully abolish the retail sector by making all consumption collective. Both service and retail workers will play an important part in the socialist system of planning, accounting, and distribution. This reveals a very important fact about socialism: it gradually breaks down the very distinction between industrial and service workers. Because socialism involves the gradual transfer of ownership and management to the working class, every worker will perform both physical and service labour. A steel worker will not just be an expert in everything related to steel but be trained in socialist management techniques and integrated into the planning agencies. Steel workers will learn significant scientific knowledge and computer programming skills so that the management of production can gradually be transferred to them. Steel workers will visit schools to teach young pupils the art of welding, invite students to the factory, and teach them the science behind steel production. This does not mean that all students will become steel workers, but only that production will be fully integrated into basic education. New literature and art will be produced that focuses on the lives of steel workers, their hopes and their dreams, and how socialism has liberated them from the chains of capitalist exploitation. A good indicator of the progress of a socialist revolution is how much it has succeeded in breaking down the division between service and industrial worker. At an advanced stage of socialism, the very category of service worker will disappear entirely, which will make every worker both an intellectual and a producer. Workers will cease to be wage-slaves of capital but become teachers in their workplace and at schools. Students will learn both the great literature created by bourgeois society, and the new socialist writing produced by working class people.

International socialism as I have defined it is therefore the only solution to the struggles faced by service and retail workers. While it is important to fight for reforms under capitalism, it is more important to struggle for socialism. As this requires a socialist revolution—not the election of more social democrats—it is vital to win service workers over to socialist ideas. Because they are a significant section of the workforce, socialists need to devote time to organising service workers to take up Marxism. One way to do this is to demonstrate how socialism would improve their lives by passing management over to them and raising their educational, cultural, and material level. Even if a small minority of cleaners, baristas, cooks, plumbers, bus drivers, and electricians take up Marxism, this will significantly strengthen the entire socialist movement. Although prior socialist countries such as the USSR and the GDR were unable to progress very far, they are full of examples that one can use to show how socialism transforms people's lives. While we should rigorously criticise the Stalinist deformations of Marxism, we should also learn how former socialist countries distributed food, organised housing management, and thought about domestic labour. This experience, combined with Marxist theory, can provide service and retail workers with a genuine alternative to the misery that they face under capitalism. It is not hard to explain to a worker at Starbucks or a cleaner at Molly Maid that their low-wage, unfulfilling jobs are only an effect of the capitalist division of labour and could be significantly transformed with socialist relations of production. When a group of Starbucks workers learn that a socialist state can enable them to take over their café and reorganise production, this can empower them to fight for socialist revolution. An outsourced cleaner at Molly Maid or Bidvest-Noonan who works forty hours a week with no job security or career prospect would be happy to learn that socialism will abolish outsourcing and create meaningful opportunities for them to live happy, fulfilled lives. Socialists are needed to construct an inspirational vision of a socialist future, so that working people take up Marxism as their ideology.

Unless socialists do the difficult work of discussing Marxism with service and retail workers, it is unlikely that a revolution in the advanced capitalist centres will occur. This book, which places the service and retail worker in a dignified light, can serve as a starting point to constructing a vision for a socialist future. It is common to hear socialists argue that we must fully subordinate propaganda activity to factories and sites of industrial production. They argue that because their labour process is collective, it is easier for them to take up the management of industry and perceive the necessity of socialism. As I have shown, hospitality workers, cleaners, and retail employees work are no less capable of self-management, nor is their labour process any less collective than industrial proletarians. The task of socialists is to organise *all* working people while adopting specific strategies and tactics for *different* sections of the workforce. It is vital that socialists arm workers with a revolutionary socialist internationalist consciousness, which enables them to unite with workers around the world. The primary task should be to stimulate a strong desire for socialism in the working class combined with an identification with the international proletariat. Workers in stage one and stage two need to be organised into an international united front against imperialism and monopoly capitalism. In this way, socialists will really serve the people by organising the forces need to bring down the capitalist system and create a socialist society, which is more just, fulfilling, and egalitarian than capitalism.

CHAPTER 12

Afterword

In his *Communist Manifesto*, Marx says that revolutionary socialists represent the *entire* working class and formulate a political programme that defines the strategy needed to make a socialist revolution. He emphasises that revolutionary socialists should represent all working people rather than a small segment. Unfortunately, Marxism after Marx has sometimes only represented the industrial sections of the working class centred at the point of production. Revolutionary socialists have not devoted enough theoretical work to understanding service and retail workers, which has resulted in a lack of Marxist influence among them. This book has attempted to amend this problem by showing how service workers produce surplus-value, and the important role that retail workers play in the realisation of surplus-value.

As I have demonstrated, workers employed by industries that produce service commodities—cleaners, administration, maintenance work, bus drivers, etc.—are productive workers who are exploited just like workers who manufacture physical goods. Neoliberalism has caused significant maintenance tasks to be outsourced, resulting in new sites for profitable capitalist investment. Furthermore, because of deindustrialisation and imperialism, the production process is often geographically divided into two stages. As I have shown, the production of physical goods is primarily located in the periphery, while the realisation of the surplus-value contained in these goods is situated in the imperialist centres. The dislocation that results from the geography of imperialism has caused socialists to neglect attempts to unify workers in the two stages. So long as retail employees in stage two are alienated from workers in stage one, it is unlikely that they will be capable of fully breaking free of corporate propaganda and organising themselves into a militant force. While some might occasionally organise trade unions and make demands for higher wages, they will be very limited so long as they remain confined to their local social formation. Proletarian internationalism holds the key to strengthening the ability of all working people to fight for their interests and become a militant political force.

In order to be capable of representing the entire working class rather than only one of its segments, revolutionary socialists must seriously begin thinking about how to organise service and retail workers. Most socialists would probably agree that cleaners, hospitality workers, and retail employees are part of the working class because they make a living from wage-labour. However,

 | DOI:10.1163/9789004469624_013

unless they become aware of how these workers relate to surplus-value, their demands will not go beyond trade union campaigns for higher wages and more secure employment contracts. While these campaigns—such as the Fight for 15—contain important lessons for organising service workers, they do not go beyond reforms to the capitalist system. Without the clarity of Marxist theory, it is unlikely that socialist activism around service workers will go beyond trade union demands. Marxism can show how a service or retail worker relates to the entire capitalist system, revealing the strategy needed to make them a force that disrupts capitalism's systemic features. For example, socialists who understand that retail workers are integral to the realisation of surplus-value could organise a campaign that seeks to disrupt the surplus absorption process. They then could then explain to the retail worker how their life would be different under socialism and begin organising them into a revolutionary force that is united with workers in stage one.

More research into service workers will be needed for revolutionary socialists to adequately grasp the dynamics of exploitation in the service and retail industry. In this book, I have only attempted to show how Marxism could inform such research and what a service sector would be like under socialism. Future research and case studies into the labour processes of service workers would greatly improve the ability of Marxist theory to provide an account of the exploitation faced by working people. Studies that explore labour-processes of workers in the care sector, tourism, privatised hospitals, video game industry, and entertainment are especially needed. An entire book could be written about the extreme levels of exploitation faced by adjunct professors and temporary lecturers in American, British, and European colleges.

My hope is that this book has equipped socialists with the tools to begin thinking about how to get service and retail workers to take up Marxism. This book is a starting point, but much work remains to be done. What is certain is that while the composition of the working class has changed in the twenty-first century, the future of human society remains bound up with its liberation. The CEO's and managers of large corporations, the capitalist bankers, neoliberal ideologues, and capitalist politicians have nothing to offer society except stagnation, imperialism, and war. It is the cleaners, hospitality workers, plumbers, electricians, retail employees, teachers, steel workers, bus drivers, and other working people who will take humanity to a more advanced level. These people hold the key to a bright and happy future, which puts an end to the exploitation of man by man and ends the oppression of the working class. Revolutionary socialists should thus invest their time into organising service workers and equipping them with the tools needed to make a socialist revolution. If this book has inspired a few people to devote themselves to service and retail workers, then it will have succeeded in its primary aims.

Bibliography

Alexander, Michelle. 2010. *The New Jim Crow.* New York: The New Press.

Alimahomed-Wilson, Jake and Immanuel Ness, (eds.). 2018. *Choke Points: Logistic Workers Disrupting the Supply Chain*. London: Pluto.

Althusser, Louis. 2014. *On the Reproduction of Capitalism.* Trans: G. M. Goshgarian, London: Verso.

Amin, Samir. 1974. *Accumulation on a World Scale.* One Volume Edition. Trans: Brian Pearce. Sussex: Harvester Press.

Amin, Samir. 2018. *Modern Imperialism, Monopoly Finance Capital, and Marx's Law of Value*. New York: Monthly Review.

Armstrong, Charles. 2015. *Tyrrany of the Weak*. Ithaca: Cornell University Press.

Asia Floor Alliance. 2019. *Precarious Work in the H&M Global Value Chain.* Online: https://asia.floorwage.org/wp-content/uploads/2019/10/Asia-Floor-Wage-Alliance-H-M.pdf.

Baran, Paul. 1957. *The Political Economy of Growth.* New York: Monthly Review.

Barnes, Jack. 2019. *The Turn to Industry: Forging a Proletarian Party*. New York: Pathfinder.

Bettelheim, Charles. 1976. *Class Struggles in the USSR, Volume 1.* New York: Monthly Review.

Berry, Joe. 2005. *Reclaiming the Ivory Tower: Organizing Adjuncts to Change Higher-Education*. New York: Monthly Review.

Bidvest-Noonan. 2020. Financial Statement for 2019. Companies House. Accessed 3 September, 2021: https://find-and-update.company-information.service.gov.uk/company/05049403.

Boltanski, Luc and Eve Chiapello. 2018. *The New Spirit of Capitalism* (New Edition). Trans: Gregory Elliot, London: Verso.

Booth, Adam. 2015. "The Sharing Economy, the Future of Jobs, and "Post Capitalism". *In Defence of Marxism*. Accessed 1 April 2021: https://www.marxist.com/the-sharing-economy-the-future-of-jobs-and-postcapitalism-part-one.htm.

Braverman, Harry. 1974. *Labor and Monopoly Capital.* New York: Monthly Review.

Brennan, Joe. 2017a. "South Africa's Bidvest snaps up Noonan Services for €175m" *Irish Times*. Mon, Jul 31, 2017. Online: https://www.irishtimes.com/business/retail-and-services/south-africa-s-bidvest-snaps-up-noonan-services-for-175m-1.3172201.

Brennan Joe. 2017b. "Noonan Services bosses score €20m-plus payday with BidVest deal" *Irish Times*. Tue, Aug 1, 2017. Online: https://www.irishtimes.com/business/retail-and-services/noonan-services-bosses-score-20m-plus-payday-with-bidvest-deal-1.3172781.

Brittain, James. 2010. *Revolutionary Social Change in Colombia.* London: Pluto.

Brooks, Andrew. 2019. *Clothing Poverty* (New Edition). London: Zed.

Bryer, Robert. 2017. *Accounting for Value in Marx's Capital*. London: Lexington Books.

Bukharin, Nikolai. 1929. *Imperialism and World Economy* [*1915*]. Trans: Mirovoe Ivanovich, New York: International Publishers.

Bukharin, Nikolai and E. Preobrazhensky. 1966. *The ABC of Communism* [*1923*]. Ann Arbor: University of Michigan Press.

Cant, Callum and Jamie Woodcock. 2020. "From disorganisation to action in the service sector" *Capital and Class*. Vol. 44, No. 4.

Cope, Zak. 2019. *The Wealth of Some Nations*. London: Pluto.

Daley, Jason. 2011. "Capital Ideas" *Entrepreneur,* October.

Daszkowski, Don. 2018. "Molly Maid Franchise Review" *The Balance, Small Business*. 7 August, 2018. Online: https://www.thebalancesmb.com/molly-maid-franchise-review-1350258.

Davis, Angela. 1982. *Women, Race and Class*. London: Women's Press.

Davis-Blake, Alison and Joseph P. Brochak. 2009. "Outsourcing and the Changing Nature of Work" *Annual Review of Sociology*: Vol. 35 (April):321–340.

De Brunhoff, Suzanne. 2015. *Marx on Money*. Trans: Maurice Goldbloom. London: Verso.

De La Motte, Bruna and John Green. 2015. *Stasi State or Socialist Paradise?* London: Artery Publications.

Douglas, Dorothy. 1972. *Transitional Economic Systems: The Polish-Czech Example*. New York: Monthly Review.

Economics Institute of the Academy of Sciences of the U.S.S.R. 1957. *Political Economy,* London: Lawrence & Wishart. Online: https://www.marxists.org/subject/economy/authors/pe/index.htm.

Ehrenreich, Barbara (ed.). 2003. *Global Woman: Nannies, Maids, and Sex Workers in the New Economy*. London: Granta Books.

Elson, Diane (ed.). 2015. *Value: the Representation of Labour in Capitalism*. London: Verso.

Emmanuel, Arghiri. 1972. *Unequal Exchange*. Trans: Brian Pearce. London: NLB.

Fine, Ben and Alfredo Saad-Filho. 2016. *Marx's Capital, Sixth Edition*. London: Pluto.

Foster, John Bellamy. 2014. *The Theory of Monopoly Capital* (New Edition). New York: Monthly Review.

Foster, John Bellamy and Robert McChesney. 2012. *The Endless Crisis*. New York: Monthly Review.

Frank, Andre Gunder. 1967. *Capitalism and Underdevelopment in Latin America*, New York: Monthly Review.

Garcia, Ana (ed.). 2015. *BRICS: An Anti-Capitalist Critique*. London: Pluto.

Ghodsee, Kirsten. 2018. *Second World, Second Sex*. Durham: Duke University Press.

Grossman, Victor. 2019. *Socialist Defector*. New York: Monthly Review.

Gruss, Bernard and Natalija Novta. 2018. "The Decline of Manufacturing Jobs: Not Necessarily a Cause for Concern" IMF Blog, April 9, 2018. Accessed: 17

June, 2020: https://blogs.imf.org/2018/04/09/the-decline-in-manufacturing-jobs-not-necessarily-a-cause-for-concern/.

Hart-Landsberg, Martin. 2013. *Capitalist Globalization: Consequences, Resistance, Alternatives*. New York: Monthly Review.

Hart-Landsberg, Martin and Paul Burkett. 2005. *China and Socialism*. New York: Monthly Review.

Harvey, David. 2007. *A Brief History of Neoliberalism*. New York: Oxford University Press.

Harvey, David. 2006. *Limits to Capital*, New Edition. London: Verso.

Harvey, David. 2010. *A Companion to Marx's Capital* London: Verso.

Harvey, David. 2013. *A Companion to Marx's Capital: Volume 2*. London: Verso.

Haug, W.F. 1986. *Critique of Commodity Aesthetics*. Trans: Robert Block, Cambridge: Polity.

Haywood, Harry. 1978. *Black Bolshevik.* Liberator Press.

Hristov, Jasmin. 2014. *Paramilitarism and Neoliberalism.* London: Pluto.

Indeed. 2018. Job Reviews. Accessed 25 October, 2019: https://uk.indeed.com/.

Indeed. 2019. Job Reviews. Accessed 21 July, 2020: https://uk.indeed.com/.

Kearsey, Joe. 2020. "Control, camararderie and resistance: Precarious work and organisation in hospitality" *Capital and Class*. Vol. 44, No. 4.

Keeran, Roger and Thomas Kenny. 2010. *Socialism Betrayed*. iUniverse.

Koblar, Simon and Luka Mladenovic. 2020. "Calculating the speed of bus trips" *Urbani Izziv*, Vol. 31, No. 1, June.

Kosová, Renáta and Francine Lafontaine. 2010. "Survival and Growth in Retail and Service Industries: Evidence From Franchised Chains." *The Journal of Industrial Economics*, Vol. 58, No. 3 (September), p. 543.

Kuusinen, Otto. 1963. *Fundamentals of Marxism-Leninism*. Trans: Clemens Dutt. Moscow: Foreign Languages Publishing House.

Lenin, Vladimir. 1913. *Three Sources of Marxism*, in *Collected Works, Volume 19*. Moscow: Progress Publishers, Available Online: https://www.marxists.org/archive/lenin/works/1913/mar/x01.htm.

Lenin, Vladimir. 1914. *Karl Marx: A Brief Biographical Sketch*, in *Collected Works, Volume 21*. Moscow: Progress Publishers. Available Online: https://www.marxists.org/archive/lenin/works/1914/granat/index.htm.

Lenin, Vladimir. 1916. *Imperialism: The Highest Stage of Capitalism*, in *Collected Works, Volume 22*. Moscow: Progress Publishers. Available Online: https://www.marxists.org/archive/lenin/works/1916/imp-hsc/.

Lenin, Vladimir. 1917. *Letter on Tactics*, in *Collected Works, Volume 24*. Moscow: Progress Publishers. Available Online: https://www.marxists.org/archive/lenin/works/1917/apr/x01.htm.

Lenin, Vladimir. 1919. *A Great Beginning*, in *Collected Works, Volume 29*. Moscow: Progress Publishers. Available Online: https://www.marxists.org/archive/lenin/works/1919/jun/19.htm.

Lukacs, Georg. 1967. *History and Class Consciousness*. Trans: Rodney Livingstone. London: Merlin Press.

Luxemburg, Rosa. 2003. *The Accumulation of Capital*. Trans: Agnes Schwarzchild. New York: Routledge.

Machin, Stephen Mark Stewart and John Van Reene. 1993. "The Economic Effects of Multiple Unionism: Evidence from the 1984 Workplace Industrial Relations Survey" *The Scandinavian Journal of Economics*. Vol. 95, No. 3 (Sept.), pp. 279–296.

Magdoff, Harry. 2000. *The Age of Imperialism* (New Edition). New York: Monthly Review.

Mandel, Ernest. 1978. *Late Capitalism*. Trans: Joris de Bres. London: Verso.

Marx, Karl. 1955. *Poverty of Philosophy* [1847]. Trans: Institute of Marxism-Leninism. Moscow: Progress Publishers. Available Online: https://www.marxists.org/archive/marx/works/1847/poverty-philosophy/.

Marx, Karl. 1969. *The Communist Manifesto* [1848], Trans: Samuel Moore, in *Selected Works, Vol. One,* Progress Publishers, Moscow.

Marx, Karl. 1976. *Capital, Volume 1* [1867]. Trans: Ben Fowkes. London: Penguin.

Marx, Karl. 1977. *Early Writings*. Trans: Rodney Livingstone. London: Penguin.

Marx, Karl. 1978. *Capital, Volume 2* [1885]. Trans: David Fernbach. London: Penguin.

Marx, Karl. 1981. *Capital, Volume 3* [1894]. Trans: David Fernbach. London: Penguin.

Mavrakis, Kostas. 1976. *On Trotskyism*. Trans: John Macgreal, London: Routledge.

McFarlane, Bruce and E.L. Wheelwright. 1970. *The Chinese Road to Socialism*. New York: Monthly Review.

Menezes, Fino. 2019. "Should Children Clean Their Own Schools? Japan Thinks So" Good Blog, 07/02/2019. Online: https://www.good.is/articles/japan-children-clean-schools Accessed 18 March 2021.

Mitchell, Willian and Thomas Fazi. 2017. *Reclaiming the State*. London: Pluto.

Molly Maid UK. 2016. Financial Statements. Companies House: London. Online: https://beta.companieshouse.gov.uk/company/09654170/filing-history.

Moran, Caitlin. 2021. "Why Does Cuba Have So Many Classic Cars?" The News Wheel, Accessed 23 March, 2021: https://thenewswheel.com/why-does-cuba-have-so-many-classic-cars/.

Nove, Alec (ed.). 1972. *Socialist Economics*. London: Penguin Books.

Odlyzko, Andrew. 2010. *Collective Hallucinations and Inefficient Markets: The British Raily Mania of the 1840's.* Online: http://www.dtc.umn.edu/~odlyzko/doc/hallucinations.pdf.

Peet, Richard. 2003. *Unholy Trinity: the IMF, World Bank, and WTO*. London: Zed Books.

Perez, Laura. 2016. "The Uber Controversy Reveals the Rottenness of the Taxi Industry" In Defence of Marxism Website. Accessed 1 April 2021: https://www.marxist.com/uber-controversy-reveals-rottenness-of-taxi-industry.htm.

Piketty, Thomas. 2013. *Capital in the Twenty-First Century*. Cambridge: Harvard University Press.

Potorti, Mary. 2014. "Feeding Revolution: The Black Panther Party and the Politics of Food" *Radical Teacher*. No. 98, Winter. Online: https://radicalteacher.library.pitt.edu/ojs/radicalteacher/article/view/80.

Poulantzas, Nikos. 1978. *Classes in Contemporary Capitalism*. Trans: David Fernbach. London: Verso.

Poulantzas, Nikos. 2008. *The Poulantzas Reader.* Ed. James Martin. London: Verso.

Prahad, Vijay. 2008. *The Darker Nations*. New York: the New Press.

Prashad, Vijay. 2014. *The Poorer Nations*. London: Verso.

Reuters. 2018. "Life in Communist East Germany Was Almost Comfortable at Times" 8 November, 2018, Accessed 25 December, 2020: https://www.reuters.com/article/us-germany-berlinwall-merkel-idUSKBN1XI287.

Rodney, Walter. 2018. *How Europe Underdeveloped Africa* [1972]. London: Verso.

Rubin, I.I. 2010. *Essays on Marx's Theory of Value*. Trans: Milos Samardzija and Freddy Perlman, Delhi: Aakar.

Saad-Filho, Alfredo. 2019. *Value and Crisis*. Leiden: Brill.

Saad-Filho, Alfredo and Lecio Morais. 2018. *Brazil: Neoliberalism Versus Democracy*. London: Pluto.

Saul, John. 2014. *A Flawed Freedom: Rethinking Southern African Liberation*. London: Pluto.

Schmidt, Ingo and Carlo Fanelli (eds.). 2017. *Reading Capital Today*. London: Pluto.

Senin, M. 1973. *Socialist Integration*. Moscow: Progress Publishers.

Smith, John. 2016. *Imperialism in the Twenty-First Century*. New York: Monthly Review.

Standing, Guy. 2011. *The Precariat*, London: Bloomsbury Press.

Starbucks Financial Report. 2018. Company's House UK. Accessed 6 March 2021: https://find-and-update.company-information.service.gov.uk/company/02959325/filing-history.

Suwandi, Intan. 2019. *Value Chains: The New Economic Imperialism*. New York: Monthly Review.

Sweezy, Paul. 1970. *The Theory of Capitalist Development* [1940]. New York: Monthly Review.

Sweezy, Paul. 1972. *Modern Capitalism and Other Essays*. New York: Monthly Review.

Sweezy, Paul. 1980. *Post-Revolutionary Society*. New York: Monthly Review.

Sweezy, Paul and Leo Huberman. 1960. *Cuba: Anatomy of a Revolution*. New York: Monthly Review.

Sweezy, Paul and Paul Baran. 1966. *Monopoly Capital*. New York: Monthly Review.

Szymanski, Albert. 1979. *Is the Red Flag Flying*. London: Zed Books.

Therborn, Goran. 1978. *What the Ruling Class Does When It Rules*. London: Verso.

Thomas, Clive. 1974. *Dependence and Transformation*. New York: Monthly Review.

Transnational Information Exchange. 2011. "Workers Exchange Between Germany and Bangladesh". Online: http://www.exchains.org/exchains_newsletters/ExChains_%20NL_14_2011_BD_eng.pdf.

Transnational Information Exchange. 2017. "The H&M Experience: Organizing Retail Workers in the Age of Precarity", 18 Jan 2017. Online: https://www.transnational-strike.info/2017/01/18/the-hm-experience-organizing-retail-workers-in-the-age-of-precarity/.

Tregenna, Fiona. 2010. "How significant is intersectoral outsourcing of employment in South Africa?" *Industrial and Corporate Change*, Volume 19, Number 5, 1431.

Tregenna, Fiona. 2011. "What Does the 'Services Sector' Mean in Marxian Terms?" *Review of Political Economy*,Volume 23, Number 2 (April), 281–298.

Trotsky, Leon. 2020. *The Permanent Revolution & Results and Prospects.* [1929] London: Wellred Books.

Trotsky, Leon. 2004. *The Revolution Betrayed.* [1937] New York: Dover Book.

United Voices of the World Union. 2017. "What Sort of An Organisation is Noonan Services Group" Accessed April 2020: https://unitedvoicesoftheworld.squarespace.com/blog/2017/5/8/what-sort-of-an-organisation-is-noonan-services-group-the-facilities-management-company-that-the-london-school-of-economics-lse-employs-to-operate-its-cleaning-services.

Webster, Andrew. 2018. "Nintendo is Slowly Erasing the WiiU From Existence" The Verge, 1 May 2018. Accessed 13 September 2020: https://www.theverge.com/2018/5/1/17301860/nintendo-switch-ports-wii-u-obsolete.

White, Alan. 2017. *Who Really Runs Britain*. Edinburgh: One World Books.

Wood, Ellen M. 2017. *The Origins of Capitalism: a Longer View*. New York: Verso.

Wood, Alex. 2020. "Beyond Mobilization at McDonald's: Towards networked organising" *Capital and Class*. Vol. 44, No. 4.

Woodcock, Jamie. 2016. *Working the Phones*. London: Pluto.

Woodcock, Jamie. 2019. *Marx at the Arcade.* Chicago: Haymarket Books.

Wren, Anthony. 1972. "Bus Scheduling". *Operational Research Quarterly*, Vol. 23, No. 2 (June), 224–226.

Wright, Erik-Olin. 1978. *Class, Crisis, and the State*. London: NLB.

Wright, Erik-Olin. 1985. *Classes*. London: Verso.

Yates, Michael. 2003. *Naming the System: Inequality and Work in the Global Economy.* New York: Monthly Review.

Zizek, Slavoj. 2007. *How to Read Lacan*. New York: Norton.

Index

Printed in the United States
by Baker & Taylor Publisher Services